The Writer's Portable Mentor

Also by Priscilla Long

Fire and Stone: Where Do We Come From? What Are We?
    Where Are We Going?
Minding the Muse: A Handbook for Painters, Composers,
    Writers, and Other Creators
Crossing Over: Poems
The Writer's Portable Mentor: A Guide to Art, Craft, and the
    Writing Life (First Edition)
Where the Sun Never Shines: A History of America's Bloody
    Coal Industry
The New Left: A Collection of Essays (Editor)

THE WRITER'S PORTABLE MENTOR

A Guide to Art, Craft, and the Writing Life

SECOND EDITION

Priscilla Long

UNIVERSITY OF NEW MEXICO PRESS
ALBUQUERQUE

© 2010 by Priscilla Long
All rights reserved. University of New Mexico Press edition
    published 2018 by arrangement with the author.
Printed in the United States of America

Library of Congress Cataloging-in-Publication Data
Names: Long, Priscilla, author.
Title: The writer's portable mentor: a guide to art, craft, and
    the writing life / Priscilla Long.
Description: Second edition. | Albuquerque: University of
    New Mexico Press, 2018. |
Identifiers: LCCN 2018006286 (print) | LCCN 2018007812
    (e-book) | ISBN 9780826360069 (e-book) |
    ISBN 9780826360052 (pbk.: alk. paper)
Subjects: LCSH: Authorship—Handbooks, manuals, etc.
Classification: LCC PN147 (e-book) | LCC PN147.L66 2018
    (print) | DDC 808.02—dc23
LC record available at https://lccn.loc.gov/2018006286

Cover illustration: © Donna Huntriss
Designed by Lisa C. Tremaine
Composed in Sabon

Writing is a labor, shot through with delight.

—*Scott Russell Sanders*

CONTENTS

PREFACE TO THE SECOND EDITION

I am a reader and following from that, a writer. So to be able to contribute this work to other writers and to those who want to write is a privilege for which I am profoundly grateful.

I shaped the original pages of *The Writer's Portable Mentor* for fifteen years, using the evolving manuscript in my writing classes. I did (and still do) the exercises many times over in relation to my own works in progress. Let's say I am on intimate terms with its alchemical effects. And I've had the gratification of witnessing other writers blossom under its aegis.

So why a second edition? I'm in excellent health and not so very old, but I want *The Writer's Portable Mentor* to live on beyond me. The venerable University of New Mexico Press, with its stunningly competent staff (as I learned when the press published my book of poems) makes a perfect home for the second edition of *The Writer's Portable Mentor*.

For the second edition I wanted to switch most of the model sentences, paragraphs, and pieces, to replace them with new ones. Why, since I adore the models in the first edition? Partly for selfish reasons. I felt greedy for a fresh palette, a novel cuisine, a new wardrobe. And I fancy that devotees of the first edition will relish these new goodies as well. It's my hope that old and new readers alike will find these models as revelatory as I have.

The replacement process required an intense year of reading, for my practice is to read all of any work from which I pick out a sentence or paragraph. Reading is what I do, but this year's marathon has been a benison. How could I possibly thank all the authors, past and present, who have—through their literary works—given such richness to our culture and to our lives? And by *literary* I am not referring to some genre but to artists ranging from crime writer James Ellroy to poets Mary Oliver and Gwendolyn Brooks to novelists Annie Proulx and

Viet Thanh Nguyen to classic giants like James Baldwin. The novels, stories, essays, and poems by these and other writers have been my mentors, my teachers, my tutors, my taskmasters. I am forever in their debt.

Other changes in *The Writer's Portable Mentor* reflect changes in the world of reading, writing, and publishing that have occurred since the first edition appeared in 2010. This includes everything from the number of words in an average-length short story to reflections on the decision on whether or not to self-publish to the findings of neuroscience on what our brain does while we write by hand versus what it does while we tap keys.

To those I thanked in the first edition: I must thank you again—all of you. My workshop, including writers and visual artists, began some twenty-seven years ago and is still going strong. I am grateful to Jack Remick, M. Anne Sweet, Geri Gale, Gordon Wood, Sadato Hosoda, and Anna Bálint. The folks at HistoryLink.org, the online encyclopedia of Washington state history, have kept on keeping the faith that comprehending the past will help us to shape a future we will want to live in.

I am grateful to Sharon Oard Warner, novelist and longtime founder/director of the Taos Summer Writer's Conference, for providing me with the opportunity to teach prose style in Taos and Santa Fe every summer for close to a decade. I am grateful to Hugo House—Seattle's center for writers—for creating such a warm and stimulating community in which we writers can write and teach and learn and perform and listen.

I must thank the team that coalesced around creating the first edition of *The Writer's Portable Mentor*. We have remained a team, evolving into one whose purpose is mutual aid and support for the endeavor of getting our works out into the world. Thank you to Andrea Lewis, Susan Knox, and Waverly Fitzgerald. I am grateful to Ms. James Kessler whose hard work and competence as editorial assistant has been invaluable to this book. I am grateful to Scott Driscoll, Kate Trueblood, Laura Kalpakian, and Maya Sonenberg for good advice and kind support. I could not do without my loyal but critical first readers including my dear friend Bethany Reid, my sister Pamela O. Long, and brother-in-law Bob Korn. Great thanks to Liz Long, David Messer-schmidt, and Jay Schlechter, without whom I would be a mess.

Lastly I am grateful to Elise McHugh and the staff at University of New Mexico Press, for taking on *The Writer's Portable Mentor* with love and enthusiasm and for making it their own. Thank you.

A Writer's Practice

For writers dedicated to their craft, learning the craft never ends. Yet the pleasure in it deepens as we achieve, upon occasion, a virtuoso sentence, a virtuoso page of writing. This book is for writers who strive for virtuosity. It is designed to mentor you, first, in practices that catalyze productivity—for basic productivity underlies everything else. And second, in craft moves that will aid you in your quest to deepen the work and carry it forward.

I wrote and rewrote *The Writer's Portable Mentor* during years of teaching both apprentice writers and writers who are seasoned and quite well-published but who want to deepen their skills and extend their range. It is for you if your goal as a writer is to develop faster, become more skilled, or go in new directions. My goal is to help you realize beautiful and accomplished works on a regular basis and to get them out into the world. *The Writer's Portable Mentor* is particularly oriented toward writers of creative nonfiction (or, as some prefer, literary nonfiction) and short stories. But poets, novelists, and magazine writers may profitably thumb it for the reason that a well-stocked toolbox of craft strategies and creative approaches can be taken into any genre or form.

And we writers do proliferate forms. Some of our best essayists are poets; our best poets write novels upon occasion. Creative nonfictions use the techniques of fiction, and in the world of literary culture, hybrid forms are rampant. The best magazine writers play words as if they were notes, just as poets do. The best essayists can out-jump-cut the best short-story writers: film has entranced us all. And so it goes.

I am a writer in several of these genres: poetry, creative nonfiction, fiction, and essay, including history and science. My own history has been to cross genres: my poet's ear gets into my prose, and subject matters mutate from poem to paragraph.

The Writer's Portable Mentor is here to guide you through six areas of vital concern to the practicing writer:

basic productivity
language work
training in observation
grasping and employing deep story structures
developing sophisticated (rather than habitual) sentencing skills
the regular practice of completing works and publishing them

Here's what you can expect from each of these areas:

Basic Productivity. Creative work is, first of all, work. The artist, wrote Katherine Anne Porter, "must roll up his sleeves and get to work like a bricklayer."* We writers commit to a work process—a daily work process—without any guarantee of artistic or commercial success (except of course we expect to be paid for commissioned work). Creativity studies have shown that high-achieving creators produce not only more masterworks than do average creators, but also more duds.† Even Picasso produced duds. In other words, high-achieving creators produce more. They have learned how to work. This interesting fact should encourage us to give priority to the daily work habit and to push away anxieties about whether or not this piece will be any good.

But the more skilled we become at our craft, the better we get at realizing works—completing them and making them good. "Nothing we create," writes the novelist Walter Mosley, "is art at first. It is simply a collection of notions that may never be understood. Returning every day thickens the atmosphere. Images appear. Connections are made."‡

* Quoted in Tufte and Stewart, *Grammar as Style*, vii.
† Simonton, "Historiometric Perspective," 122.
‡ Mosley, "For Authors, Fragile Ideas," 163–64.

The Writer's Portable Mentor utilizes timed writing in a note-book—called writing practice or discovery writing—to guarantee productivity. In this practice, developed by Natalie Goldberg in *Writing Down the Bones* and by Peter Elbow in *Writing Without Teachers*, the writer writes continuously without stopping for an amount of time (five minutes, ten minutes, a half-hour) set on a timer. Writing practice can be used to observe, to question a character ("What do you want?"), to write a scene, to conceptualize the next step or the next work, to write a character's backstory, to write from the point of view of a non-point-of-view character (to discover how this character actually views the situation rather than just faking his or her dialogue lines), to uncover memories, to write the entire draft of a book review, essay, or chapter. And despite how wired we all are, there are good reasons—from lack of distractibility to how much more of our brain we use when writing by hand versus tapping keys—to keep using (or start using) an old-fashioned writer's notebook along with our computer.

Language Work. If you love literature, if you aspire to art, then the clay you work is language. *The Writer's Portable Mentor* contains practices that will get you nearer to language and help you gather more language to work with. This is not about strutting big words, but about working with clicks and knocks (sound), pewter and copper (color), the vowel scale. To work with language is to make like Adam and put a name on a thing. Is that a tree or is it a black walnut tree? To work with language is to reach back in time to get a word root, to thus deepen the felt layers of meaning. A *flagrant* violation (from Latin *flagrare*, to burn) has fire in it. It is a conspicuous violation—it burns brightly. Feeling the heat of the old fire burning inside *flagrant*, we can then start to play with the word. Something flagrant is neither subtle nor hidden nor moderate. It may be hot; surely it is not frozen. We might speak of flagrant red hair or a flagrant display of hubris in launching a rogue war, but flagrant ice cream is oxymoronic and a flagrant bonfire is redundant. Just so, *mellifluous* (L. *mell*, honey; flowing) has honey in it. We writers collect words. We work with sound.

We repeat words as if they were notes. We look up the root, and then, given the word's ancient meaning, we play.

Training in Observation. Visual artists train themselves to see by drawing whatever is in front of their eyes. Some visual artists, including abstract painters not known for drawing, draw for years and years. As writers we can likewise train ourselves to see by writing whatever is in front of our eyes. The Here and Now assignment, in which you sit and write what your sense organs receive, without opinion or comment, comes to us from the visual arts. It can be used to observe a street, a person, a river, a jazz band. Other observation exercises in *The Writer's Portable Mentor*, such as Observing Gesture, are variations of the Here and Now assignment.

Good writing incorporates acute observation. It renders concrete detail in place of received opinion and general language. Good writers can become better writers by training themselves in observation as visual artists do.

Deep Story Structure. There's a dynamic—a dialectic if you will—between writing freely and continuously in your writing-practice notebook to discover what it is you have to say and writing into a specific structure (a dramatic narrative structure, say, or a twenty-part collage) to create a finished piece. You want that structure, even though you may be clueless as to what it will be when you begin. (Alternatively, you can assign yourself a given structure, much as a poet assigns himself or herself to write a sonnet. Prose can be as formal as poetry. If you begin with a given form, then the job is to find among your own concerns the content that feels right for that form.)

But let's say you know what you want to write, but you don't know how to shape it. To write without a structure is to be lost in the woods. It's okay to be lost, but not for long. The skilled, prolific, professional writers among us are writing into structures. That is the way to save yourself from years of frustration.

The Writer's Portable Mentor explores four different "story structures" (applicable to short fictions and nonfictions) including the dramatic story structure. This dramatic structure is still common and many professional writers spend their careers exploring its protean possibilities. But in our era, other structures are also proliferating. Here we take a look at three other structures: the theme structure, the collage structure, and the A/B (two-strand) structure. Beyond these specific forms, we strategize on how to go about structuring anything you might be writing, from essay to cookbook to memoir to novel.

I myself love to work on assignment. I complete the assignments I give to my classes, which comprise adult writers, and hand in my homework to class members as they hand in their homework to me. Often, in the Advanced Short Forms Seminar, these are structure assignments: write a collage, write a story using the dramatic structure employed by Steve Almond in his short story "A Dream of Sleep," write a one-sentence story that is one thousand words long. One way to advance the project of creating a body of work is to take each suggested structure as an assignment, perhaps putting each form to use two or three times. But note this: the word *assignment* does not mean doing a piece for practice. We do our assignment (and *do* get our practice). Then we go on to revise the piece, send it out, and ultimately see it published.

Sentencing Skills. Consciously shaping sentences to reflect and intensify their meanings is a high skill that most of us could stand to further hone. The great writers have mastered the sentence forms—simple, compound, compound-complex—and use them fluidly. I am thinking of William H. Gass and Maya Angelou. I am thinking of Cormac McCarthy. I am thinking of Mary Oliver and John Berger and James Baldwin. I am thinking of Robert Bringhurst.

This work is about manipulating the form of the sentence so that it both says what it means and performs, incorporates, or enacts its meaning. Here a nasty fight takes place in a boxing ring. As the boxers jab, so the sentence jabs:

> They charge. Their heads jab like boxing-gloves. They kick and spit and bite.
>
> (Jean Toomer, *Cane*, 67)

What difference does syntax make? Who cares whether you use a fragment or a simple sentence or a compound sentence? The answer is that a sentence emits a feel that derives in part from its structure. Consider this compound sentence from the Book of Psalms:

> The Lord is my shepherd; I shall not want.
>
> (Psalm 23)

To my ear the biblical sentence (like those found in the sacred writings of many faiths) carries a kind of solemn authority. What is the craft technique behind this solemn authority? It is, I believe, the form of the compound sentence.

The process of composing sentences consciously tends to begin slowly, involve a few frustrating moments, and become increasingly pleasurable—even gratifying—as you see your work gain in muscle and clarity.

Completing Works and Publishing Them. At a certain point, beginning to publish is an essential component of doing creative work. And that means sending it out, exposing it. We all get rejections. But work never sent out is never finished. Hidden from the world, it remains safely (and sadly) on the writer's shelf. There are strategies and values that inform the process of putting work into the world. The last section of *The Writer's Portable Mentor* considers effective practices toward becoming a published, visible writer, a writer whose work takes its place in the world.

Throughout all this work, our core strategy, our quintessential tool, is to learn craft from models of virtuoso writing. We read because we are readers, but we reread because we are writers. We scrutinize sentences, beginnings, deep structures, ways of bringing characters onstage. Robert Louis Stevenson said, "I have played the sedulous ape to Hazlitt, to Lamb, to Wordsworth, to Sir Thomas Browne, to Defoe, to Baudelaire, and to Obermann. . . . That, like it or not, is the way to learn to write."* In this way we keep learning, down through all our years of writing. Our best teachers are the masterworks we scrutinize.

But what, you may ask, is the difference between this and plagiarism? Particularly because we are looking so closely at models, it's important to be excruciatingly conscious of acquiring technique while leaving alone image, word, and idea. I may write using a compound sentence (a form, a deep structure), but I may not use *your* compound sentence. I may read Tom Andrews's masterpiece seventy-six-part collage titled "Codeine Diary," and thus inspired, set out to write one myself. I will look closely at how he carries forward in chronological order a single childhood story, intermixed with hospital and dirt-bike experiences.

But in my writing, I will not use any word or phrase or idea appearing in his work. His work is my teacher for the moment, but the subject matter I choose to do my work in will be worlds away. And in the end, my collage may well end up with forty parts or with eighty-three parts because it will begin to exert its own demands.

Will constant close reading weaken or sabotage your own voice? Only if you read one or two writers exclusively and try to write like them all the time. "Raymond Carver" voices were common during the 1980s. But these Carver imitators did not love Colette (an opposite sort of voice). They were reading Carver and not reading Maya Angelou. Not to mention not reading Alice Adams, Tobias Wolff, or Jean Rhys. No matter what your own aesthetic, whether minimal or maximal, whether spare or lush, or some of each, it helps to read beyond it into other aesthetics and even to dabble in other aesthetics in your own writing.

To develop our own voice, we write truthfully, and in detail. We strive for extreme accuracy. We use our own material, whatever we discover that to be. We write about whatever is central to who we are

---

* Quoted in Hendrickson, *Literary Life*, 3.

in this world. We work out our own thoughts in our own words, not to please, not to impress, but to discover what it is that we have to say.

From models we take strategy, structure, and technique. The fact that we are working our own most urgent material acts as counterweight to the model and ultimately allows us to pull it away altogether, with only scents or hints of the model extant in the new work.

Writing is hard work, but the more you sink into it, the more pleasurable it becomes. The more absorbing it becomes. Yes, there are times of frustration. Perhaps the essay you are working on refuses to lie down. Perhaps twenty publishers have rejected your memoir. Perhaps your novel has bogged down and you're clueless how to finish it. Ambition is always fraught with anxiety. But the more you work along, steady as a gardener or a baker or a cake decorator, the more writing repays you. It takes on its own life. It's a way of looking at the world, a way of living in the world. On some days—despite all the talk of sweating bullets and opening veins—it becomes its own kind of happiness.

HOW TO USE THIS BOOK

If you are like me, you will read the last chapter first. Then you will read the acknowledgments, then maybe chapter 3. This is the way to begin. But after reading *The Writer's Portable Mentor* in whatever order suits you, you may feel a bit overwhelmed. There's a lot here.

I suggest first rereading chapter 1 and taking it to heart: basic productivity underlies everything else. Then take the chapters one by one. *Actually do the exercises!* Actually begin doing the Here and Now practice. Actually begin your Lexicon. Actually write that list of ten compound sentences.

But—and this is crucial—do every exercise in relation to some piece you are working on. Don't just make up sentences on the fly, out of your head. Instead, in your writer's notebook, write out a paragraph from the piece you are working on as it currently exists. This is your "before" paragraph. Then work the paragraph, using whatever craft technique you are currently deepening (as well as any others). When you get an "after" paragraph you like, type it back into the piece.

Work on sentences the same way. Compose your list of ten sentences using, say, the adverbial clause of manner. Shape every one from the material in your piece. Make your sentences not just formally correct, as if you were taking some sort of remedial English class, but as dazzling as the model sentences you are looking at. Then fit some of these recast sentences back into the piece you are working on.

Actually doing the exercises is what will move your craft skill up to the next level. Keep in mind that it will take time to develop your ear to make a move new to you sound right. Read your new passages out loud and work on them until they sound good to your ear. No matter what level you are working at now, you will start to see your writing get better. And what a pleasure that is.

Note: For the most part, I drew the model sentences and paragraphs in *The Writer's Portable Mentor* from the works of other writers. On rare occasions I composed a passage to fit the form under discussion, and any model sentence with no author ascribed came from my own hand. Sources for all passages quoted, chapter epigraphs, and footnotes may be found in the bibliography.

PART I

Your Move

Care of the cow brings good fortune.
—*The I Ching*

I.

Daily Writing

*Practice is something done under all circumstances,
whether you're happy or sad. You don't become tossed
away by a high weekend or a blue Monday.
It is something close to you, not dependent on
high-tech gyrations or smooth workshop leader talk.
Writing is something you do quietly, regularly, and in
doing it, you face your life.*
—Natalie Goldberg

Writing every day is the key to becoming a writer. Writing every day is the key to remaining a writer. It is the only secret, the only trick. Don't despise the fifteen-minute write. Don't despise writing in your journal. Don't despise writing down your complaints for fifteen minutes before going to work. Any writing counts.

Keep a timed-writing (or writing-practice) notebook. In it, write for fifteen minutes every day. Of course on some days you will write for longer than fifteen minutes. But—and this is important—a long session one day does not apply to the next. The day after a long session, sit down once again to your fifteen minutes. Decide the night before when those fifteen minutes will be. The next day, when the time arrives, say at four o'clock in the afternoon during your coffee break, stop whatever you are doing and write. This advice does not originate with me—I got it from Dorothea Brande's *Becoming a Writer*. Ever since I read that inspiring book some thirty-five years ago, I have written every day (excepting one or two migrainous days per year). I write early in the morning, in the silence of dawn, soon after pouring that indispensable mug of strong hot coffee.

Write without stopping. Do not be concerned about being good, interesting, or correct. Writing is a discovery tool that belongs to you. If you can't think of the next thing to say, write your hesitations, write "okay, let's see, what else, well, maybe . . ." Do not lift your pen into the air. (What would happen to a bird in flight if it stopped flapping its wings?) Do not rush, do not stop. Write continuously for fifteen minutes. You can continue if you want, or you can stop. It is not better to continue. It is not better to stop.

Writing in your notebook for fifteen minutes a day is a practice that continues no matter what article or book you are working on, no matter where you are with that poem or novel. In other words, the timed writing in the notebook is not superseded by work undergoing revision on the computer.

Writing practice in your notebook underlies all your other writing. It keeps you connected to your writing no matter what else is going on in your life. It keeps you connected to the external world and to your interior life. It provides you with a resource base, ever expanding, out of which you produce finished pieces.

It keeps you generating new writing. It forever eliminates the sporadic work habit. It recognizes that generating new work is qualitatively different from rewriting, and that both need consistent attention. The fifteen-minute write makes the difference between being a writer and wishing to be a writer. It makes the difference between being an author who no longer writes and a writer who may also be an author but who still takes up the pen every day, for better or for worse. Writing practice moots the concept "writer's block."

I have found that fifteen minutes is not a token span of time. I once had a client who wrote for two hours every day for about five years. She was really making progress! But then she underwent a major, exciting career change and took on massive new professional responsibilities. There was no way she could get to her two hours. Sadly, she stopped writing for a decade. Fifteen minutes is obtainable. It's obtainable whether you are a physician with a grueling schedule or a working mom with three toddlers (or both).

The fifteen minutes is not token, I've found, because it keeps you connected to what you are working on, no matter what your current circumstances. In a busy life, a week and then two weeks can go by in no time at all, with little or no writing done. The practice of writing for fifteen minutes per day simply deletes this problem.

Why a notebook? Why not a computer or your device? I argue that we writers should keep on using or begin to use a nonelectronic notebook, that quaint old thing with pages sewn together that asks to be written in by hand. We should keep using our computers and devices of course. But we should also carry a notebook.

A notebook is quiet. It does not ding or ping. It does not deliver texts. It does not serve as a phone, calendar, clock, weather forecaster, or means to chat. It does not enable you to interrupt yourself to look up something on the internet, leading to something else, leading to . . . we all know how that goes. It does not provide access to social media. Writing in a notebook, we are with our own thoughts, our own words, our own observations, our own spellings, our own hesitations, our own ways of saying things. Time in the notebook is quiet time, time with our own plans, dreams, thoughts, lists of plants or types of dogs seen on the walk today. A notebook has no spcllchcck. It cannot reformat. It cannot be lost in the cloud (it can be lost on a bus). And later you can sit quietly and turn its pages (different from scrolling) and underline interesting ideas or observations for later use. A notebook allows for a different type of thought process. And shaping letters, writing words by hand, actually activates more parts of the brain than does tapping a key, according to the latest neuroscientific findings.*

Mind you, I am quite wired. I have bonded with my laptop. Even though I write daily in a notebook, I have some eight thousand Word files containing my writing, all on my laptop. I also carry and use a

---

* For starters, see Maria Konnikova, "What's Lost as Handwriting Fades," *New York Times*, June 3, 2014, D-1; May, "A Learning Secret."

device. I am subject to the dings, the texts, the urge to look it up. I know the territory.

But I also savor the daily connection of hand to page, body to page, breath to page that comes from writing by hand. Norman Mailer said, "It's hard to explain how agreeable it is to do one's writing in longhand. You feel that all of your body and some of your spirit has come down to your fingertips."* A quick internet search brings up numbers of writers who compose by hand—Joyce Carol Oates, John Irving, Andre Dubus III, to mention three. The brilliant Lauren Groff composes the first ten to twelve drafts of a novel by hand.† So, despite the electronics revolution, we writers, many of us, still compose by hand. And not just the old, the Luddite, the clueless.

I encourage you to purchase a notebook, a nice notebook, not too heavy, one that opens flat and has pages you like. Then you must purchase the perfect pen. Now you are all set to write in that notebook every day.

The writing done in writing practice can be about anything. It can be a journal-write (here I differ with one of the originators, Natalie Goldberg). It can be an observation exercise. It can be work on an essay, story, article, or scene. It can be used to conceptualize new work. ("The story I want to write next is . . ." Set your timer and write.)

Often I hear, "I'm sick of moaning and complaining in my journal." There is no need to moan and complain (I enjoy doing so once in a while) and there is no need "to journal" at all if you are sick of it. Writing in your journal can involve describing what is in front of you. Describe the gooseneck lamp, the pile of books, the turned mahogany-wood mug bristling with pens. Do a recapitulation in which you detail the previous day from beginning to end (an exercise from Ira Progoff's *The Journal Workshop*). Or set the timer, begin a short essay, and write it straight to the end for a fast first draft. Or write for fifteen minutes

---

*   Mailer, "Generations," 5.

†   Charlie Rose interview with Lauren Groff, January 20, 2016, https://www.youtube.com/watch?v=90t3Qo3to3g.

a single unpunctuated sentence that begins, "What I want to do with my life is . . ." That's what Buckminster Fuller did before going on to become Buckminster Fuller.

There are ways to shape your writing practice so that it better serves your own goals.

- In your notebook, begin each practice session on a new page. (Do not run the sessions into one another.) Date each session and when you're finished, if obvious, give the writing a descriptive title or label (Thoughts on Cloning, Remembering Susanne). These labels become clarifying when you are looking back through your notebooks for themes, concerns, bits of writing.
- If you are working on a story, essay, review, or other piece in your writing-practice notebook, type what you've written as soon as you can, the same day if possible. Soon after you've handwritten a scene, type that scene. Then draw a line through the handwritten version. You can still read it but you know it's typed—superseded.
- Observation exercises should be part of every writer's practice. Every time you go to a new city or a new country, do the Observing the Here and Now exercise (see page 38). Spend fifteen minutes describing your teenager. If you are a teenager, spend fifteen minutes describing your parent. Go to a coffeehouse and do the Observing Gesture exercise (see page 49), an exercise that trains you to observe and describe body language.
- Plan. Conceptualize new work. Organize your day. Where would you like to be as a writer a year from now? What pieces or chapters do you plan to complete this month?
- Join or start a writing-practice group, which is entirely different from a critique group.

The Writing-Practice Group. Every Tuesday and Friday at Seattle's Wayward Coffeehouse at 65th and Roosevelt, at 2:00 p.m. or a bit after, the writers gather. Everyone is welcome. (We buy coffee, or have lunch beforehand. We want this establishment to stay in business.) Seattle authors and master-teachers Jack Remick and Robert J. Ray, friends of Natalie Goldberg, established this writing practice (at a different coffeehouse) nearly thirty years ago.

Each arriving writer writes a start line on a piece of paper and puts it on the table. For example: "Her lips were blue" or "He slammed the door" or "I lied." At 2:30 sharp the writers begin writing, all using the same start line. (You soon discover that you can quickly go from any start line to any piece you want to work on.) When the timer goes off, each writer reads, in turn. There are no comments and there is no feedback—different from a critique group. After the writers read exactly what they have written, in all its roughness, the timer is reset and the writers resume writing. There are several cycles of this, and then everyone goes home or back to work.

Writing-practice groups vary start lines and vary the segments of writing time. One way is to write for five minutes, ten minutes, twenty minutes, and then five minutes. In another way, the writers begin, "Today I am writing about . . ." and proceed. Everyone writes for forty-five minutes. To make the reading time manageable, this group might split into two reading groups.

You can do writing practice with one or two buddies. One of my writing buddies and I used to meet at a café to write. We alternated making up assignments for ourselves. One time we decided to describe for one hour without stopping a philodendron that sat between us. We did so, and we were astonished at how much there was to see in this common household plant.

The above-mentioned Jack Remick and Robert J. Ray have written several entire books during writing practice, scene by scene, chapter by chapter. After writing practice they go home and type up what they have written, and work on it further. I think I should repeat that. After writing practice *they go home and type up what they have written* because they are using writing practice to produce completed, polished, and ultimately published work.

Use your writing-practice group to further your own purposes. Don't write passively, don't write to please others at the table. Write to play or explore when that's what you want to do. Other times, work on your story, novel, essay, or review. Then go home and type.

Hands On: Jump Starting an Essay or Story

Do this exercise today. Do not put it off. Do it to give yourself the next thing to work on as you are working through the rest of *The Writer's Portable Mentor*. This exercise will plunge you into the work of writing a piece. No more chewing on the pencil. No more staring at the page or the computer screen. In the space of an hour, the exercise generates a rough draft, gives you something first to type and then to work on. In this exercise you set the timer and write through your hesitations. Do this by yourself or do it with a writing buddy or in a writing-practice group. Write continuously without stopping. If you become stuck, write, "I am stuck" or write out your hesitations: "Let's see, what else do I want to say, perhaps . . ." Don't stop writing and don't worry about being correct or neat or about whether or not it's going to be any good. Just write without pausing or lifting your pen from the page.

1. Five minutes—I want to write an essay (story) on . . . (In this write, spin out a number of ideas.)
2. Five minutes—The essay that attracts me most right now is . . .
3. Ten minutes—List ten items, in no particular order, that I certainly would want to cover in this essay. Note that this one is not precisely a writing practice because you are making a list, and you can pause.
4. Five minutes—Take the most interesting thing on the list and write on it for five minutes. Then take another item and write on it for five minutes. Then another.
5. Five minutes—Does this piece have a central dramatic

conflict? If so, what is it? Who is the antagonist? What is at
stake?

6. Five minutes—If the piece has a dramatic conflict, write a
   trial opening paragraph that contains this conflict.

7. Five minutes—How is the conflict resolved?

8. Five minutes—What does the main person in question (protagonist if it's a story, the "I" if memoir) *do* to resolve the
   conflict?

9. Ten minutes—What important questions emerge from this
   subject matter? (If this is fiction, what are the character's
   questions? What are your questions about the character?)

10. Now go home and type up these "writes." Leave a good
    amount of space between each paragraph—put them in
    chronological order if you want—but at this point you have
    not necessarily discovered an order.

This exercise will give you a draft of a story or essay to work on.
In the space of an hour or two you will be much further along than
you would be by chewing on your fingernails for that same amount of
time. You're on your way!

2.

Working with Language

And so in the last light, at the end of the day, what
matters is language.
—*Eavan Boland*

It is remarkable how many virtuoso prose writers are also poets. I am thinking of Mary Oliver, Anne Carson, Seamus Heaney, Amit Majmudar, Eavan Boland, John Haines, Maya Angelou, John Updike, Anne Michaels, Thomas Lynch, et al. These poets collect words the way some numismatists collect coins. They work sounds constantly and consciously. The music in their prose functions as a magnet to draw readers into their thoughts, memories, reflections, reports. The music vibrates in the lines but it's not rock music; it's a subtext, a whisper that runs along under the text, inaudible to readers with no need to concern themselves with the technical aspects of writing they love.

This chapter is about how to get nearer to language. It is about how to vastly increase your resource base in the language, and how to play words like music.

GATHERING WORDS

I have known writers who have worked hard for years doing pretty good work. They may aspire to art, but the writing never comes close to the most brilliant writing being done today. All that hard work should give more back to the writer, yet the quality of writing remains merely competent.

Often this hard-working writer is approaching language passively,

different from the way Barry Lopez or Arundhati Roy or Ben Okri
approaches language. This writer is using only words that come to
mind, or words he grew up with, or words she stumbles upon while
reading the *New York Times*. Naturally this writer looks up the occasional unfamiliar word in a dictionary, as any educated person would
do. But he strives for expression with rather general, conventional diction that has little to offer in the way of echo, color, or texture. Unlike
J. A. Baker:

> The northern slope is open woodland, rusty with winter
> bracken, silvered with birches, green with mossy oak.
>
> > (J. A. Baker, *The Peregrine*, 79)

Nothing fancy here, but Baker's concrete language and his use of color
make the sentence glow.

The writers of deep and beautiful works spend real time gathering
words. They learn the names of weeds and tools and types of roof.
They work to overcome plant blindness—the tendency to see plants
as green background instead of as individual organisms, each with a
name. They make lists of color words (ruby, scarlet, cranberry, brick).
They savor not only the meanings, but also the musicality of words.
They are hunting neither big words nor pompous words nor latinate
words but mainly words they like. They are not "improving their
vocabulary" or studying for the SAT or the GRE. They are not trying to be fancy or decorative. This is a different kind of thing. Annie
Proulx:

> I use an old Webster's unabridged. I do collect dictionar-
> ies, and I do read them, and I do keep word lists, and I do
> make notes of language. I have big notebooks, page after
> page of words that I like or find interesting or crackly, or
> whatever. And from time to time I will also, if I feel a section
> is a bit limp, take a couple of days and just do dictionary
> work and recast the sentences so that they have more power

because their words aren't overused. Often the search for the right word can consume a lot of time, but usually it can be found.*

First-rate writers get an enormous amount of capital out of putting accurate names on things. Take a glimpse of the third-floor walk-up where Leo, a character in a Don DeLillo story, lives with his ex-wife:

> There was the long metal bar of the old police lock set into its floor niche inches from the front door. There was the tall narrow radiator, a relic, unscreened, with a pan set beneath the shutoff valve to collect the drip. At times he stared into the columns of the radiator, thinking whatever he was thinking, none of it reducible to words.
> There was the cramped bathroom they shared, where his broad bottom could barely wedge itself between the tub and the wall and onto the toilet seat.
> (Don DeLillo, "The Starveling," 189)

DeLillo's language gets its freshness from its accuracy. I like *long metal bar of the old police lock* and *floor niche* and *radiator* and *pan* and *shutoff valve*. Not to mention Leo's broad bottom . . .

Here, Arundhati Roy, in her first novel, portrays the grandmother. She is sitting in the old house on the hill, at the dining table, rubbing a cucumber:

> She was wearing a limp, checked seersucker nightgown with puffed sleeves and yellow turmeric stains. Under the table she swung her tiny, manicured feet, like a small child on a high chair. They were puffy with edema, like little foot-shaped air cushions.
> (Arundhati Roy, *The God of Small Things*, 21)

---

* Upchurch, *Glimmer Train Guide*, 248.

Roy specifies seersucker, puffed sleeves, yellow turmeric stains. The tiny swollen feet, which, it turns out, the grandmother is quite proud of.

Open any anthology of excellent stories or essays. How many town names, street names, restaurant names, dog names, actual prices, actual dates, proper names of person or place do you see? Yet these pieces eschew writing that is merely decorative. They are vibrant with nouns and verbs:

> The first time I saw her she was walking on Sunset between
> the XXX Movie Theater and the Saigon Restaurant.
> (Dagoberto Gilb, "Brisa," 103)

DICTION PRIMER

Concrete words are words that can be perceived through a sense organ: eyes, nose, skin, tongue, ears. You can always specify *which* sense organ has perceived a concrete word (*yellow*: eyes; *rotten eggs*: nose). Proper names are concrete. A proper name can turn general words like *street* or *river* into specific concrete words: *Everett Avenue*; the *Nooksack River*. Because you are perceiving through one of your sense organs, what you are perceiving is typically one thing. You can't see "rivers." You *can* see the Duwamish River. You can see the Snake and Columbia rivers at their confluence. You can't see "cities" but you can see Chicago.

Abstract words like *love* or *inscrutable* or *freedom* cannot be perceived through a sense organ.

There are, it seems to me, degrees of concretion. Thus *yellow* is concrete (you perceive it through your eyes). But *mustard-yellow* or *yellow ocher* are more concrete (the words make a closer match to the actual color).

To put a person or place on the page, we amass concrete words that pertain to that person or that place. Here is Jonathan Raban, writing (by pure linguistic coincidence) about Concrete, Washington, a small industrial town north of Seattle. Raban is writing in 1995 in the ecologically aroused Pacific Northwest. Concrete returns him to the 1970s:

> Concrete people were still smokers. In the bars, drifts of pungent violet fog threw the pool players into soft focus. The Saturday-night crowd of broad-beamed folk put one in mind of corn dogs, Jo-Jos, and tubs of chocolate-chip-cookie-dough ice cream. The bars were monuments to local sport and industry. Their walls were hung with rusty two-man saws, with mirrors advertising the Winchester Repeating Arms Company alongside Michelob and Budweiser, with antlers, stags' heads, and the pinned-out skins of wildcats. No bar in Concrete was properly a bar without a stuffed lynx or bobcat, its back arched, its right-hand foreclaws raised against the viewer, its jaws wide open for the kill.
>
> (Jonathan Raban, "Last Call of the Wild," 209)

Less skilled writers tend to use many more abstract, general words like *gentle* or *abuse* than do first-rate writers. But concrete details put in for their own sake can be distracting. Sometimes a character can simply get in a car and drive away; to learn that the car is a red Honda Civic coupe may do nothing to further the story. Some writers—I think of the poet Mark Strand—use *car* and *tree* to great effect.

Think of a detail as an index to something else—a situation, a character trait, an era. A man's mismatched socks may index his lifestyle (up early to do the milking, nobody here but the cows). A town's boarded-up Main Street—hard times. A sweetgum tree's red and orange leaves—autumn.

How much language to use is the writer's choice, always. But to use a limited vocabulary because in reality you only command a limited vocabulary produces a result entirely different from what you might produce in a spare style spun out of an ample and ever-growing word list.

WHERE TO FIND GOOD WORDS

No writer should be without a Very Large dictionary. Would you hire a carpenter to build you a house who had for tools a single pair of pliers? Would you begin a cross-country road trip with one gallon of gas in the tank? No you wouldn't, but many writers go for years with nothing more in hand than their little college dictionary.

Hint for the true fanatic: The very largest Very Large dictionary, and the most delicious, is *Webster's New International Dictionary*, Second Edition, Unabridged, with a 1934 copyright. Note that it's the second edition we want. (The sensible, cost-conscious, and ever so *reasonable* editors of the third edition dumped one hundred thousand words.)

The 1934, second edition of this dictionary has six hundred thousand words. It has words like croodle, which is mildly obsolete but which feels comfortable with cradle or crook and which can be brought back into use. This dictionary even has extra words on the bottom of each page, and numerous words come with elaborate illustrations (a wooden sailing ship, with every rope, spar, and crossbeam named). It can be had for a fairly large chunk of change on the used-book market. (Some time in 2005 I bought mine for $60, a steal. I bought another as a wedding gift for two dear writer friends for $125.)

As you know, *The Oxford Dictionary of the English Language* is also an indispensable resource. This dictionary traces a word back to when it first entered English (a Germanic language that came into existence in the centuries after Germanic tribes, including Angles, invaded England in the fifth century and suppressed the Celt-speaking Britons). The dictionary gives instances of a word's use from its earliest appearance to the present. The verb *to write* for example can be found in an old English sentence of the year 835: "This mid episcopus rodetacne [ic] festnie & write." Many university and public libraries subscribe to *The Oxford Dictionary of the English Language*. The Seattle Public Library, for example, provides it online to anyone who has a (free) library card.

At least one ample, argumentative grammar-and-usage book is a necessity, since most dictionaries describe but do not prescribe. Usage manuals prescribe. They fight to retain the difference between *insure* and *ensure*, between *that* and *which*, between *alumnae* and *alumni*. They insist and recapitulate that *and* and *but* are excellent ways to begin a sentence, favored by first-rate writers the world over, approved and even advocated by even the most conservative grammarians. The original Fowler's (*A Dictionary of Modern English Usage* by H. W. Fowler) is an entertaining and enlightening read. For a contemporary work, I would not be without my *Garner's Modern American Usage* by Bryan A. Garner. It is also essential to have a grammar book. One I like is *The Deluxe Transitive Vampire* by Karen Elizabeth Gordon.

What guidebooks are to the world traveler, dictionaries, grammars, and usage manuals are to the writer. But gathering words should take you beyond these reference works to other compendiums of words. Clothing catalogs name clothes (chinos, cords, boot-cut jeans). Tool catalogs—try leevalley.com—name tools (ripsaw, bucksaw, coping saw, band saw). Go to an art store for types of brushes and names of pigments (bone black, burnt umber). Go to the United States Geological Survey for geographical features (shrub-steppe, bog, slough) and for spooky proper names such as the Great Dismal Swamp. You get the idea.

THE LEXICON PRACTICE

For most virtuoso writers, collecting words is a definite, specific, regular habit. Leonardo da Vinci ended up with more than nine thousand words in his lexicon.* James Joyce gathered words and phrases in a fat notebook: after he used one in the book he was writing—*Ulysses*—he would cross it out.† Mary Oliver ventures outdoors with pen and pad,

---

* Gelb, *Leonardo da Vinci*, 73.
† "Ireland Buys a Trove of Joyce Notebooks," *New York Times*, May 31, 2002, E5.

ready to record any bug or old bone. If such writers do their lexicon work, so also should we.

What I call the Lexicon Practice is the specific process by which you put actual time—regular time—into collecting words and phrases. There are two parts to the practice. One is to make your own Lexicon (word book) and the other is to collect words and phrases in a list that pertains to the piece you are currently working on. I call this second part the word trap, because trapping words is like trapping fish in a net. The words are out there. Time to bring them in.

I have been teaching these practices for two decades and what impresses me is how I can, years later, read the writing of a former student and tell whether or not she is doing the Lexicon Practice. I can tell by her writing. Writers who do the Lexicon Practice have left in the dust what I call "conventional received diction." Writers who don't do it in one way or another are pretty much stuck with television words, newspaper words, cereal-box words.

Conventional received diction is the language of belief rather than the language of recorded sensory experience. For example, to speak of "buying a home" rather than "buying a house" or better, "buying a California bungalow" is to speak in the conventional diction of the real-estate business. This term is based not on sense perception but on an agenda: if we long for a home then we will be more likely to "buy a home" than to "buy a house." To speak of hair color as blonde (or blond) is often to wander into the beige-curtained suburb of convention and stereotype rather than to put a specific person's head of hair on the page:

> Into the bay window came a woman. Stout, bleary-eyed,
> elderly, though her hair was dyed a squid-ink black.
> (Lauren Groff, *Fates and Furies*, 322)

I discovered my own form of Lexicon Practice in the following way. For twelve years during the 1970s and early 1980s, I worked as a printer in Boston. During those years I began getting up at 4 or 5 a.m. to write before leaving for work at 7. My thermos of hot strong coffee was at the ready. I would sit to write in my nightgown and robe; my big old black-and-white cat, Frisky, would jump into my lap and curl up and watch my moving pen with intense interest, occasionally batting it with his paw. My then-husband, Peter Irons, would be fast asleep in the next room. A carpenter friend had made me a simple, built-in, L-shaped desk with a black-Formica handwriting surface and, to my right, when I swiveled the chair, a place for my IBM Selectric typewriter. I will never forget the pleasure of those silent mornings of writing.

At the time I had written nothing about my childhood growing up on a dairy farm on the Eastern Shore of Maryland. That part of who I was was put away: perhaps I was not ready to face the traumas of childhood. In any case my friends, pals, coworkers, comrades, and various buddies had all emerged from radically different backgrounds. Childhood was for me a distant country. But for unknown reasons, words began coming to me, and I began entering them into a black-and-white composition notebook. I titled my notebook *Memories of Underdevelopment* after the great Cuban film of that name. During a season of winter mornings I filled the notebook with the language of my childhood, words with no currency whatever in my postchildhood life—greenbriar, dirt road, Neil Lindsey's pig, 4-H Club, teats, stanchions, silage, milkers, mastitis, calf barn, gutter, manure pile, manure spreader, marsh grass, muck, eels, eel trap, watermen, field hands, tizzylish cake . . . What amazed me was how the words themselves held that time and that place. I went on to remember small stories, which became "Snapshots: The Eastern Shore of Maryland," which ultimately appeared in *North Dakota Quarterly*. That first lexicon was for me a turning point as a writer.

And the point is that every childhood has a lexicon. Place names, certain trees and buildings, the toys of 1934 versus the toys of 1964 versus the toys of 1984, they all make vivid a particular place, a particular era, a particular person, a particular experience. It is astonishing how much language itself holds, with no meanings added by the writer, no interpretations, no sentences, no writing.

Hands On: Make Your Own Lexicon

Buy a small bound and sewn blank book, with fine paper. This is your Lexicon.

Put in words you like, words that strike your fancy, words you want to own. I suggest giving each word half a page. Put in the word—lickspittle—and draw a horizontal line dividing the page in half. This way you can put in a word and look it up later. (Under lickspittle write: a contemptible, fawning person; a flatterer or toady.) You will end up with two words per page.

This is not a typical vocabulary list full of horrible latinate words you don't know and don't want to know.

The rule is, put in only the good words, the juicy words, the hot words. From time to time, savor this book. Look up words you've put in (something from your reading) and haven't looked up yet. Be sure to investigate the root. Put in familiar words along with new words. Play with sounds, right in your Lexicon: kitchen matches, cord/weird/word, fired/turd.

From time to time read a big dictionary hunting for a new word, a good word, any word that strikes your fancy: galoot.

On some pages make word lists. Fiddle parts—peg box, button, side rib, bridge. Words for blue—cobalt, woad, sapphire, smalt. Words from an art exhibition you especially loved—bone, tin plate; cotton, cord, silk ribbon, silver, galloon; coconuts, shells, ostrich eggs (from Moscow Treasures).

Put down things you don't know the names of. Do you know the parts of a window? (Muntin? Sash? Top rail?) Do you know the parts of a rocking chair? Draw or describe the thing in your Lexicon and then set about looking (in a book on house repairs or on furniture) for splat or spindle or stile. Do not order your list in any way. If you try to order it alphabetically, you will have nowhere to put words that sound good together and you will have nowhere to draw an object—a tool or roof or chair—that you will later put a name to. Do you know the names of the weeds in your garden? Look in Alexander C. Martin's

Golden Guide to Weeds. Identify the ones you see—spatterdock, chickweed, pokeweed. Write them in your Lexicon.

Do nothing more. Do not try to force the words into your writing. Just work on the Lexicon on a regular basis, as a form of play. It is remarkable how the words you put in your own Lexicon have a way of creeping into your writing.

Your Lexicon becomes part of the resource base you create for yourself as a writer. We writers accumulate large vocabularies that are constantly expanding. We take pleasure in learning the names for things. The Lexicon holds new words and words that please you. It forever ends the in-one-ear-out-the-other problem as it pertains to putting a name on a thing.

The Lexicon is a blank book with a pleasing feel, a permanent little book that you keep beside your dictionaries. Eventually you will accumulate several Lexicons. It's fun to play with them, of an evening, to look up a word, to list the kinds of stones or guns or stars or brooms.

Hands On: Make a Word Trap

The second part of the Lexicon Practice is to make a word trap—a list of one hundred or more words or phrases—for every story or essay, not to mention novel, you work on. Most items on the list should be concrete words like *tomato* or *horse manure* that can be perceived by one of the senses. Begin by writing one hundred numbers on one hundred lines in your writer's notebook. The numbers will stretch you to keep going—past thirty words, past forty-three words. We make the word trap in the notebook because it starts out being too messy for the Lexicon, and besides, we don't necessarily want all these particular words in our Lexicon.

I work on my list before I begin a piece and during the whole time I am working on it. The list comprises language—not big words or necessarily even new words—associated with that time and place, that trade or event or person. Just making the list will help you sink deeper into the subject matter. After you've completed the list in the notebook, type it. Then work on it some more. Put words together that sound good. Keep naming things more and more accurately. And when you've finally completed the piece that this word trap pertains to, write your favorite words in your Lexicon for future reference.

For an essay called "Housekeeping" (set in my own house), I list objects in my house, for example:

> dropleaf table
> blender
> black buckram covered journal books
> lamp

Working on the list means naming things more accurately and working with sounds: I added a hyphen too, which pleases me.

> Pembroke table
> Osterizer blender
> black buckram-bound journals
> black metal gooseneck lamp

The second part of making a word trap trains your ear and gets good sounds going. Write twenty-five numbers on twenty-five lines. Each numbered item in the list will end up with two or three or four words taken from your first list. Here's the beginning of my list for a piece I am writing called "Composition in Yellow":

> 1. yellow, pall, pillowcase
> 2. yearning, urine, yams
> 3. "yellow peril," pearls, pee
> 4. sulfur, turmeric, yellow toad
> 5. pear, peach, yellow pansy
> 6. Yellow Springs; Yellowstone Park, yellow brick road
> 7. mildew, mold, buttermilk

These items sound good together. Individual words within items have no need to connect with each other in any narrative sense. I like the way *turmeric* chimes with *yellow toad* and have no clue as to whether one or both or neither will end up in the piece. The list has no need whatever to make any sense whatever.

Can a verb be concrete? Conventionally, a concrete word is a noun and indeed the usual phrase is "concrete noun." But I include verbs because I think that to *trudge* to work is more vivid and more concrete than to *go* to work or to *walk slowly* to work.

Persons have lexicons. The list alone can evoke a person with remarkable vividness. My Grandfather Henry: ice water, salted butter, Pennsylvania Dutch, "the wooden hill" (staircase) . . .

Places have lexicons. The Pacific Northwest: crow, Puget Sound, Steilacoom Tribe, western red cedar, Smith Tower, Emmett Watson's Oyster Bar, Starbucks, Northwest jellyfish, geoduck (pronounced *gooey duck*), Stillaguamish River . . .

Indeed, any subject matter is rich in lexicon, if you will but go after it, hunt it down, gather it up. Here is Sue Allison on measurement:

> A yard, a pace, a foot, a fathom. How beautiful the language
> of measurement is, and we're not even talking iambs yet.
> A fifth, a finger, a jigger, a drop, a dram, a grain, a scruple.
> A scruple is twenty grains, or twenty barley cornes. It is as
> small as a pebble.
> (Sue Allison, "Taking a Reading," 1)

Every craft, trade, profession, or job has a lexicon. You are reading a book: books have a lexicon. Here book geek (bookseller, book sales rep, book writer, book reader) Lewis Buzbee recalls how his employers at Upstart and Crow, the bookshop of his first job, sat him down to teach him the history of the book and its parts:

> First, they told me about the book itself. The right page was
> the recto, the left the verso. The pages of a hardcover were
> bound in groups called signatures; the pages of a paperback
> were cut flush and glued to the spine in a process called

perfect-binding. Gutter, colophon, deckled; the words and
terms spilled out.

(Lewis Buzbee, *The Yellow-Lighted Bookshop*, 49)

An interesting exercise is to take a passage that attracts you and
from it make a reverse lexicon—a list of its most quirky or interesting
words. This can lay bare the effects of diction (word choice) on the
piece. A reverse lexicon for Buzbee's passage would include:

book	glued
recto	spine
verso	perfect binding
hardcover	gutter
signature	colophon
flush	deckled

WORDS AS NOTES

Whenever we write, we work with sound. Every word, every sentence
emits sound. The question is, is it a musical sound, whether plain or
ornate, or is it the interminable drone of a washing machine?

Here is a sentence composed by William H. Gass:

Neat people are fascists of the mop and bucket, the tight
sheet, the silver chest.

(William H. Gass, "Lust," 291)

How neat that *neat* and *sheet* are perfect rhymes and that *people*
picks up that long *e* sound. And listen to the assonance (echoing vowel
sounds) of *mop* and *bucket*, and the swishing of *fascist* and *chest*.
Finally, we take in the tintinnabulation of terminal *t*'s in *neat*, *bucket*,
tight, *sheet*, and *chest*. Such a short sentence. Such a lot of sound work
going on.

Working sound is about creating echoes and resonances. Resonance:

intensification and prolongation of sound, especially of a musical tone, produced by sympathetic vibration.

Here's a passage from the poet Mary Oliver:

> In the lyrical poems of Robert Frost there is almost always something wrong, a dissatisfaction or distress. The poet attempts an explanation and a correction. He is not successful. But he has, often in metaphorical language, named whatever it is that disquiets·him. At the same time, in the same passages, the poem is so pleasant—so very pleasant—to read or to hear.
> (Mary Oliver, "A Man Named Frost," 49)

Listen to the alliteration (same first consonant) in *dissatisfaction, distress, disquiet*. Listen to the chime in *distress* and *successful*, to the repeated "shun" sound in *dissatisfaction, explanation, correction*. Note how repeating is one more way to make an echo. For Mary Oliver, language is a musical instrument.

And for Cormac McCarthy:

> They were starving right enough. The country was looted, ransacked, ravaged. Rifled of every crumb. The nights were blinding cold and casket black and the long reach of the morning had a terrible silence to it. Like a dawn before battle. The boy's candlecolored skin was all but translucent. With his great staring eyes he'd the look of an alien.
> (Cormac McCarthy, *The Road*, 129)

Listen to *right, ransacked, ravaged, rifled*. And to *crumb, cold, casket, black, candlecolored*, the *k* sound alliterating but also echoing within *casket* and *black* and *candlecolored*.

Here is Thomas Lynch, funeral director and poet:

> The moments spent before the mirror while tending to my toilet did nothing to lessen the lessons that Time is certainly

not on our side, nor does it heal more wounds than it opens.
The ever-retreating hairline, the whitening of one's beard
and mustache, the bleeding gums, the basal cell carcinomas,
the boils and blisters and bags under the eyes, the belly gone
soft, the withering member, the hemorrhoids and hematomas, the varicosities and local edemas, the puff, the paunch,
the wrecked version of one's former self that presents itself
most mornings, are enough to render most men suicidal.
                    (Thomas Lynch, "Sweeney Revisited," 41–42)

Listen to the wordplay in *lessen the lessons*. Listen to the alliteration
in *tending, toilet*, and *Time* and in *bleeding, basal, blisters, bags, belly*,
and further in *hemorrhoids* and *hematomas*. Listen to how *hematomas* and *edemas* assonate. What a lot of sound work going on in a
short passage.

Here is a simple sentence from Jean Rhys's masterpiece novel:

The black and gilt clock on a shelf struck four.
                        (Jean Rhys, *Wide Sargasso Sea*, 125)

The sentence sticks to plain words. But clacks the *k*'s and trills the *l*'s.
Its stark power derives in part from the fact that every word comprises
one and only one syllable.

SOUND EFFECTS

Poets know what a slant rhyme is, and poets, at least the lyrical poets,
know alliteration, assonance, the vowel scale, and various other ways
to make words echo. Here are some main types of sound effects that
are just as effective in prose, when used with a good ear. (See ahead for
a note on how to develop that good ear.)

Slant Rhyme
Slant rhyme, also called off rhyme or imperfect rhyme or near
rhyme, is not new. Emily Dickinson—who was of course way ahead

of her time—used it a lot. She would put together words like *vio-let* and *light* or *Heaven, even, given.* Slant rhyme can sound more modern than perfect rhyme (*white, height*) and modern poets use it profusely.

Here are examples of perfect rhymes followed by a slant rhyme:

some/hum	home
cash/flash	flesh or wish
flood/blood	glad or Trinidad or mood
blue/shoe	blow, maybe shawl
dust/rust	roost
change/range	orange or hinge
word/bird	bored

Alliteration

Alliteration occurs when first consonants make the same sound and thus set up an echo. Many slogans alliterate: *Power to the People.* Alliterating can be overdone and sometimes, once you begin enthusiastically alliterating, it is necessary to tone it down, to revise against it. But first, do alliterate. Here's a sentence by the novelist John Dufresne, speaking of the writer's need to keep a notebook:

My job is to jot.

(John Dufresne, "Holdalls," 116)

Assonance

Assonance is the echoing of vowel sounds. In Dufresne's sentence above, *job* and *jot* alliterate but they also assonate.

Here Barry Lopez speaks of the desert:

The last thing you will notice will be the stones, small bits of volcanic ash, black glass, blue tourmaline, sapphires, narrow slabs of grey feldspar, rose quartz, sheets of mica and blood agate.

(Barry Lopez, *Desert Notes; River Notes*, 28)

See how the *a* sounds echo in *ash, black, glass, sapphires, slabs,* and *agate* (the first *a*). That's assonance. Lopez also alliterates: *bits, black, blue,* and *blood.*

The Vowel Scale

Sounds have frequency.* Sound travels in waves that come at more frequent or less frequent intervals. The shorter the wave, the higher the frequency. Eek! is a high-frequency sound. The longer the wave, the lower the frequency. Blue is a low-frequency sound.

It is useful to think of the high-frequency vowels as high-energy vowels. Pie in the sky! Let's get high! Dream on! Scream! Hey, hey! In his great villanelle, Dylan Thomas makes conscious use of vowels high on the vowel scale: "Rage, rage against the dying of the light."

Low-frequency vowels are low-energy vowels. They bring us down. We have the blues (not the greens). We are lonely. We feel moody, we moon about, we moan and groan. We feel low.

Certain words are riveting because (I think) they combine lowest- and highest-frequency sounds and thus contain both shadow (low) and light (high): *moonlight.*

Here's your primer:

Lowest Frequency	Highest Frequency
long *o* (boo)	long *e* (bee)
long *o* (bone)	long *a* (bay)
short *o* (book)	long *i* (buy)

The Scale from Low to High
boo
bone
book
aw (thought)

---

* I am indebted to John Frederick Nims (*Western Wind*, 160–61) for the insights in this section.

oi (boy)
ow (bough)
ah (bar)
bud
bird
bat
bet
bit
buy
bay
bee

We all use the vowel scale semiconsciously (it may be partly physi-ological), but it is a delight to begin using it consciously. If your char-acter has the blues, try revising the diction of her thoughts to lower on the vowel scale. For an excited, high-energy feel, try making more words shriek naked in the night trees.

Hands On: Working with Sound

Begin working with sound. Try all kinds of sounds. Many poets eschew blatant perfect rhymes (slow, blow, show), but some writers can make them work. If this is your cup of tea, try putting the rhymes here and there rather than only at the end of lines. And use slant rhymes too. In prose and poetry, try all the sound effects. It will likely feel awkward at first, but gradually your ear will improve. The point is not to go fancy or to indulge in false rhapsody or fussy hyperdescription. The simplest-sounding prose can be playing words as notes.

- Develop your ear. Read, reread, and read out loud the lyrical writers, including the prose and poetry of lyrical poets. Keep in mind that poetics in our culture is vastly diverse: Some poets write against conventional lyricism and strive for an antilyrical voice. Other poets use engines other than sound to drive their

poems. Besides which, there's such a thing as a "prosy" poem
with diction dull and gray. This is a common fault of unrealized
poems but it may be a technique of some writers. Whatever the
case, reading them only deadens your ear. To train your ear,
read the lyric poets. Gerard Manley Hopkins is a must. Try William Butler Yeats and John Haines. Try Muriel Rukeyser. Try
Theodore Roethke, Kenneth Rexroth, and Gwendolyn Brooks.
Lyric poets all.

- Develop a keen awareness of word roots, and include them in
your Lexicon. You can chime and ding Old English words—
wood, God, bed, clock, work—much easier than latinate
words—approximately, judicious, interim, attention. But there
are no absolute rules. Use latinate words whenever you want to,
but do so with cognizance and consciousness.

- Learn the rudiments of sound effects in language. A short list
would include the vowel scale, slant rhyme, assonance, alliteration, sibilance (the s sound), and repetition. Music is related to
echo. No need to master the names of the sounds that echo in
thick and *smoke*, but find them and use them.

- Sentences that have lists in them are a prime place to work
sound. Consider this one composed by Ben Okri. Note how
weird, *wounded*, and *wonderful* alliterate and how *d* sounds
echo:

> The bar saw its most unusual congregation of the weird,
> the drunk, the mad, the wounded, and the wonderful.
> (Ben Okri, *The Famished Road*, 89)

- Take something you are working on, that you have on your
computer. Take one of your paragraphs and write it by hand
back into your writing-practice notebook. Consider it a
"before" paragraph. Now work it to hone sound (and accuracy). Then type the changes back into the piece itself. Keep
on doing this, paragraph by paragraph. Here is a paragraph I
worked about the German Expressionist artist Gabriele Münter.

Before
A forceful and original artist, Münter was socially inse-
cure, and in her relationship with Kandinsky, lived outside
what would have been her preferred (and more protected)
way of life within a marriage.

After
Gabriele Münter was a forceful and original artist, but
socially diffident and emotionally dependent on Kandinsky. She was too Bohemian or too conventional or too
timid to tell him outright that she longed to marry him.

Much better, or so it seems to me.
- Take a paragraph that holds a lot of emotion. Make that a
  "before" paragraph. Then work on an "after" paragraph that
  pushes the words lower in the vowel scale (for a sad scene) or
  higher in the vowel scale (for a tense or exciting scene).

REPETITION

Good writers delight in repeating good words. Poor writers, timid writers, average writers, many teachers including writing teachers, and some
editors despise a repeated word. Their philosophy is: use once and discard. To them words are like dental floss, toilet paper, chewing gum.

To first-rate writers, a good word is a note to be chimed. Begin
looking for repetition in your reading; you will see it everywhere:

> The house smelled of **old** beer, **old** grease, **old** smoke.
> (Daniel Woodrell, *Winter's Bone*, 53)

> She was a **poor** person, I was her **poor** child, and no one asks
> **poor** people if they want war.
> (Viet Thanh Nguyen, *The Sympathizer*, 3–4)

Here's a sentence voiced by a character who is a writer:

Anyway, **work** is not the word I would apply to what I do. **Work** is too large a term, too serious. **Workers work.**

(John Banville, *The Sea*, 30)

In this tiny passage Banville repeats *work* four times and bears down even harder by echoing *w* sounds in *way, work, word, what, worker.*

Now look at a passage composed by Lidia Yuknavitch:

Sienna Torres was a **troublemaker** young woman from a **troubled** household making **trouble** wherever she went. She **broke** the rules at school, she **broke** them at home, she **broke** them at Albertson's and Nordstrom and 7-Eleven, and she **broke** them at swim practice.

(Lidia Yuknavitch, *The Chronology of Water*, 135)

Yuknavitch morphs the word *trouble* into three forms, *trouble, troubled,* and *troublemaker,* a rhetorical devise known as polyptoton (pronounced *polyp-TOE-ton*). The effect, I think, is to further convince us of how much trouble this troublesome troublemaker was. The sentence, instead of moving on, bears down. And then we break into *broke*: She broke . . . she broke . . . she broke . . . she broke. . . . As Sienna's actions (breaking rules) repeat, so the word *broke* repeats. The sentence does more than state its meaning; it enacts its meaning.

Here Lewis Buzbee reflects on a life spent working in bookshops and reading books:

Books are **slow.** They require time; they are written **slowly,** published **slowly,** and read **slowly.**

(Lewis Buzbee, *The Yellow-Lighted Bookshop*, 5)

And here the novelist John Olson repeats the word *escape* twice and the word *desire* four times in a thirteen-word sentence:

You can't escape **desire**: even the **desire** to escape **desire** is a
desire.

(John Olson, *In Advance of the Broken Justy*, 85)

Anne Carson's character is lying alone in a tent with her sleeping
boyfriend and her thoughts. The relationship is in trouble. The couple
is about to break up.

Drops of water from a leak in the roof of the tent are hitting
my forehead one after another like items on a list. I am **bad**
at building a fire. **Bad** at folding the tent. **Bad** at driving
the truck. **Bad** at sticks. **Bad** at snakes. **Bad** at coffee. **Bad**
at clothesline. **Bad** at knives. **Bad** at water fetching. **Bad** at
unpacking. **Bad** at packing. **Bad** at shortwave radio tuning.

(Anne Carson, *Plainwater*, 194–95)

Rick DeMarinis's character Jack feels overcome with pointlessness:

I felt **blue**. Worse than **blue**. Sick. I felt incurable—ridden
with the **pointlessness** of just about everything you could
name. The farm struck me as a **pointless** wonder and I found
the idea depressing and fearsome. **Pointless** bugs lay waiting
in the fields for the **pointless** crops as the **pointless** days and
seasons ran on and on into the **pointless** forever.
   "Shit," I said.

(Rick DeMarinis, "Weeds," 48)

Oliver Sacks contemplates time:

I had found myself thinking of **time**—**time** and perception,
time and consciousness, **time** and memory, **time** and music,
time and movement.

(Oliver Sacks, *On the Move: A Life*, 350)

Listen to the prologue to Jack Remick's California novel *Valley Boy*:

> **When they came out of the dustbowl,** they carried **things** on
> their backs. The **things** they couldn't carry they left behind
> for the thieves and the looters of antiques. **When they came
> out of the dustbowl,** there was nowhere to go but west
> because the fruit was in the West and ranchers needed **hands**
> to pick it.
>   They had **hands.**
>   **When they came out of the dustbowl,** his mother was
> three years old and she had one pair of shoes and one dress
> and the dress was sewn from a Gold Medal flour sack.
>   **They came out of the dustbowl** into the West **to get to**
> the sea, **to get to** wet land, **to get to** the oranges, **to get to**
> peaches and pears and apricots, **to get to** grapes and almonds
> and the cotton.
>
> (Jack Remick, Valley Boy, prologue)

Finally, Lorrie Moore:

> Her nervous collapse was subtle. It took the form of trips
> to a small neighborhood park, for which she dressed all in
> **white: white** blouses, **white** skirts, **white** anklets, shoes flat
> and **white** as boat sails.
>
> (Lorrie Moore, "Two Boys," 3)

Hands On: Learning to Repeat

If you have trained yourself not to repeat, learning to do the opposite
takes practice and it takes developing your ear. Hint No. 1: Three is the
magic number. Repeating a word once looks like you ran out of words.
Repeating it twice signals confidence and intention. Hint No. 2: Repeat
a word as soon as possible after you first use it. Immediately is better
than soon.

Now try this. Do a five-minute writing-practice session describing a place or person. Circle the hot words and put them in a list.

What is a hot word? Hot words zing. They hold what may be emotionally strong, emotionally hot. Use impulse and instinct to find your hot words.

Now that you have circled the hot words, choose one, and do the practice again, writing on the same subject. Write for a full ten minutes. In every line of writing, force yourself to repeat the word you have chosen.

I repeat, in every line of writing, force yourself to repeat the hot word. I did not say repeat the word in every sentence. I said repeat the word in every line. Every time you return with your hand to the left side of the page, you are obliged to repeat your hot word before you get to the end of the line. Now, at a certain point you will become desperate. Keep writing anyhow. Past the point of desperation lies inspiration.

This exercise is fascinating. In a group of ten writers we do the exercise, and then read what we've written. Invariably there are amazing passages that go deeper and deeper into the emotion of the situation.

Now take what you have written and compose a paragraph. Try repeating more than one word, as do many of the models presented in this chapter.

Read aloud the passage you have written. Work on it for sound. Read it aloud again, and then again, until it sounds just right.

The practice of repeating, though, requires a cautionary note. Soon after you begin, you will hit the wall of teachers, editors, and peer writers who wish to stamp out repetition. Admit that your passage may not be well-rendered—yet—and keep on working your ear. Show your peer writers passages by Lorrie Moore and other virtuoso writers and ask if they think these writers were in error. Show them this part of your *Writer's Portable Mentor*.

As for teachers and editors, it depends on your relationship. Don't fight with them. Go ahead and trade your repetitions for a grade or a paycheck. But in your other work, keep the faith and keep on perfecting your skill at repeating words.

VERB WORK

Verbs carry the action, they carry the story, they carry character, feeling, a sense of doom, a sense of hope. Question every adverb because adverbs modify verbs. Consider whether "She ate her soup noisily" could be changed to "She slurped her soup."

The simple act of circling and questioning every verb in a passage you have written can result in radical improvements.

> My colleague and I **went backfiring** out of Savannah at dusk in his old Buick.
>> (Melissa Fay Greene, "On Writing Nonfiction," 232)

> The visionary political vocabulary of three centuries has been **garbaged**.
>> (John Berger, "Wanting Now," 7)

> Aunt Sallie had lost the two loves of her life in a few short months, but she chose **to peacock** her grief, wearing Thai silk dresses in jewel colors, dyeing her hair blueblack.
>> (Lauren Groff, *Fates and Furies*, 220)

At least once in every piece you write, consciously make a sentence using multiple verbs:

> I **kicked** and **thrashed** and **screamed**.
>> (Ben Okri, *The Famished Road*, 20)

> The lights **changed**, brakes **screeched**, and traffic **halted**.
>> (Rosamunde Pilcher, "The Tree," 29)

E. B. White, that master essayist, here speaks of his dog:

> He never just lay and rested. Within the range of his tether, he

continued to **explore, dissect, botanize, conduct post-mortems, excavate, experiment, expropriate, savor, masticate, regurgitate.**

(E. B. White, "Bedfellows," 83)

And finally, here is Jonathan Raban on the second day of a vacation in Bandon, Oregon, a place that overlooks the Pacific Ocean:

The next morning, the foghorn was still **mooing** and the sky lay on the sea in wreaths and coils of smoke.

(Jonathan Raban, "The Waves," 185)

Hands On: Working Verbs

- Take a page of a piece you've written. Circle the verbs. Question each one. Change at least one verb per page.
- Circle every adverb. (Adverbs modify verbs.) Can you take out an adverb by making the verb do more work? (Change "She cut vigorously" to "She whacked." Change "He ran fast" to "He raced" or "He sprinted." Change "She turned around quickly" to "She spun around.")
- In every piece, write at least one sentence with multiple verbs.

꙳

This is more than you need to know to begin working with sound.

You can begin to practice your vowel scales. You can make consonants clack and sibilants swish. You can ring words like bells, ding the hot words.

But don't forget truth and don't forget accuracy. That is your brake on flowery, overalliterated, hyperdecorative, false language. Don't forget image. Eschew adjectives. Adore verbs and nouns. Keep it simple. *Omit needless words.*

3.

Writing to See

Your beliefs will be the light by which you see,
but they will not be what you see and they will not be
a substitute for seeing.
—*Flannery O'Connor*

We write to bring insight to the page. We hope to be perceptive. We hope to discern the essential nature of the matter at hand. Very well. The truth is that insight begins with sight—with seeing what is there. Perception, writes Joan M. Erikson in *Wisdom and the Senses*, begins with sense perception.

Sense perception requires really looking, really listening, really paying attention. It requires time. Henry James famously said that a writer is one upon whom nothing is lost. But, writer or not, it's easy to become one upon whom most everything is lost as we rush to get to work or get the kids to school on time. Our days full of duties and distractions, not to mention way too much attention paid to the small screen in our hand, tend to dull our senses. Under these circumstances, it's a good idea to spend regular time each week training ourselves in observation. For a writer, observation becomes a habit and a way of life. And it really can't be cranked up for special circumstances (such as the piece you happen to be working on) and then let drop.

A visual artist may attend a life class and sit and draw the figure for an hour or two hours a week. John Berger describes the drawing process this way: "For the artist, drawing is discovery. And that is not just a slick phrase, it is quite literally true. It is the actual act of drawing that forces the artist to look at the object in front of him, to dissect it in his mind's eye and put it together again; or, if he is drawing from memory, that forces him to dredge his own mind, to discover the content of his own store of past observations."*

The Here and Now exercise is the writer's version of drawing.

OBSERVING THE HERE AND NOW

Go to a café. Or go to a park. Or go to a library. Or go down to the river. Write for fifteen minutes at a steady pace without stopping. (Use a timer, or write down your start time.) Describe what's in front of you. You can describe the whole scene, or just one object.

Don't write about anything except what you see, hear, touch, taste, or smell. Don't write your feelings, opinions, or reflections. Write color and shape. Write sound. You might describe the damp air or the hard desk. The taste of coffee. The smell of exhaust fumes. No feelings. No opinions. No thoughts.

These writings connect you to the world, to where you are. The more you do them, the more aware you become. They are pure training in sensory observation; you can also type them and compose them into settings, poems, pieces of essays. They are concrete-word farms.

Doing this exercise, you will inevitably come across objects, gizmos, thingamajigs, doohickeys, and doodads, not to mention any number of plants, that you can't put a name to. Write these down in your Lexicon, not the word, which you don't know, but the thing that awaits its word. Write "the vertical center piece in the back of a straight-back chair." In your Lexicon you can also draw the chair. The definition will be there waiting for the word *splat*.

Now a warning: when you first do the Here and Now exercise, and then compose it into a setting or a poem, you may have a rather adjective-laden paragraph. First do your lexicon work (make that chair into a ladder-back chair, make the table a Pembroke table).

---

*   Berger, "Drawing," 10.

Then work at reducing adjectives and increasing concrete nouns and verbs. Make a list sentence, and make the list a list of nouns. Work to make the nouns more specific: not *small house*, but *cottage*; not *roof*, but *mansard roof*; not *container*, but *Mason jar, flowerpot, rucksack*. Work to make the verbs contain their adverbs: not *slowly walk*, but *stroll*.

You can do the Here and Now exercise from memory. Write continuously but slowly to recall every detail of a kitchen, an evening at the movies, a family meal. Here's a scene from *A Scanner Darkly* by Philip K. Dick:

> He found himself confronting an all-white room with steel fixtures and steel chairs and steel desk, all bolted down, a hospital-like room, purified and sterile and cold, with the light too bright. . . . Two deputies regarded him, both in full uniform of the Orange County Sheriff's Office, but with medical stripes.
>
> (Philip K. Dick, *A Scanner Darkly*, 108)

And here is the Sprague mansion in James Ellroy's spooky crime novel *The Black Dahlia*:

> The entrance foyer was as Spanish as the outside of the mansion was Tudor: tapestries and crossed wrought-iron swords on the whitewashed walls, thick Persian carpets over a polished wood floor. The foyer opened into a giant living room with a men's club atmosphere—green leather chairs arranged around low tables and settees; huge stone fireplace; small Oriental throw rugs, multicolored, placed together at different angles, so that just the right amount of oak floor bordered them. The walls were cherrywood, and featured framed sepias of the family and their ancestors.
>
> (James Ellroy, *The Black Dahlia*, 141)

Hands On: Training in Observation

- Look over the piece or pieces you are working on. Can you go to an actual setting and capture it in your notebook by setting your timer and writing it down? Do so.
- Set your timer and do a Here and Now from memory: capture every detail you can remember of a childhood kitchen, a drugstore, a street, or a classroom.
- On a regular basis, do the Here and Now exercise just to train your capacity to observe. Look and write and look again. Or write while looking.
- Try this: for thirty days in a row, do the Here and Now exercise for fifteen minutes a day in the same place. Do lexicon work each day so that gradually you can put a name on everything you are looking at. I once did this in my living room. At first it was interesting. Following that: excruciating boredom. I wrote through that and one day, like magic, I saw the room in a new way, its wood and earth colors glowing, a glint of sunlight on the maplewood rocker turning it almost white . . .

SEEING COLOR

Look up from this page. Look around you. What colors do you see? What if you were to paint the scene before your eyes, just as you see it? What pigments would you squeeze from the tube? Look at your hand. How many colors do you see? Can you put them into words?

We've heard the phrase "gray prose." Gray prose is general prose, colorless prose. We could do worse than to color our prose. Some nouns—rubies, urine, blueberries—carry color onto the page without further elaboration. These concrete nouns are good because nouns are stronger than adjectives, and in becoming aware of color you don't want to inadvertently begin proliferating adjectives. Remember the color verbs: to blacken, to yellow, to purple.

To comprehend what it could mean to become acutely cognizant of color, we can turn to Vincent van Gogh's letters to his brother Theo. Here he writes from the coast of southern France:

> The Mediterranean has the colouring of mackerel, change-
> able I mean. You don't always know if it is green or violet,
> you can't even say it's blue, because the next moment the
> changing reflection has taken on a tinge of rose or grey.
> (Vincent van Gogh, *The Letters of Vincent van Gogh*, 267)

Or, we can turn to that lyrical classic of the Harlem Renaissance, *Cane*, by Jean Toomer. *Cane* is more than color—it's metaphor, music, mojo—but colors glow on every page.

> Gray slanting roofs of houses are tinted lavender in the
> setting sun.
> (Jean Toomer, *Cane*, 73)

Here is Leslie Marmon Silko. Does it surprise you that she is a painter as well as a writer?

> The Catalina Mountains were heaped with blue rain clouds
> so the light of the rising sun was diffuse and luminous—a sil-
> ver blue shimmered in the jade green of the jojoba and palo
> verde, and greasewood.
> (Leslie Marmon Silko, *The Turquoise Ledge*, 97)

How is your color lexicon? Go to any art-supply store. Purveyors of pigments such as the firm Winsor & Newton provide sample sheets with daubs of paint painted on. These sheets name the pigments, which have over the centuries evolved stable names (burnt umber, Payne's gray, yellow ochre), unlike the colors of house paints and printing inks, which are dyes named by advertising writers. The hue of a house paint by Pittsburgh Paints called "Twilight Purple" or one by Benjamin Moore called "Autumn Purple" are not traditional and there's no way to know what they look like without looking at them. Burnt sienna, though, refers to a traditional pigment, a clay containing the red iron oxide and manganese oxide. Burnt sienna is burnt sienna no matter who manufactures it.

Any common object, substance, or living thing that has a stable color can be used as a color word. In a home-furnishing catalog a washcloth may be "wheat" or "blackberry." But you can't color something "river" and you really can't color something "stone" (although it's done anyway), because rivers continuously change color and stones come in reds (iron oxide), grays (granites), blues (bluestone), and yellows (calcite). Ebony, that hard, blackish heartwood of *E. ebenum* originating in Asia and Africa, has a stable color and it has become a common color word. Color words warm and they brighten:

> As the long orange afternoon drew on, he thought, as he
> often did, about the rest of his life.
> (Shirley Hazzard, *The Great Fire*, 119)

One of the pleasures of writing color is searching for color words outside a short list of red, green, yellow, and blue. Here Joe Wilkins writes of his Aunt Edith, a printmaker:

> With her full, calloused hands, hands nearly as big as a
> man's, she pulls the wet print from the face of the wood—
> all orange and fishbelly and pale blue, maybe the scab hills
> south of Billings at daybreak—and she studies then the
> colors and densities and textures, and finally hangs the print
> up with the others to dry.
> (Joe Wilkins, "Eleven Kinds of Sky," 37)

Note that lovely color word *fishbelly*. Keep in mind that colors derived from objects or living things become instantly metaphorical in that they compare one thing to another. Instantly then, the writer must work to make the metaphor intensify the character or setting or situation rather than detract from it. Wilkins's *fishbelly* fits the Yellowstone River of his Montana memoir.

Just look at the wardrobe A. S. Byatt gives to Dr. Gerda Himmelblau, her story's dean of women students:

> She wears suits in soft dark, not-quite-usual colours—
> damsons, soots, black tulips, dark mosses—with clean-cut
> cotton shirts, not masculine, but with no floppy bows or
> pretty ribbons—also in clear colours, palest lemon, deepest
> cream, periwinkle, faded flame.
>   (A. S. Byatt, "The Chinese Lobster," 94)

Here's a passage I wrote about my childhood:

> They stink of hay and sweat. The father is there, his face
> burnt dark-orange like a Jersey calf. And the twins, with
> their pale yellow braids and pink faces. They get paid a quar-
> ter an hour by the father's boss. The field hands, Neil Lind-
> sey and Buck Washington, have worked on the farm longer
> than anyone. Neil is a coppery-dark man, large and kindly,
> who lives at the end of the lane. Buck is bony and reserved,
> with dusty black skin the color of a bible.
>   (Priscilla Long, "Snapshots: The Eastern
>   Shore of Maryland," 98)

To state the obvious, had my father been a Wall Street lawyer, I would not compare his face-color to a Jersey calf. If Buck Washington had been a Buddhist, I would not compare his face-color to a bible.

Color connotes. Here, Ray Bradbury has no need of the word *sinister* to describe a stranger just arrived in a small town.

> His vest was the color of fresh blood.
>   (Ray Bradbury, *Something Wicked This Way Comes*, 73)

Speaking of connotation, it's considered disrespectful to compare the skin color of people of color to foods—chocolate or coffee or caramel. A person is not a snack. And to sexualize a person (by suggesting that he or she is edible) in a nonsexual context is to demean. I mention this because it can be done in innocence and without intending harm.

Hands On: Writing Color

Do the Here and Now exercise, this time paying close attention to color. Write slowly and mention the color of everything you see. Use as many different words for colors as you can think of. Words meaning brown: dun, auburn, burnt sienna, umber, chocolate, turd-colored, straw-colored. Her hair the color of rust.

Run comparisons. Write thinking of objects in the world that are the same color as this person's eyes. You might write in your notebook: "His eyes were blue sort of like the sky, no—brighter, maybe like blue thistles or maybe robin's eggs. Bleach." Later, choose the most accurate one for color but also for the character, the situation. A character with steel-blue eyes will differ considerably from one with pale blue eyes.

Finally, remember this: Nouns and verbs are strong. Adjectives and adverbs are weak cousins, hangers-on. Do not use your color practice to proliferate adjectives in your writing. Use color verbs: dusk reddens the sky. Use nouns that emit color—walnut, eggplant, cherrywood. Add a color adjective, but force it to earn its keep by deleting two adjectives and one adverb.

OBSERVING PERSONS

We prose writers are always writing persons, whether a historical figure, a fictional character, or the shopkeeper down the street. No doubt it's one of the first things we learn to do. Still, it's easy to neglect one or more aspects of putting a person on the page. As a writer, I need these reminders, and I hope they are useful to you.

To write a telling portrait is to observe a person closely, to recognize who that person is. It is to observe the person in his or her body as well as in his or her actions, opinions, achievements, or derangements. It is to hear the quality of voice, to remember his or her habitual expressions or startling expressions. Portraits, even brief ones, usually include body type, dress, gesture (body language), and color (hair, skin, neon-pink spikes). Whenever a person comes on stage, he or she needs some kind of portrait (unless you are writing from his or her point of view). Call it a visual. Writing is a visual art.

Here, in a Rosamunde Pilcher story, is Edwin, ancient relative and dinner guest of Ian and Jill, a young couple unhappily obliged to cancel weekend plans when he turns up.

> Edwin was coming up the steps from the street, with Ian behind him. Jill had not seen him since last Christmas and thought that he had aged considerably. She did not remember that he had had to walk with a cane. He wore a black tie and a relentless dark suit. He carried no small gift, no flowers, no bottle of wine. He looked like an undertaker.
> "Edwin."
> "Well, my dear, here we are. This is very good of you."
> He came into the house, and she gave him a kiss. His old skin felt rough and dry and he smelt, vaguely, of disinfectant, like an old-fashioned doctor. He was a very thin man; his eyes, which had once been a cold blue, were now faded and rheumy. There was high color on his cheekbones, but otherwise he looked bloodless, monochrome. His stiff collar seemed a good size too large, and his neck was stringy as a turkey's.
>
> (Rosamunde Pilcher, "The Tree," 38)

Edwin has body type, coloration, clothing. A common strategy is to compare the person being portrayed with some iconic figure in the culture. Edwin is likened to an undertaker, to a doctor.

A portrait can be quite short, even just a line or two:

The bartender, a small woman with Mohawked black hair
and eyes lined with glitter, filled a shot glass. Vincent noticed
her leather vest with silver and turquoise buttons and he
noticed the tight sleeveless T-shirt and what it covered.

(Jack Remick, *Trio of Lost Souls*, 6)

The very split-second a character (whether fictional or actual) enters
the page, he or she should get a portrait. Think of it as theater. When
an actor makes an entrance you can *see* the character.

The more important a character is, the more space on the page he
or she might occupy. But even in a brief appearance, a character has a
body type. He or she dresses and moves.

Here is Alberto, in a story by Ben Fountain. Alberto commands a
guerrilla army in a South American country. The protagonist, Blair,
a graduate-student ornithologist, has been kidnapped. The guerrillas
must decide whether or not to execute him as a spy:

Seven or eight subcomandantes were seated along the wall,
while Alberto, the *comandante máximo*, studied Blair with
the calm of someone blowing smoke rings. He resembled a
late-period Jerry Garcia in fatigues, a heavy man with steel-
rim glasses, double bags under his eyes, and a dense brillo
bush of graying hair.

(Ben Fountain, "Near-Extinct Birds
of the Central Cordillera," 4)

And here is Oliver Sacks. The year is 1961. His motorcycle breaks
down, a trucker gives him a ride, and he finds himself at Travel Happy,
an Alabama truck stop. This is "another trucker's" only appearance:

A few minutes later, another trucker shambled up, a short fat
man wearing the floral shirt of the "Tropicana Orange Juice
Co. Fla.," half-unbuttoned to expose a hairy pudding belly.

(Oliver Sacks, *On the Move: A Life*, 90)

A portrait can be intermixed with lines of dialogue. Dialogue spoken by non-point-of-view characters should include gesture (body language) and other visuals—body type, clothing, color. In this story by Tim Gautreaux, Julian, a repairer of obsolete typewriters, has inherited an abandoned, derelict mansion. He has deluded himself that he can afford to restore it. He drives to the nearby town of Poxley to purchase, on time, a few items of furniture:

> Mr. Chance Poxley, a soft, liver-spotted gentleman in a
> white shirt and skinny tie, also showed him a small used
> refrigerator.
>   "You can't live without no icebox," Mr. Poxley told him.
> "You'll leave a can of potted meat out too long on the windowsill and think you can eat it the next day. Then you'll get
> to throwing up all over the place. You'll get the sick headache." Mr. Poxley raised a blue-veined hand to his forehead.
>   (Tim Gautreaux, "Idols," 5)

Later in the passage, Mr. Poxley scratches the back of his head. He squints.

In this story Julian is the point-of-view character. We look at the world out of his eyes and he is not of course looking at himself. A point-of-view character can peer into a mirror or someone else can remark on his appearance ("You haven't shaved for days—is something wrong?"), or she can choose a dress ("She pulled on her skimpy, slinky red dress"). Only in such ways can a point-of-view character view himself or herself. Reserve most of your portrait work for your non-point-of-view characters.

Hands On: Putting Persons on the Page

In this practice you separate a person's or character's qualities in order to focus on each one in turn. Do each timed write in the spirit of exploration. Allow yourself to stall and stammer in the writing in order to dwell, in order to stay with something. ("He waves his arms when he talks, sort of up and down, like he's trying to flag a taxi or something, or give signals to an airplane, what do you call that . . .") Write for three to five minutes on each element. If you feel stuck, use negatives: she's not obese, not short, not a redhead. Then move in closer: her hair is the color of a Chestnut horse.

- Write down one hundred concrete words associated with this person. The words might pertain to clothing, foods, hobbies, occupation or trade, books read.
- Give a macroportrait: In quick strokes give an overall picture of the person you are going to portray: "a short fat man wearing a floral shirt . . ." The macro includes body type, and then simply the most noticeable things about the person at first glance.
- Coloration: Color of hair, skin tones (everyone's skin has coloration and no person's skin has only one tone). Use comparison as you write; slow down in order to dwell. Write: "His face was reddish, not like strawberries but maybe more like raw beef, pink beef, well, there is a purple splotch, like purple grapes on the side of his nose. The red is a sunburned red, it has rust in it, I'm thinking of the red stones in New Mexico but it's darker . . . His hair is the exact color of an Irish setter." And so on. Expand your range of color description by using comparisons to common (and uniformly colored) fruits, dogs, birds, gems, vegetables, horses, etc.
- Body language: Put the person's habitual gestures on the page. The way the person walks, moves his or her hands, weeps, laughs, talks. Consider open and shut, looseness and tightness, defended and undefended. Consider energy, agitation, stillness. The foot tapping. Arms hanging to the sides motionless.
- What the person said: exact words, exact phrases.
- Dress the person. Dress reveals character. The way people dress reveals who they are or who they think they are.
- Write for ten minutes to reflect on this person or character. What insights can you come to?

- Write a ten-minute biography of the person.
- Now compose a portrait of the person, using the most telling attributes from each of the various categories. It can be long or short, two lines or two pages.

OBSERVING GESTURE

Body language, or gesture, is as ubiquitous as speech. More ubiquitous, because it continues through silence, and in dialogue it's a form of speech. Body language can either contradict or intensify what is said verbally:

> "What do you mean?" His lips quivered.
> "What do you mean?" He slammed the book down.
> "What do you mean?" He knit his brow.
> "What do you mean?" He grinned at her.

Or this:

> "I love you," she said, and turned away.
> "I love you," she said, and raised the gun.
> "I love you," she said. Tears streamed down her face.

Body language can hold things not consciously felt by the speaker:

> "I'd love to go," she said, looking at the ground.

Excellent writers use body language at every turn. Here's a passage from a Rick DeMarinis story. The protagonist's temporary girlfriend "had a way of looking at things that he could envy if he could believe it." She states that she has stopped living her life for other people. All her obligations were voluntary.

> He'd shrugged his shoulders at first, then laughed. She threw a fake karate punch at his chest. "You prick," she said, laughing.

"I guess I'm just not a subtle person," he said. She gave him a
sidelong pickerel smile, her small teeth needle-sharp, then made
a machine gun of her arm and shot him dead. They collapsed
into each other, in the direction of the bed.

(Rick DeMarinis, "Seize the Day," 288)

The shrug, the laugh, the fake karate punch, the sidelong glance, the
mock shooting, the collapse into the bed, all are as vital to the dialogue
as the spoken words.

Hands On: Writing Gesture

- Go to a café or to some other place where people hang out and
  you can write about them. Choose two people sitting together.
  You are going to open your notebook, set your timer for fifteen
  minutes or a half-hour, and observe them while writing continuously. Observe their postures and gestures, the way they
  hold themselves, the way they move their hands, where they
  place their feet. Use this strategy taken from the visual arts:
  Look, memorize what you see, then turn to the page and write.
  Then look again. Note position of hands, torso, elbows. Note
  movements (jiggling foot, smiling, eyes, position of hands). Just
  detail the body language, no opinions, no speculations. And
  don't worry. You'll become a pro at averting your eyes just as
  your subject looks over. People are utterly absorbed in their
  own affairs: it's remarkable how easily you can write on and on
  without being observed.
- Only *after* you've completed the observation exercise without
  opinion or speculation, *then* see if you can arrive at any insights
  on the body language you have observed. Decide on degree
  of intimacy. Decide who has more power. (Defended? Wide
  open? Leaning back? Leaning forward?) Give evidence for your
  decisions. Record how far apart or close the pair sits within a
  half-hour period. Is there a space barrier (how wide is it?) or
  has the barrier been crossed? Think about:

tension vs. ease
defended vs. open
happy vs. depressed
wary or aware vs. oblivious
intimacy vs. distance
power relations: Who has more power? Or, are they equals?
low self-esteem vs. centered, confident

Gesture work begins to give you a vocabulary of body language. The task is to work on rendering stances and gestures, to learn to name body parts—Is it "put out her hands" or "turned up her palms"?—and to become adept at including body language in dialogue and portrait.

Gesture work is character work. One man, when he talks, strokes his beard and looks into the distance. Another stares solemnly into your eyes. Yet another looks anywhere *but* into your eyes.

OBSERVING VOICE

Particular people have particular voices. Particular characters have particular voices. Certain works of fiction and nonfiction are entirely voice-driven. But even essays and stories not voice-driven are given authenticity by voice. People do not have neutral voices, just as they do not always say what they mean. Voices have age and region, but also individual characteristics. Paying attention to voice in the grocery store and in your reading will repay you many times.

No writer is better at voice than Grace Paley. Look at any story:

> I was popular in certain circles, says Aunt Rose. I wasn't
> no thinner then, only more stationary in the flesh. In time
> to come, Lillie, don't be surprised—change is a fact of God.
> From this no one is excused.
>
> (Grace Paley, "Goodbye and Good Luck," 3)

And here is Annie Proulx, another master of voice:

In the spring of his final year of school he drummed his
fingers on Wallace Winter's pickup listening to its swan-
necked owner pump up a story, trying for the laugh, when a
knothead they knew only as Leecil—god save the one who
said Lucille—walked up and said, "Either one a you want
a work this weekend? The old man's fixin a brand and he's
short-handet. Nobody wants to, though." He winked his
dime-size eyes. His blunt face was corrugated with plum-
colored acne and among the angry swellings grew a few
blond whiskers. Diamond couldn't see how he shaved without bleeding to death. The smell of livestock was strong.

"He sure picked the wrong weekend," said Wallace. "Basketball game, parties, fucking, drinking, drugs, car wrecks,
cops, food poisoning, fights, hysterical parents. Didn't you
tell him?"

"He didn't ast me. Tolt me get some guys. Anyway it's
good weather now. Stormt the weekend for a month." Leecil
spit.

(Annie Proulx, "The Mud Below," 48)

Finally, here's the opening to a Dagoberto Gilb story:

I've got two sports coats, about six ties, three dressy pants,
Florsheims I polish *a la madre*, and three weeks ago I bought
a suit, with silk lining, at Lemonde for Men. It came with a
matching vest. That's what made it for me. I love getting all
duded up, looking fine, I really do. This is the thing: I like
women. No, wait. I *love* women. I know that don't sound
like anything new, nothing every guy wouldn't tell you. I
mean it though, and it's that I can't say so better. It's not like
I do anything different when I'm around them. I'm not like
aggressive, going after them, hustling. I don't play that.

(Dagoberto Gilb, "Maria de Covina," 3)

How do you write distinct voices, whether in stories or nonfiction pieces? Partly, it's a matter of learning to hear voice. Once again, observation deepens insight. In your carry-about notebook, write down exact scraps of talk you hear at the office, in a café, on the bus, in your own kitchen. On an airplane, one flight attendant asks another, "Tom, did you talk to the overwing exits?" That's flight-attendant lingo (passengers sitting beside exit doors must be willing to perform certain duties in an emergency). On this flight my 23-year-old niece Joanna said to her mother, "Don't you just love the scene in *The Red Violin* where the old man unravels the sweater?" "Don't you just love . . ."—that's voice. Think about it. Would your grandfather ever say, "Don't you just love?" Place, time, gender, generation all influence a person's voice.

Listen for voice, and write it down. Do not plan to do anything else with such scraps, just accumulate them. You will begin listening in a new way. You will begin to hear voice.

Here's a voice I captured of a middle-aged, white, bulky, rather jovial construction-worker type. He and I were both waiting for our appointments in a clinic. He had just explained that on a construction job-site he could remember the names of all 748 men on the job (his job involved meeting with each one each week). But, he said: "Sittin' down at school and tryin' to learn out of a book, I'm no good at it."

Lee Gutkind, writer and editor of the journal *Creative Nonfiction*, advises that when conducting an interview for an article, the most important things to write down are the interviewee's specific expressions. You will remember the gist of the conversation very well, but actual speech—the housepainter reminding the homeowner to "exercise the windows," the bridge engineer speaking of excavating "in the dry"—tends to slip away. Yet that expression more than any gist captures that person and her world.

Hands On: Writing Voice

Do writing practices to capture voices you know well:

- Fifteen minutes—Write a bitter complaint in your own most colloquial voice.

- Five minutes—"My father always used to say . . ."
- Can you capture the voice of one of your friends or family members? Try. Then, next time you get together, check it out. Try again. Now use elements of what you've learned in a story or essay.
- Do a writing practice in which you tell something that happened to you in the most colloquial version of your own voice. Make this into a story.

Continue to observe the voices of people around you. Write it down. Can this voice (especially if it's a voice you know well) be turned into a character's voice?

A final word. Writing regional and ethnic voices is a nice skill, easier if the voice is one you grew up with. Study the masters. Study the works of Grace Paley, Tim Gautreaux, Annie Proulx, Dagoberto Gilb, Maya Angelou, Cormac McCarthy. Note how the great majority of words in these voiced sentences are actually written in Standard English. There is something about a sentence in which every word is bent out of standard that makes it seem caricatured.

4.

Object and Setting

The gathered, crumpled, slewed sheet, its folds like gray
twigs woven together to make a nest, and its highlights
like falling water, is unambiguously eloquent about what
has happened on the bed.

—John Berger, on a Frans Hals painting of a nude

In real life, objects and settings carry strong meanings. No knick-knack, no set of car keys, no room is neutral or random. Compare your own living room with that of your great aunt or your best friend. The chair, the rug, the photos speak—even if obliquely—about who that person is. If you've ever had occasion to deal with a person's effects after death, you know how powerfully these trinkets and packets of letters and ironed cotton handkerchiefs bare a particular person's particular life. And so it is with fictional characters. Rooms stand for lives; objects hold history.

Compare two characters, portrayed through their respective suppers. The first is the ex-convict Socrates, the protagonist in Walter Mosley's *Always Outnumbered, Always Outgunned*:

> He boiled potatoes and eggs in a saucepan on his single hot
> plate and then cut them together in the pot with two knives,
> adding mustard and sweet pickle relish. After the meal he
> had two shots of whiskey and one Camel cigarette.
>
> (Walter Mosley, *Always Outnumbered,*
> *Always Outgunned*, 69)

Now here, in *After the Stroke*, is May Sarton partaking of her supper:

> The table looked beautiful with a white cloth strewn with violets—the pattern is violets—two deep red roses in the center with the silver candlesticks and tall white candles. The tenderloin roast about which I felt terribly anxious turned out perfectly.
>
> (May Sarton, *After the Stroke*, 226)

Though one supper is fiction, the other fact, the techniques of detailing the suppers are identical. Far from taking up room as meaningless description, the objects—the single hotplate, the silver candlesticks—stand in for the characters themselves. Socrates with his hotplate is no corporate lawyer. May Sarton with her silver candlesticks is no ex-con cooking on a hotplate. We can take our own work to the next level by giving our character objects that represent his sorry past or her essentially European aesthetic or whatever lies at the heart of who he is.

Settings work to intensify the emotion of the story, and settings characterize. Here is an alley, seen through the eyes of the above-mentioned Socrates:

> The sun was just coming up. The alley was almost pretty with the trash and broken asphalt covered in half-light. Discarded wine bottles shone like murky emeralds in the sludge.
>
> (Walter Mosley, *Always Outnumbered, Always Outgunned*, 13)

The alley holds tranquility. It also holds the character of Socrates. The alley is beautiful not because trash is beautiful but because this is a man who, despite his hard life, can see the beauty in things.

Places mirror lives. Here's a workplace whose denizens, we instantly grasp, do not hobnob among the Wall Street elite:

He worked with Daisy in the clerical department of a filthy
.   secondhand bookstore on the Lower East Side of Manhattan. The department was a square-tiled space between
morose gray metal stacks of books and a dirty wall with
thin white pipes running along the bottom of it. There were
brown boxes of books everywhere, scatterings of paper, ash-
trays, Styrofoam cups, broken chairs, the occasional flashing
mouse.

(Mary Gaitskill, "Daisy's Valentine," 10)

If you merely list out words here—filthy, morose, gray, dirty, thin, ash-
trays, Styrofoam cups, broken—you can see what powerful vehicles
they are for carrying the lives of Mary Gaitskill's wasted (though win-
some) characters.

Settings ought to do double duty to intensify a story emotionally.
Here's a story whose characters are depressed and damaged, being
"treated" at a mental-health facility named Pond House:

Donna looked out the window at the street below. You
couldn't open the windows. A tree outside was struggling to
burst into bloom but had been compromised heavily by the
parking area. Big chunks of its bark had been torn away by
poorly parked cars.

(Joy Williams, "The Visiting Privilege," 273)

Because objects occur in settings, settings and objects are interre-
lated. It is useful to speak of them in the same breath. They resonate
metaphorically: Socrates's rudimentary room and his hotplate stand
for themselves but they also stand for Socrates's circumstances, his
history, his occupation. I read somewhere that the great Russian writer
Isaac Babel, understanding how revealing objects can be, used to pay
women to show him the entire contents of their pocketbooks.

Here is Ayemenem House, the setting at the center of Arundhati
Roy's masterpiece novel *The God of Small Things*:

Filth had laid siege to the Ayemenem House . . .

Midges whizzed in teapots. Dead insects lay in empty vases.

The floor was sticky. White walls had turned an uneven gray. Brass hinges and door handles were dull and greasy to the touch. Infrequently used plug points were clogged with grime. Lightbulbs had a film of oil on them. The only things that shone were the giant cockroaches that scurried around like varnished gofers on a film set.

(Arundhati Roy, *The God of Small Things*, 84)

The house, once beautiful, is a filthy ruin, as could likewise be said of the once-prosperous family that inhabited it. But one room, kept by one who has just returned, one who does not accede to the status quo, differs:

It was like a room in a hospital after the nurse had just been. The floor was clean, the walls white. The cupboard closed. Shoes arranged. The dustbin empty.

(Arundhati Roy, *The God of Small Things*, 87)

Shoes arranged. Dustbin empty. The psychoanalyst Christopher Bollas perceives objects as expressions of self. In *Being a Character* he suggests that we evoke "self experiences" by choosing objects. You might choose to order your shoes. You might choose to pick up a softball mitt on one occasion, a sonnet on another. A different person will pick up a flat of petunias or a pistol. We choose not only an activity but also the self we want to inhabit while carrying out that activity. What object does our protagonist pick up? Does the object tend to change as our protagonist changes?

Objects carry both history and desire. Fêng shui is greatly concerned with objects, and fêng shui coach Karen Rauch Carter writes in *Move Your Stuff, Change Your Life* that again and again she encounters relationship-seeking single women whose walls are covered with images of solitary, single women. She advises replacing these with images of couples and coupling. The idea is to portray not the reality but the intention and the desire. We writers might concern ourselves with what our protagonists put on their walls. Does this taxidermed moose-head represent who the character is or does it represent what he wishes to be?

Did I mention that settings and objects carry strong meanings? A room can stand for a character's mood—it can look dreary or the dust can dance. Objects carry cultural meanings as well as personal meanings less accessible to an outsider. If you walked into my house you would see on the mantelpiece a carved African bowl. It was carved in Liberia some time during the mid-1960s. Considered at length it may raise cultural and historical questions and suggest a lot of history. For me personally it is also a relic of my late sister, who brought it back from the Peace Corps long ago. Does your character possess a relic of lost love or a memento of a distant place?

We writers can deepen our work by observing settings and objects— deeply and at length—and using them to enrich every page.

Hands On: Objects and Settings

Make objects do work. Make settings do work. What is that blue bowl on that yellow tablecloth good for? Why is that room dusty and why does that dust darken that room? Make settings carry the emotion, the drama, the mood, the character's situation or past or wish.

- Describe a room of your house. Describe it from the point of view of someone who is totally depressed, has lost the love of his life, his money, his home, his wallet, his job, etc. Do not mention any of these circumstances. Only describe the room. Now describe the same exact room again, from the point of view of a happy person. (This is, essentially, John Gardner's exercise from *The Art of Fiction*.)
- Now describe your character's kitchen. Make the kitchen say

everything about your character's life. Open your character's bottom drawer, the drawer where she keeps mementos. What are they? How do they carry her past?

- Make a list of objects for each of the characters in your novel (or memoir or story). Specify the objects to the utmost. Not just chewing tobacco but Elephant Butts chewing tobacco.

PART II

Finding a Structure

I copy what I admire. I pinch. I read not only for pleasure,
but as a journeyman, and where I see a good effect, I
study it and try to reproduce it. Like an actor will study
a senior character and learn an effect of make-up or a
particular slouchy walk for a role he's not thought of
himself. He doesn't regard that as being particularly
influenced by the actor, but as a trick of the trade which
he owes it to himself to pick up.
—*Lawrence Durrell*

5.

Thinking Structure

The search for models, in my terms, becomes a search for
alternatives.
—C. D. Wright

Work Habits of Highly Successful Authors was the title of an
excellent panel at the July 2004 Pacific Northwest Writers
Association Conference. Sitting on this panel were three hyperproductive writers: Carolyn See (six novels, three nonfiction books, and coauthor of five more books), Donald E. McQuinn (nine novels), and Terry
Brooks (twenty-three novels). These many-book authors had never
before met and neither did they cheat and compare notes to get their
stories straight. Their advice was identical. They each did two things.
They wrote one thousand words every day (with, I think, one day off a
week). And they wrote into a structure. Write every day, each advised,
one after the other. And, each elaborated, write into a structure.

Does writing into a structure (setting aside for a moment the question of *what* structure) conflict with writing practice—writing continuously without stopping until the timer goes off?

It doesn't conflict because you can write into a structure in the
writing-practice manner. Besides, writing into a structure should be
done in tandem with "discovery writing," that is, writing to learn what
you have to say, writing to work out your thoughts, writing to find
out what your antagonist thinks (by writing from her point of view in
your notebook, even though in the finished story you are never going
to be in her point of view).

Skipping discovery writing, deciding on a structure, and then forcing material into it like stuffing a sausage may result in writing that is too thin, with a forced or contrived feel. Discovery writing—a term coined by Jack Remick and Robert J. Ray—in the writing-practice notebook makes the work richer, more layered, and more insightful. But doing writing practice endlessly with no structure in mind puts you on the road to Never Never Land—never finishing, never publishing.

You write in your writer's notebook to find out what you have to say and then you deliberate on how to structure it and then you write it again, into its structure. In the midst of shaping and revising you may go back to your notebook to explore another aspect or to write for a second or third time to get to the bottom of it. There are writers who write entire novels, scene by scene, in their writer's notebook. Then, of course, they go home and type.

Writing to a form strikes some writers as a strange idea. But think of an assignment to write a sonnet. There are hundreds of sonnets, poems structured the same way, but which differ radically from one another in subject matter, language, image, tone. The form is the vessel. What goes into it is up to the writer.

These chapters on structure offer four prose structures, with models to illustrate each one. For each type of structure, we'll take a close look at a model and work through the steps of separating its structure from its content. This is a core skill that, with practice, will enable you to comprehend the structure of any piece of writing, much as an x-ray makes visible the skeleton, leaving in the dark all that these bones support.

Our four structures are:

1. Theme Structure
    Ira Sadoff, "Ben Webster"
    John Olson, "Home"
2. Collage Structure
    Eula Biss, "Babylon"
    Patrick Madden, "Laughter"

3. A/B or Two-Strand Structure
   Amit Majmudar, "The Servant of Two Masters"
   Lee Zacharias, "Buzzards"
4. Dramatic Story Structure
   Steve Almond, "A Dream of Sleep"

When I set out to write a new piece into a structure that I've extracted from a model, I spend a large amount of time cogitating on what to write about. This rumination may take as much time as generating the first draft of the piece. It is helpful to pick a subject different from that of the model, because you will be living closely with the model for some time and you don't want to inadvertently ingest image or idea. You must work on material that is truly your own, of central importance to you. These are vital moves when you consciously put yourself under the influence of another writer. When we absorb the lessons of our models we incorporate neither subject matter, nor word, nor image, nor idea, but structure and technique. That we are working our own most urgent material acts as a counterweight to the model, allowing us to ultimately pull our own piece away altogether, with only scents or tints of its influence remaining. Finally, it is important that we use as models the work of a great variety of writers, because we are in the process of exploring, evolving, and speaking in our own voices. The last thing we want is to become a weak imitator of a predecessor writer.

Nothing here is offered in the spirit of an academic exercise. Who among us has time to waste? Everything here is intended to assist you in completing and polishing excellent, original, publishable works. There is no better way to build a body of work than to give yourself the assignment of writing into a particular structure, then writing into another structure, then into another . . .

FINDING THE RIGHT ONE

How to approach this part of your learning? I suggest reading this section of *The Writer's Portable Mentor* straight through and then going back and choosing a form to write a piece into. First study the structure and then choose a subject matter from among your concerns that is both different from that of the model and might possibly fit the structure.

How to match content with structure? Think about the content. Does it suggest a narrative? That is, does it have a character in trouble or want (whether actual or fictional) with enough grit to fight his or her way out, for better or worse? If so the dramatic story structure illustrated by Steve Almond's "A Dream of Sleep" in chapter 9 suggests itself. For example, I had a character, a woman in her forties, who'd spent her life not writing her own PhD dissertation but instead helping her brilliant professor husband, who has now dumped her for another woman, a fellow professor. This is a significant complication, worthy of a story, I thought, and so the dramatic story structure seemed right. ("Living for Robert" appeared in *The Chaffin Journal*.) On the other hand, for a piece called "Stonework," I had my stone collection, my fascination with stones, the book I'd written on the rock that burns (coal), a collection of persons I might call "emotional stones," in other words, a little of this, a little of that. No real protagonist, but something to say. A collage suggested itself. Remember that this process is not arbitrary, but rather, organic. Think of molding your material into its most natural shape.

Practice abstracting the structure of works you read—essays or articles or short stories. This involves the skill of looking at the piece literally. Structure is carried in the following sorts of moves:

- What are the literal divisions—sections separated by white space, a subtitle, or a number?
- How many paragraphs does each section contain? What are the transition devices?
- Mark out the scenes. A scene takes place in one setting. If you shift settings you are writing a new scene. A scene is one episode, in which there is dialogue and/or some sort of action. Think of a scene as happening on stage in a theater. A scene

shows you what is happening, when it is happening, where it is happening. Summary is different. Summary explains, summarizes what happened, but doesn't show it happening.

- New character comes on stage (Antagonist? Helper? Protagonist?).
- What is this character's role? That is structural.
- Dialogue carries the essential dramatic action and thus is structural.
- Shifts from concrete description or narration to passages of philosophy, insight, or metaphor are structural shifts.
- Compare the beginning to the end. Does the beginning mirror the end? This is structural.
- Note all actions, whether mental or physical. Actions tend to move a story forward and are structural.

The rewards of comprehending structures are great. Consider a new structure as an invitation to write not only a new piece but, for your own body of work, a new kind of piece. Some structures, such as the seemingly simple collage structure, can be quite challenging.

How many different structures are there for short fictions or non-fictions? Impossible to say. Some writers have little interest in new structures, writing their great stories and fine essays into traditional structures. Others constantly try to find new structures, which sometimes work and sometimes begin to seem a bit gimmicky. Thinking about structure, reading *for* structure, and becoming savvier about writing *into* structures is an ongoing process that lasts for all the years of writing. The guideline, the goal for any given structure, is that it fit or even intensify its content.

INVENTING A STRUCTURE

There is no need to invent a structure. Most works that are original in their ideas and fresh in their language use a traditional structure. Original works do not require an original structure.

But it's fun to invent structures. How to begin doing such a thing? Think first of what the content is asking for. Form exists to intensify meaning.

For example, I invented a creative nonfiction titled "Archaeology of Childhood." I grew up on a commercial dairy farm where my father was employed as the dairyman. The farm was our home. We children grew up there and returned there to visit our parents for two decades after we'd moved away. We felt that the farmhouse, barns, windmill, machine shed, and silo were "ours," though not in the sense of a property right. Eventually, due to falling milk prices, the farm went out of business. The original owner died and the land was sold to a nonfarmer who used its fields, woods, creeks, and marshes for duck hunting. The duck blinds were kept in repair but the other buildings stood in desuetude.

Decades later, with the permission of the new owner, we returned to see our old place. We walked down the rutted mile-long dirt road, now impassable by most vehicles. The farmhouse was still there, overgrown with Virginia creeper, uninhabited except by field mice. The barns, too, were extant, but collapsing, roofs caving in. The milkhouse, machine shed, rusting windmill—everything was there. It was eerie, like returning in a dream to the ruins of childhood. The word *archaeology* came to mind.

To shape "Archaeology of Childhood," about our return journey to that place and its memories, I used the form of an academic archaeology article. My bookish friend Greg Lange left two shopping bags full of archaeology tomes on my doorstep. From them I took the form, which includes numbered sections, lists of artifacts, descriptive paragraphs, and so on. Within the different sections, I used different kinds of sentences, sentences that reflected the feel of that section.

The content, you see, can suggest its own form.

Francine du Plessix Gray wrote a masterpiece essay titled "The Work of Mourning." It is a big, wide-ranging piece in which, among much else, she elaborates Elizabeth Kübler-Ross's five stages of grief: denial, anger, bargaining, depression, acceptance. Gray's work is shaped in five parts. In the first part we don't even learn that the essay is actually about the death of her adored father when she was ten years old. (First stage: denial.)

I wrote a piece called "Genome Tome," which had twenty-three (very short) "chapters"—just as we have twenty-three pairs of chromosomes. The structure was not arbitrary but suggested by the content. One of the chapters comprises twenty-three questions pertaining to the meanings and implications of the Human Genome Project. The only alternative structure that suggested itself was one with forty-six "chapters," one for each chromosome (rather than *pair* of chromosomes), but that seemed a bit much.

One way to invent a form is to think of nonliterary texts. I think of Kim Adrian's "Questionnaire for My Grandfather," Michael Martone's "Contributor's Note," and many epistolary stories. I have yet to see a short-short based on milk-carton copy or cereal-box text but maybe soon I will.

STRUCTURING A BOOK

Are you writing a novel? A memoir? A how-to book? Collect ten examples of your genre (some you've read before, some new ones) and read them for structure. Write out these structures in your notebook. Then choose one that fits your story, or design a fitting hybrid. Begin your own book by employing one of your found structures, modifying as you work along. By the time you finish your own work, it will have found its own shape.

Past reading counts for nothing here. When we remember a book we've read, even recently, we typically don't remember the structure, if we even noticed it in the first place. We remember the character or a tense moment or the setting or something that happens. So, for this work, it is necessary to reread for structure. To write down the structure, start with obvious divisions—paragraphs, sections, scenes, chapters.

This work will repay you many times. Making a serious study of structure is an indispensable stage of writing any full-length book. Many nonfiction books have a rather simple structure that you can discover by looking at the Contents page. In fact writers writing a nonfiction book should write the book into a simple list of chapters. Keep in mind that a nonfiction book is an object made up of chapters. It has a title page and a Contents page. (If your book manuscript in progress has no title page and/or no Contents page, put them in immediately! To be writing a book for years with no title page and no Contents is to be structurally oblivious. You may write until death and then we could bury your one thousand–plus pages with you!) It is my own belief that it is folly to make an outline with its roman numerals, its arabic numerals, its capital letters and lowercase letters, its endless permutations and degrees of hierarchy. Instead, make a simple list of chapters. Then write the book, chapter by chapter.

Here is the structure (the Contents) of a fine book by David B. Williams titled *The Street-Smart Naturalist: Field Notes from Seattle*:

1. The Eagles
2. The Fault
3. The Plants
4. The Creek
5. The Stone
6. The Geese
7. The Bugs
8. The Weather
9. The Hills
10. The Invaders
11. The Water
12. The Crows

Each chapter in *The Street-Smart Naturalist* is essentially an essay on its topic. Each chapter comprises an interesting mix of human and natural history along with the writer's personal experience.

Certain guidebooks contain indispensable instructions on deep structure. Novelists can learn to plot from Robert J. Ray and Bret Norris's *The Weekend Novelist,* and no mystery writer should even begin without Robert J. Ray and Jack Remick's *The Weekend Novelist Writes a Mystery.* Also indispensable for novelists is Donald Maass's *Writing the Breakout Novel.* Nonfiction writers can grasp dramatic story structure from Jon Franklin's *Writing for Story.* These books will save you years of trial and error. Read them. Do the exercises suggested. Master their contents.

Developing a structure is a core task required for writing a book. Begin exploring structure as you begin doing discovery writing and research. The structure is the framework you write into, your security blanket, your assurance that all your hard work will result in a completed manuscript.

WORD COUNTS

How long should a piece be? How many words? (In the world of professional publishing, we typically speak of word count, not numbers of pages.) How long is a book? How long is a newspaper article? How long is a short story? Here are some guidelines.

The first thing to know is that articles, essays, stories, and books are getting shorter. Memoirs and literary novels tend to run from 60,000 to 90,000 words. The minimum length of a novel manuscript submitted to the AWP (Association of Writers and Writing Programs) novel award is 60,000 words. An average length for a short story or lyric essay in many literary journals is now 3,000 words or fewer, whereas it used to be more like 5,000 words. Flash fictions and flash nonfictions (under 1,000 words) are common. The famous online journal *Brevity* will take nothing over 750 words.

But there's still a place for longer pieces. Two venues that accept *only* longer pieces are *The Long Story Short Journal* (minimum length 4,000 words) and *The Seattle Review* (minimum length forty double-spaced pages). In other journals, a piece may run as long as 7,000 words or longer, but it has to be pretty spectacular to earn that much space in an issue. Our second model for the A/B structure, "Buzzards" by Lee Zacharias (see chapter 8), runs to close to 9,000 words. It originally appeared in the literary journal *Southern Humanities Review* and found a wider audience in *The Best American Essays 2008*. It is pretty spectacular.

Word count is another way to think about deep structure. Let's say you are writing a set of creative nonfictions in which personal matters intersect with science. Or let's say you are writing a book of interconnected stories about the members of a single Chicago-based family. To complete your book you need twenty 3,000-word pieces or you need fifteen 4,000-word pieces, or some other combination that gets you up past 60,000 words. What you have done here is broken down the work into manageable units.

There. You've got your assignment. Go for it!

Hands On: Writing into Structures

After you've chosen a structure to try, make a list of the model's sections and, if it is not too long, its paragraphs. If you are looking at a short story, make a list of the scenes. Now make analogous paragraphs (if an essay) or scenes (if a story) for your own piece.

Write the paragraphs one by one in your writing-practice notebook. Type them up, and then begin working your language, extending a thought, eliminating, or further elaborating. Do the necessary research, write, and rewrite. After you've completed a draft, take one last look at your structure-model to make absolutely certain that you have not unconsciously taken word, image, or idea from your "teaching" piece, your model.

Then put the model aside and work on your own piece on its own terms.

6.

Theme Structure

Working within the self-imposed discipline of a particular
form eases the prospect of having to reinvent yourself
with each new piece.
—*David Bayles and Ted Orland*

The theme structure is a common traditional form. It's a perfect salad bowl for a remarkable variety of salads. It's a simple form that often states its subject in the title. With the theme structure you can range widely while staying squarely on subject. Suppose I wanted to write a piece titled "Bald Eagle." Paragraphs might dip into eagles and their lifestyle, the eagle as a symbol of America, how bald eagles nearly went extinct (and their comeback), their eagle eye (sharp vision), their role as spirit messenger in Native American world views, my own encounter with a bald eagle, the evolution of feathers and of flight. . . You get the idea.

Let's explore the theme structure by scrutinizing Ira Sadoff's thirteen-paragraph piece on the jazz musician Ben Webster. Actually, let me rephrase that. Let's begin by reading "Ben Webster" out loud, rather slowly. This is how, in the Advanced Short Forms Seminar, we take in a new piece. We read it paragraph by paragraph, each taking a turn to read. To skim a piece is to get its gist but to miss its structure. So we read out loud, as if we were schoolchildren. Read "Ben Webster" this way with a buddy or read it out loud to yourself.

"Ben Webster" by Ira Sadoff

He's almost as wide as he is tall. His forehead is broad as an anvil. His eyes are red, alcohol red, and he glides onto the stage absentmindedly, as if he were on the way to somewhere else. He wears a worn-to-shine brown double-breasted suit and a porkpie hat. He doesn't know we're out there, any of the ten of us, in a small Amsterdam café in 1973. He may not know blacks and whites can use the same bathroom everywhere now, that the Vietnam War is winding down, that people may want to hear his music again. He was chased here a decade ago, by racial prejudice, by the lack of work, by television and rock and roll, by free jazz. He's archaic as Keats; he's a relic of jazz history.

He snaps his finger and nods to the white Dutch rhythm section. They're out of tune, they don't play together, they play figures and chord changes from the fifties (they learned everything they know from old Charlie Parker records), they're a little too loud, and worst of all, they're bored. He's done these same tunes night after night and they want to play something more modern, more dissonant.

He growls at them and keeps snapping his fingers until they pick up the beat. Then he lifts up the saxophone, opens his eyes as if for the first time, and moves to the edge of the stage, where a Dutch girl is drinking coffee and talking with her boyfriend. He moves the sax in her direction; he serenades her. He plays "Prelude to a Kiss," a ballad he learned with the Ellington band forty years before. It makes you want to wince, until he's eight notes into the melody. Then you find you're hypnotized by the pure beauty of his instrument, by the remarkable voice, by the wordless story the melody tells. By the unrelenting melancholy, the history of the familiar tune played as if you've never heard it before. This is Ben Webster, two months before he dies, on September 9, 1973. He's the musician who can always move you, who's a relentless bastard, who beats up on his piano player, who drinks himself sick. Who knows the secret of melody. Who, like many of our artists, like most of our black artists, dies alone and impoverished and completely unappreciated.

Jazz is an expression of the history of a people, because every musician must understand its history before being able to play. No one can come to "Confirmation" without bowing to Charlie Parker;

no one can play "Well, You Needn't," without absorbing the irony of Thelonious Monk.

But rather than exalting the individual imagination, rather than exalting the perverse notion that complexity and eccentricity are themselves a virtue, that design and pure intellect prove the greatness of the art, jazz depends upon improvisation and community. A familiar tune, a tribal tune, really, is given an interpretation. The individual experience of the artist intersects with the community. Call and response, originated in West Africa, lets artists interact with each other, respond to each other's ideas. They can break in on one another, they can cut each other up, they can alter the whole tone and rhythm of a piece.

When I listen to the music of Ben Webster, though, I forget all the intellectual justifications for jazz; those rules simply don't apply. Webster reduced me to pure feeling, to mood and attitude. I don't care what tune he plays and I don't often care who's playing with him (only with Ellington, Hawkins, and Benny Carter are Webster's cohorts more than time-keepers, tapping feet). I can't claim to hear notes I've never heard before; I don't hear configurations, inventions of melody I've never imagined. Instead I hear a voice. A human voice. A timbre, an imagination, a way of playing that comprehends the nuance, the suggestion of phrase. His tone is thick and reedy, throaty, almost as full of air as note. He keeps his instrument in the lower register until he wants to reach for some emotional statement on a melody: then the notes will come slowly, full of associational logic, sparsely decorated. Our understanding requires patience. He might play a series of quarter notes and then suddenly linger on the penultimate or final note of a phrase as if to say, "Look at what's inside this note." Sometimes the note will bleed onto the next phrase, the next chord change. But always Webster's signature—the raspy sound and the deliberation of phrase—gives a ballad the texture of what Rahsaan Roland Kirk would call "the inflated tear."

Webster moves me by the sheer force of personality. I see the torchy ballads in small, dimly lit cafés; I see the streetlight and cigarette smoke. I imagine a life that's full of hurtful memories. And I can see a lonely figure holding back his rage. The outsider who knows that love is the only possible salvation, but salvation is only something to long for. You only have to listen to his renditions of "Where Are You?" or "When Your Lover Has Gone," to follow the quest and be consoled by the experience. And though his tone darkens over his forty-year career, though he chooses gruffness over grace, the tunes change only in minor ways. He might cross out a note, a phrase, stretch or compress it, and although the change might represent an improvement, the change is not essential. Webster's greatest gift as an artist is his ability to inhabit the tone of a tune each time he gets up on the stand.

We live in a culture where innovation is more highly valued than interpretation. Pound's "make it new" has become a cry for eccentricity. It's as though life would be entirely too boring if we didn't change our clothes every day, if there weren't some new electronic gadget to amuse us, if we couldn't love someone new after a few years. We also have little patience for grief. My students tell me they hate Nathanael West because he's too depressing. Producers in Hollywood won't make "down" movies. We have a short, happy attention span. Loss is un-American. These are nostalgic grievances, but it shouldn't surprise anyone, even those who love jazz, that Webster is not quite tragic enough—he's not a drug addict; his connection with his race is implicit rather than explicit; he doesn't quite provide an heroic enough image to become the martyr America requires of its artists.

Webster's born in 1909 in Kansas City, he comes from a middle-class black family, he picks up the violin before he picks up the tenor saxophone. He plays with Andy Kirk's band in 1929. He meets up with the first great tenor player, Coleman Hawkins, and learns to make the saxophone growl, he learns how to make it run, how to sing. But it is not until the forties, in the great Ellington band in the middle war years, when he's on the bandstand with Johnny Hodges (who has the sweetest tone of anyone who ever lived) that he develops his unmistakable tone and approach to the ballad. Then Charlie Parker, also from Kansas City, arrives and changes the quarter notes to eighth notes, changes swing to be-bop, learns to twist the melody out of shape the way Picasso can distort a face. Webster, who's obstinate, who knows who he is, never gives be-bop a try. He's not hostile, he's just not interested. And in a few short years, one of the most prominent tenor players of the swing era is forgotten. He becomes a sideman, he plays in various bands, but basically he's obsolete.

Then, in the mid-fifties, like a number of older players, he's resurrected. He backs up Billie Holiday in a series of Verve recordings when Billie's voice is gone and when she's never been so expressive. People remember them both. Verve signs Webster to a recording contract, and Webster makes a half-dozen of his most unforgettable recordings. A set of records with Oscar Peterson, J. C. Heard, and Alvin Stoller, mostly ballads (now re-released in a double album called Soulville); these recordings are Webster at his purest, his most melancholy, and his reputation as an artist could stand on them. He makes two recordings with Coleman Hawkins and their voices are so intertwined, so alike in mood, so opposite in personality—Hawkins grumbles, runs, stutters, vibrates in the lower register, while Webster is sweet, slow, pure, one note at a time—that one marvels at the illogic of recording producers . . . why were they never put in the same studio again? Why, because the producers believed, perhaps rightly so, there was no real market for these old fogies when there was Miles Davis and John Coltrane. So in a few years, after a last degrading record made to sell in 1964, "Ben Webster at the World's Fair," after the British Invasion, after the Five Spot Café is turned into a pizza parlor and then a used-clothing store, Webster takes off to Amsterdam. That's where Dexter Gordon lives, that's where Eric Dolphy lives, that's where tens of great American black artists live, because they're fed up with American commerce and race.

In those last years Webster records sporadically, and his last recordings, equivalent to Holiday's recordings of the fifties, are made for obscure Dutch labels. One set of recordings, an Affinity two-fer featuring those Duke Ellington songs that made him famous, is particularly poignant. The notes are not so different, but the tempos are slower, the emotional effect is of greater pain, the nostalgic grace of the playing reminds me of Mozart's great Clarinet Concerto, K. 622, composed shortly before his death. Every note is an elegy. And that, it seems to me, is the legacy of Webster's last recordings.

There are other lessons, confused and contradictory, in the art and life of Ben Webster. He perservered, maintained his style regardless of fashion. He died unappreciated, though his art was great and though he kept at it every day of his life. He could be a generous man but when he drank, and that was often, he'd senselessly start fights. He was a relentless womanizer. He seduced women with his instrument. He saved the best part of himself for his work.

Webster reminds us that grief is ennobling, though not necessarily transformative; that we're made more human by our suffering, though not necessarily better humans. We may never recover from loss, but we can memorialize it with the imagination. Webster's art ultimately affirms, because he makes us feel that if there's beauty even in despair, perhaps, just perhaps, we can survive the world.

&

Now, how do we extract the structure—separate the structure from the content—of this piece? The key to abstracting structure is looking at the physical page—literally. "Ben Webster" has no sections, whether numbered or subtitled or indicated by an extra space between blocks of type. Duly noted.

Now we count the paragraphs. Thirteen. It's tradition to think of word count ("Ben Webster" has 1,763 words), but more useful for our work to count paragraphs.

I like counting paragraphs instead of using a word count because a paragraph is a structural unit. A paragraph has one controlling idea, more or less. You can make a list of paragraphs by making a list of controlling ideas. It's like lining up a row of canning jars, each to be filled with tomatoes, string beans, corn, or red beets. The paragraph-as-Mason-jar way of thinking about the task makes it seem manageable. It's especially effective to take a daunting subject, one that seems unmanageable because emotionally tricky or because just too big, and give yourself the assignment: write a piece on this subject in thirteen paragraphs. A big subject gives you plenty of material to work with, and thirteen paragraphs gives you a good harness within which to do that work. You have now sidestepped one big problem with many short pieces: they are too slight. A short piece need not be slight, and it need not be the last word on the subject either. Writers return to subjects again and again. So you need not worry about "wasting" your big subject on one thirteen-paragraph piece.

When "copping a structure" to use in a piece of my own, I keep strictly to the given number of paragraphs, although this might cause one or more of my paragraphs to puff out rather big in its effort to contain everything I want to say. As the last step in this process, we discard the model and shape our own piece however it wants to be shaped. At that time I break up my ballooning paragraphs into two or sometimes three paragraphs. But this makes only a minor variation on the structure: I'm still not writing a thirty-paragraph piece. To disregard the number of paragraphs at the beginning is to disregard the structure.

Indeed, because the theme structure is a nondramatic structure that lacks the driving energy of a dramatic story in which there is a protagonist to identify with and high stakes and obstacles to overcome, it may require its short length to work well. To take the thirteen-paragraph "Ben Webster" and make it twice or three times as long may doom it to the wastebasket.

Now, with your assignment in hand—to write a thirteen-paragraph theme piece—what will your subject be? A portrait of a person comes to mind. "Ben Webster" is not an interview-based profile and it's difficult to see how it could be a useful model for an interview-based profile. Sadoff's piece includes a physical portrait of the man, his biography, a deep knowledge and ample description of his art, and reflections on the world in which he has carried out his work—the history and context of jazz.

For our piece based on this model we want to assiduously stay away from a jazz musician or, really, any sort of musician. Our goal is to learn from and use Sadoff's deep structure while producing an original piece of our own. The goal will be well-served by keeping a good distance from Sadoff's subject matter to avoid unconsciously taking words or ideas from his work.

So, our assignment is to write a thirteen-paragraph piece on a person. And, the person represents something that is somehow core to our own concerns and experiences. This is a good guideline in any case, but it's especially important when we are deliberately putting ourselves under the influence of another writer.

Let's now return to Sadoff's piece. We list the paragraphs in terms of what they contain.

Paragraph 1: Portrait (body type, clothes, coloration, gesture). Time and place, and the opening paragraph immediately answers the question, what does this writer have to do with this material?

Paragraph 2: Continuing portrait including gesture ("snaps his fingers") and the context of jazz (the bored band prefers Charlie Parker).

Paragraph 3: Observing the man in action—body language ("He growls at them and keeps snapping his fingers"). His work in action (plays "Prelude to a Kiss"). The personal reaction of the writer. The summing up: Who is this? When is this? The context of the musician as a black man.

Paragraph 4: Short generalizing statement characterizing Ben Webster's context—jazz ("Jazz is an expression of the history of a people").

Paragraph 5: Second paragraph elaborating Webster's context of jazz ("jazz depends upon improvisation and community").

Paragraph 6: Personal response to the music, using "me" and "I" ("reduces me to pure feeling"). Characterizes the quality of Ben Webster's music, a "here and now" of sound ("thick and reedy, throaty").

Paragraph 7: Further personal reaction including a riff comparing the music (the work) to a different mode (verbal images such as streetlight and cigarette smoke). Again, use of "I"—the writer inserts himself into the piece. The phrase "over his forty-year career" backs you up enough to see a life. Paragraph ends with a continuing characterization of the work ("He might cross out a note").

Paragraph 8: Statement in the universal "we" that characterizes our society as context for Webster and his work ("We live in a culture where"). Why, given what we are like, Webster has not received due recognition.

Paragraph 9: Webster's biography, given in present tense. Includes early career.

Paragraph 10: A long paragraph detailing his music career, how he was resurrected, who he plays with, his recordings with Coleman Hawkins, and the demise not of his music but of his fame and status, ending with the move to Amsterdam.

Paragraph 11: Elegy paragraph. The last recordings.

Paragraph 12: Lessons his life gives us, as a creator.

Paragraph 13: Larger meanings that this creator and his music give us.

As we study "Ben Webster," we keep in mind that as writers we are not here to opine on whether or not we like the piece (we may like it or dislike it). For the moment, "Ben Webster" is our teacher. What are its technical moves? Which of Sadoff's strategies can we adapt for use in our own very different piece? After reading the piece out loud, we go paragraph by paragraph listing these out.

Here are a few thoughts. The metaphorical images are fitting. Webster's forehead is "broad as an anvil," an anvil also being an old, archaic thing. Also, for Sadoff to write that Webster is "archaic as Keats" is to pay him a high honor, to give him world-class status as an artist. Sadoff gives us date and place, and also the context of the era, Vietnam, the situation of African Americans at that time. And for Sadoff language is a jazz tune: *archaic/Keats/relic*.

Beginning with the second paragraph Sadoff saturates his piece on one musician with his deep knowledge of the history of jazz—this one musician's context. The suggestion here is to place our subject within his or her larger world. Note how many other musicians Sadoff mentions by way of placing Webster in context—Charlie Parker, Duke Ellington, Thelonious Monk, Coleman Hawkins, Benny Carter, Johnny Hodges, Billie Holiday, Oscar Peterson, J. C. Heard, Alvin Stoller, Miles Davis, John Coltrane, Dexter Horton, and Eric Dolphy.

Also, Sadoff gets to issues beyond music—the making of art, the life of this black musician in the context of racism, loss and grief and how our culture avoids them. He gets to this larger world, along with the history and context of jazz, through the lens of one man, one artist. He covers a lot of territory without digressing.

In paragraph 8, Sadoff characterizes our society using the universal "we." ("We live in a culture where innovation is more highly valued than interpretation.") Speaking in the universal "we" is a practice and it is a skill. It is to claim authority, to speak without diminishing or undercutting your statement with phrases like "at least that's my opinion." I encourage you to learn to do this. To articulate, occasionally, for our larger culture. To characterize our own society. When you first try it, your pronouncement may end up sounding clichéd or overgeneralized or arrogant (often writers shun this move out of fear of arrogance). The work is to strive for accuracy and to work for a nonjudgmental tone.

We note the technical moves of Sadoff's sentences. His repetitions. His changes in tense and in person (from "I" to "you" to "he" to "we").

This is Ira Sadoff's piece. Now, how do *I* proceed?

I want to write a piece (as of this writing, not yet written) on the visual artist Agnes Denes, someone I've never met. Why her? She's engaged with environmental issues and with science, as I am. She's been compared to Leonardo da Vinci—that interests me. My own subject matters include art and the creative life and artists (including and even especially women artists).

So here goes. How might I organize this piece? I will start with Sadoff's thirteen-paragraph structure. This is not carved in stone but it gives me a direction for writing a complete draft.

1. Opening should include a physical portrayal of her. I will use a photograph, the famous one of her in the wheatfield she created in lower Manhattan. What do I have to do with this subject matter?

2. Context of conceptual art and Denes's place in it. Her performance piece in which she buries the only copy of her Haiku in a time capsule to be opened in a thousand years. Time as a material she incorporates into her work.

3. Another work described—her exquisite drawings based on mathematics? Include personal reaction.

4. Short statement about conceptual and environmental art. What is it, when did it start?

5. Elaboration of context of conceptual and environmental art. Name other artists.

6. Take a particular artwork and do a Here and Now on it and my reactions. (The strength piece: she extracted words connoting strength from a fat dictionary and made them into an artwork, a process that took her seven years.)

7. Take an environmental piece and do the same. Tree Mountain (in Finland, an artificial mountain with eleven thousand trees planted on it).

8. A statement about our culture and Denes's place in it. Here try a "we" statement. "We are a society devoted to consuming" or something.

9. Biography: a Hungarian immigrant become artist. Loss of language. A beautiful woman working to be taken seriously. In present tense?

10. Her career and its vicissitudes including her works, in chronological order more or less. Include Denes's writings and the "Book of Dust"—human bones and dust and writings concerning "the beginning and end of time and thereafter" and our place in it.

11. Her latest works (as I write this Denes is in her eighties).

12. Lessons of her life as a creator. Going her own way. American artist as immigrant. As refugee from world disasters.
13. Larger meanings this creator and her art give us. (Her view of artist as seer.)

Here I have a structure to write into. It's not rigid. It could change. I am also in the process of doing the lexicon work and doing research. Studying her writings and her works. Should I try to meet her? I suppose so. But I don't see the piece as being largely interview-based. In any case, my work is nicely laid out. This is no longer a vague something-or-other on Agnes Denes. It has a direction. I have a harness. And trust me. Even before it is written I can tell you it will look nothing like Ira Sadoff's marvelous piece on Ben Webster.

Now let's look at John Olson's very different theme piece. Let's read it out loud.

"Home" by John Olson

I didn't see the rain yesterday. Our blinds were drawn. They're new blinds, not brand new, relatively new, and already broken. Our cat managed to balance herself on the back of the computer desk and swat at the cord and chew the tassel so that it had to be rethreaded. Rethreading, however, did not go as planned. The tassel is dicey. It will endure several gingerly executed pulls, but pull too hard and it comes undone. The easiest solution is to not lift the blinds. This is easily accomplished, as we have no great view, and enjoy our privacy.

Our window is flush with the ground. We overlook dirt, and a few bedraggled plants. I prefer this. I like being partially underground. It gives me a secure feeling. I feel grounded.

I'm not into views. I once lived on the upper floor of an apartment with a panoramic view of Seattle's Lake Union, downtown Seattle, and the east side of Queen Anne Hill. I looked at sailboats, white caps on windy days, and the seaplanes from Kenmore Air come and go. It wasn't long before I lost interest. I prefer dirt.

The place where I truly feel at home is in a book. This is where the real panoramas are. The landscapes of the human imagination.

Oceans, raging rivers, philosophies, forests. Language is a wilderness and books are their reserves.

If I'm in line at the DMV and I open a book I feel at home. If I'm at the airport, dentist office, hospital waiting room, coffeehouse or bench at the city park and I open a book I feel at home.

Home is a sensation. Shelter, yes. Home is definitely shelter and I love that aspect of it. I say a prayer to the gods of electricity and running water every day. I do not take them for granted. A power outage that lasts more than eight hours is a reminder of how dependent we are on services to give that sheltering aspect of our homes real meaning. It makes me wonder what the hell libertarians are thinking when they squawk about the unnecessary burdens of municipal and federal agencies that ensure clean water and safe roads and standards for electrical wiring and outlets.

That said, home is quintessentially a feeling. The expression "I feel at home here" is indicative of that. I've lived in a lot of places over the years. I've lived in a school bus, hotel, boarding house, and garage. Some places felt naturally good and some places remained cold and unaccepting.

My first home was a human body. A female. My mother. I have absolutely no memory of ever being a zygote, tadpole, or humanoid floating in amniotic fluid. But I spent the first nine months of my existence living like that, rent free. It would be an interesting exercise to figure out at what point in human development a sense of self first begins. It's that sense of self that is our true first home. No sense of self, no home.

Some people are at home in themselves and some people (my tribe) never completely feel at home in themselves. There's always something inside agitating, churning, ruminating, preventing me from that idyllic sense of being comfortable in one's own skin. Sometimes a good feeling comes along and I will feel completely at home in my body, muscles relaxed, brain relaxed, my nerves flickering like little scented votive candles in a quiet Mexican church. It can be encouraged. It can be enhanced with a little wine, a little Vicodin, a little Xanax. Meditation helps, as does exercise. That boil inside can be brought down to a nice little bubbly simmer. Feelings can be mellowed. Attitudes can be softened.

Votive candles lit, confessions made, prayers recited.

The *Agenbite of Inwyt*, subtitled *Remorse (Prick) of Conscience*, is a confessional prose work written in Middle English by a Benedictine monk named Michael of Northgate sometime in the thirteenth century. The work did not garner a large and enduring audience but is most notable because James Joyce borrowed the title for referencing states of inner agitation and pain in *Ulysses*.

Remorse is awful. I hate remorse. I never cease obsessing about building a time machine and going back to edit my life, undo all the horrendous mistakes made, horrible things said, wrong turns made, opportunities lost, bad choices made. People always say "let go." You can't go back, you can't do anything, so what's the point of dwelling on it? None, obviously. I get that. I'm on board with that. I would love to let go. But how do you let go of a feeling? It's not a rope, not a wing strut, not a bowling ball. The hand has no purchase on it. It's a feeling. It doesn't have a shape, a texture, a knob or a handle. There are no levers or buttons. It's not like an elevator. I can't make it go up or down. I can't steer it. Feelings are ghosts. They're phantasmal. When we're troubled with remorse we say we are haunted by something. The mind is preoccupied, and the tenant is a shapeless, formless apparition.

Specter, shadow, wraith.

Anxiety isn't much fun either. That chronic sense of dread, of things going horribly wrong at any minute. Anxiety is a form of fear; what makes it different from fear is its irrationality, its presumption of harm where there may be no harm, its exaggeration of something scary that might not be all that bad. We just don't know. It's the uncertainty that drives us nuts. It's a fear of something that might happen, not (as for example being chased by a bear) something that is actually happening.

Psychologists give that inner discomfort a nifty little term: fight or flight. But fight what? Flee from what? If we knew the answer to that, we would be instantly relieved. We would be more at home in our bodies. We would know what to do. Resignation isn't such a bad thing either. If there's nothing we can do, if hope is more painful than helpful, surrender to a helpless situation can be liberating. It frees us from responsibility. We play a sonata on the violin while the Titanic sinks.

Or we can seek therapy. A skilled psychologist can help us to see the irrationality of a fear. The ghost will vanish. Though, as in the recent election, some fears aren't so irrational. Sometimes the things we dread do come to life. Godzilla rises from the New York harbor and starts crushing cars and buildings. A moronic fascist billionaire is elected president and critical social services are destroyed and people die.

Mortality doesn't help. Knowing one is going to die one day isn't conducive to a homey feeling inside oneself. The ship is going down. You really get that message when you turn sixty. By the time you turn seventy you're almost giddy with impermanence. Upkeep? There's no remodeling for the temple that is the body. This is where you learn stoicism.

Stoicism is a home for pessimists. Or should I say realists? Let's say realists.

Stoicism is a home for realists. The Stoics believed that we can become immune to misfortune if we cultivate certain virtues, such as developing the intellect and creating a philosophical perspective on life. But what does that mean, "philosophical perspective"? It means tapping into the idea of the universe and all beings and matter within the universe as being unified by breath, by pneuma, by Godstuff. Pneuma is breath and spirit. It is, in many ways, similar to the mindfulness movement. We minimize our pain by concentrating on our breath. By breathing in and breathing out. Our ultimate home may be breathing. Inhaling, exhaling. Letting thoughts pass through our minds like clouds. Let go let God, as they say in AA.

Logic worked for the Stoics but it doesn't always work for me. I do what I can to cultivate a philosophical perspective. Sometimes I succeed, sometimes I fall on my face. Sometimes I just thrash about like a madman, or brood like Hamlet on ghosts and revenge. I seek philosophy. I look for it wherever I can. But it helps considerably to be at home when I undertake that voyage.

❧

How do we analyze the structure of John Olson's piece? First, as always, we look at the physical page. There are twenty paragraphs. Two of them consist of one sentence only. Duly noted.

We list out the paragraphs. In doing so we are not floating high above the piece discussing its meanings. We are looking at it literally. We note the mundane paragraphs at the beginning about the blinds, the cat. We note how and exactly where this writer leaps from the material world to metaphysical, psychological, philosophical, and political worlds. We note the literary references. We follow any notion we have about the piece by pointing to the exact place in the text where this is illustrated.

Hands On: Writing the Piece

Most any idea or ideal, place, plant, animal, building, or person works within this structure. Among the theme-structured pieces I've composed are "House," "Blue Note" (on the color blue), "Composition in Yellow," "Housekeeping," "Studio," and "The Color Orange."

What might work for you using this structure? Do a writing-practice session for twenty minutes or a half-hour. If you had only five years to live, what subject matters would you certainly want to write about? After doing this discovery writing, make a list of every subject that came up. Now which of these might work as a theme-structured essay?

Choose the one that attracts you and begin writing it by "Jump Starting an Essay or Story" (page 7). And consider, Could you do one of these per month?

Finally, build your own collection of models based on this structure. You will see how delicious and commodious a form it can be.

7.

Collage Structure

The meeting of two or more distant realities on an
unfamiliar plane.
—*Artist Max Ernst's definition of collage*

In the visual arts, a collage is an amalgamation of disparate objects—
fruit labels, burlap, magazine cutouts, words printed on newspaper,
wood, a nail, a spoon. The elements composing a collage may have little or no obvious relationship before they are brought together within
the collage. Often the elements are found objects—not themselves generated by the artist. The German artist Kurt Schwitters was one of the
early masters of the form and another was Joseph Cornell with his
black-painted boxes fitted with objects hoarded from flea markets and
junk shops to reveal an inner world. The Swiss artist Meret Oppenheim, a master collagist most famous for her fur-covered teacup, is yet
another. Spend real time gazing at the work of these and other artists
to get inspired and get ideas. The found objects found in visual-arts
collages may be simulated in a literary collage (sometimes termed a
mosaic or a montage) by using quotations—words found elsewhere.

But what does "amalgamation of distant objects" mean when your
materials are words, words, and more words? Well, think of the different shapes words can take: question, reflection, poem, joke, quote,
anecdote, scripture, lecture, list.

A key quality of the collage is that its sections are short and they are
separated from each other by a space or an asterisk.

Here is a collage, "Babylon" by Eula Biss.

"Babylon" by Eula Biss

The hanging gardens were built for a homesick wife. Amytis of the Medes found the flat, dry land of Babylon depressing, and so her gardens were planted on terraces to look like hillsides.

⌁

"The air in California," my cousin once told me in New York, "smells like flowers." At the time, I took this as nostalgia for her home, but when I moved to California I found that it was true, especially in Oakland, where bougainvillea climbed telephone poles and huge hibiscus flowers poured out over the front yards of all the little houses.

⌁

The people of Babylon did not grow figs or grapes or olives, wrote Herodotus, but the land of Assyria was so rich that the fields of grain produced two hundred–fold or even three hundred–fold. He is thought to have exaggerated.

⌁

My first disappointment in California was the park. At the end of the summer it was a wasteland of brittle shrubbery. But the winter rains would make the park green, and I would learn that it was full of gardens.

⌁

Their exile in Babylon, their captivity, was, for the Jews, both a punishment and a promise. It was through this exile that God would deliver his people.

⌁

Palm trees were all I saw as my plane landed in California, and palm trees were all I could see there for a long time. The palm trees were how I knew I was a long way from home.

⌁

There was a garden in the park called the Desert Garden, where African bottle trees and pencil trees and strange succulents grew. At midday this garden was hot and still, the yellow dirt paths were pounded hard, and almost all the plants were scarred from graffiti. There were messages etched into the leaves of the agaves and up the trunks of the saguaros, between the spines. Most were declarations of love: "Edgar

R Te Amo Rosa," "Sang Love Thuy," "Victoria y Bernardo," "Lilia + Maryus," "Isidro y Blanca [heart] nuestra hija Leslie."

↵

Plants deal with their wounds differently than we do. A cut on a plant will never heal, it will simply be sealed off or, at best, grown over. On one of our first days in California, my sister picked up the bright red fruit of a cactus from the ground and its tiny spines were in her fingers, swelling, for days.

↵

"By their fruits ye shall know them," Matthew tells us. "Do men gather grapes of thorns, or figs of thistles?"

↵

My sister and I drove out into the desert, only to discover that it was not, as I had imagined, empty. It was full of ocotillos and saguaros and crucifixion thorns.

↵

I came to the fantasy of California early, twenty years before I moved there, because it was the place where my cousins lived. In third grade I wrote to the Oakland Chamber of Commerce and received, in the mail, a map of the city. This was in the eighties, when the crack houses of Oakland were still crack houses, not high-rent apartments. I pored over the map of Oakland, although the lines of it meant nothing to me then.

↵

Oakland was advertised as a "garden city" by its postwar boosters. "Workmen," read one advertisement, "find happiness in their garden-set homes. . . . Their children are healthy in the mild, equable climate." The factories wanted workers who would not leave looking for something better.

↵

But Americans always leave. We are a migrant people, a people of diasporas and exiles.

↵

The two great migrations of the twentieth century, the migrations that made the landscape I was born into, were the migration of blacks to the cities and the migration of whites to the suburbs.

In the postwar decades, industry migrated too. The General Motors
and Ford and Chevy plants left Oakland for the suburbs, and New
York's textile district emptied.

The metaphor of Babylon, already employed by preachers and
Rastafarians, entered, in the 1960s, the vocabulary of black politics.
Babylon could stand for any city—for New York, for Oakland, for
California, for the United States—for capitalism, for imperialism, or
simply for excess. "It was often an illusive metaphor," Robert Self
writes, "but it captured the profound cynicism engendered by decades
of liberal failure as well as the remarkably optimistic belief in rebirth,
in beginning again."

The fall of the city of Babylon was also the end of that particular
captivity for the Jews. A reminder that there is always some promise
in destruction.

Certain desert succulents can be forced to bloom by withholding
water. And other plants can be forced to bloom with cold, or with
cutting.

"For the Panthers and other black radicals," Robert Self writes, "the
industrial garden of midcentury had become Babylon—a false city
that had to be remade to stave off collapse."

By the seventies, landlords in New York City were abandoning their
buildings. Squatters were taking over vacant tenements on the Lower
East Side—patching roofs, rewiring electricity, building open fires, carrying buckets of water from fire hydrants, clearing the bricks and tires
off empty lots to grow vegetables. On some blocks, they simply threw
Christmas-tree ornaments full of wildflower seeds over the chain-link
fences to break on the rubble. Seed bombs, they called these. And they
called themselves homesteaders.

Meanwhile, exurbs. Penturbs. Boomburbs. Technoburbs. Sprinkler cities.

⁓

To flee within your own nation is to create a kind of captivity for yourself. A self-imposed exile. And so, the despair of the suburbs.

⁓

But to call it flight is to acknowledge only the fear and to ignore the other motivations, particularly the government subsidies—the highways, the mortgages, the tax breaks, the American dream.

⁓

I long, even now, to live in a place where I can have my own garden.

⁓

Because it is so sheltered by tall buildings, and so warmed by the "urban heat island effect," the climate of New York City is particularly suited to gardens of exile. The callaloo of Jamaica grows there, and the okra of Georgia, the peach tree of South Carolina and the tropical hibiscus.

⁓

Nonnative plants are sometimes called "invaders." Or, if we like them, "exotics." The apple tree, for one, is an exotic.

⁓

"The American traders and trappers who began settling in California as early as 1826 were leaving their country for a remote Mexican province, Alta California," writes Joan Didion. "Many became naturalized Mexican citizens. Many married into Mexican and Spanish families. A fair number received grants of land from the Mexican authorities." But when the American immigrants rebelled against the Mexican government, most of them had been in California for less than a year.

⁓

Palm trees are not native to California. They come from Mexico, from Brazil, from Australia, from Costa Rica, from China, from Africa, from India, from Cuba—from, it seems, everywhere in the world except California.

⁓

Americans began their acquisition of Mexico by simply moving there.

Even after the Mexican government prohibited American immigration to Texas, Americans continued to cross the border illegally. Stephen Austin, the "Father of Texas," urged Americans to come to Mexico, "passports or no passports."

ꝛ

After half of Mexico was claimed by the United States in 1848, thousands of Mexicans found themselves immigrants without ever having moved. In California, they outnumbered Americans by ten to one. They were made citizens of the United States, but they would, in the decades following the Treaty of Guadalupe Hidalgo, lose most of their land to drought, squatters, taxes, and American courts.

ꝛ

Now, some Americans fear a *reconquista* of the Southwest.

ꝛ

The iconic palms that line the streets and boulevards of Southern California are dying of age and disease. They were planted when the cities were young, and the cities are no longer young.

ꝛ

Oakland was once a woodland of oaks. It was named *Encinal*, "oak land," by the Spanish rancher who owned it before the gold rush.

ꝛ

In Los Angeles, the rows of dying palms along the boulevards may soon be replaced by oaks.

ꝛ

Almost two million more people left California in the 1990s than came there from the rest of the country. They went, mostly, to the mountain states, to Colorado, Montana, Idaho. "Lifestyle migrants," they were called. A native Californian who left for Idaho told *USA Today*, "I was getting tired of traffic, graffiti, dirty air."

ꝛ

But graffiti, we all know, is not a reason to leave the place where you were born.

ꝛ

"A lot of people coming in from California," observed a professor at the University of Montana, "are coming in for 'urban dread' reasons."

ꝛ

In the nineties, after New York had resisted collapse and the land on
the Lower East Side became valuable again, the city began to bulldoze
gardens on empty lots to make way for new buildings. By then, the gardens had stone paths and goldfish ponds and grape trellises and roses.

~

Graffiti is one way to claim a place you do not own. And so is plant-
ing a garden. Because we are all forever in exile, or so the story goes,
from the original garden.

~

Date palms belong to the genus *Phoenix*, and in California they rise
from the ashes of conquest. *Phoenix canariensis* is the Canary Island
date palm, brought by the Franciscan priest who founded the mission
that became San Diego, and *Phoenix roebelenii* is the pygmy date
palm, and *Phoenix dactylifera* is the true date palm.

~

Some of the community gardens of lower Manhattan had already
been razed when I moved to New York, but there was still a hanging
garden in the old meatpacking district—the elevated train tracks, no
longer in use, had grown tall weeds and wildflowers.

~

"The daughter of Babylon," Jeremiah tells us, "is like a threshing-
floor, it is time to thresh her; yet a little while, and the time of her
harvest shall come."

~

My cousin and I stood together once, by the Long Island Railroad
tracks, under a sign that read "Babylon." As I looked down the long
gray tracks netted with electric lines, my cousin looked up at the sign
and said, "Well, they call it what it is out here."

~

My grandmother keeps a garden on the graves of her parents, who
came all the way from Poland to die in New York. Her most precious
plants grow there, in the most permanent place she knows. She gave
me some lilies of the valley from that garden, and I planted them
in the shade of my father's house in the suburbs not long before he
moved away and I left for California.

~

"They tended to accommodate any means in pursuit of an uncertain end," Joan Didion writes of the pioneer women in her family, the women who went West. "They tended to avoid dwelling on just what that end might imply. When they could not think what else to do they moved another thousand miles, set out another garden: beans and squash and sweet peas from seeds carried from the last place. The past could be jettisoned, children buried and parents left behind, but seeds got carried."

I spent my first summer in New York City walking through the gardens of Far Rockaway, gardens that covered entire blocks forgotten by the city. They had paths of old carpet between rows of sunflowers. I walked through gardens in Harlem and the Bronx full of beads and candles and statues of the Virgin Mary enshrined in little wooden *casitas*. One man told me that he had everything he needed to survive Y2K in his garden.

I heard a rumor in California, which I never had occasion to test, that if you were stranded out in the desert, you could cut off the top of a barrel cactus and find a reservoir of fresh water within.

Next to the highway running through the desert outside San Diego, there were gallon jugs of water buried for those trying to make their way into the country on foot. A priest from LA had brought the jugs of water to the desert in his minivan and buried them with the help of volunteers. The water was marked with blue flags bleached by the sun, and some jugs were buried where bodies had been found. That this water had been brought all the way out there and was truly under those blue flags seemed as impossible to me as the telephone poles that persisted through the heart of the desert.

The hanging gardens of Babylon may never have existed. Herodotus never mentions them, and they are absent from the Babylonian records. But the other defining feature of the city, its immense walls, described by Herodotus as 80 feet thick and 320 feet high, were real enough to crumble with time.

After reading "Babylon" out loud, what qualities can we list out? How do we approach it as a structure? As before, we keep it literal. How many sections are there? (Forty-seven sections, 2,123 words.) A crucial characteristic is the short length of each section. Indeed, fully twelve sections consist of only one or two lines. If I'm going to use this as a structure model, I'm going to take the shortness of these short sections seriously and I am going to take a word count of around 2,000 seriously. Also, each section is separated from its neighbors by white space (often but not always including some sort of dingbat, such as an asterisk).

What makes this a collage, since every section is a short section of prose (including a few quotes)? There is no list put next to a poem put next to an anecdote put next to a quote. What makes "Babylon" a collage, I think, is that the leaps in time and place are given no connective tissue. Yet together they add up to a meditation on displacement and exile.

The form works like a weaving constructed from different colored threads. One thread is plants and gardens, mentioned specifically in thirty sections (if you count the "industrial garden" and woman perceived as a crop to be harvested). Plants are specifically associated with exile, migration, homesickness, captivity, escape, nostalgia, wounding. One might lay out the colored threads like this:

1. garden homesick (Babylon)
2. flowers nostalgia (California)
3. figs, grapes, olives, lush—vegetation exaggerated (Babylon)
4. wasteland/gardens (California)
5. Jews captivity and exile (Babylon)
6. garden and graffiti (California)—graffiti and gardens a way to make a home
7. wounded plants, wounded person
8. thorns (biblical, so in the realm of Babylon)
9. and so on, through the forty-seven sections.

It is the repeated locations (Babylon, California, New York) and the weaving of the theme-threads that give the finished piece its coherence. Note that the piece begins and ends with the hanging gardens of Babylon, providing a frame.

Using this piece as my teacher, how might I shape a piece of my own? I am working on a series of reflections on types of places, and some of my favorite places are bookshops and libraries. This might be a perfect form for that. For it would allow me to explore libraries in history and to remember libraries I've spent hours and years of time in. It would allow me to return in memory to Leary's Bookshop in Philadelphia, a three-story treasure house that became part of my childhood, the magical place where we always stopped on the way to visit our Scottish grandmother.

A form of the collage is the abecedarian, the *A* to *Z* familiar from childhood alphabet books. This type of collage has twenty-six sections, one for each letter of the alphabet. One I wrote titled "My Brain on My Mind" progresses from *A* for Alphabet, to *B* for Brain, to *C* for Consciousness, down to *Z* for Zero. Dinty W. Moore composed one on fathers, with twenty-six titled sections that include *D* for Divorce and *F* for Father Knows Best. William Boyd's abecedarians include one on the great Russian writer Anton Chekov (*A* for Anton, *C* for Critics).

What is the abecedarian good for? It is a cathedral form, a considerable space to contain and thankfully to rein in a large subject. As I began building "My Brain on My Mind," I felt the need for even more constraint, so required each section to conclude with the opening word of the following section, a move I learned from William Boyd.

When you first become entranced with the abecedarian, you will find it a bit like a puzzle. You'll have three *L*'s, four *D* 's, and no *X*'s. You keep working until the puzzle resolves. (Which *A* is most essential? Could *Alzheimer's* become *Dementia*?)

Another type of collage proceeds by means of numbered sections. (The numbered sections of a collage must be short. Many essays that are completely un-collagelike comprise rather long numbered sections.) In a numbered collage, the numbers, it seems to me, should have some bearing on the subject. Could you write a forty-part piece on turning forty?

Our second example of a collage is "Laughter" by Patrick Madden.

"Laughter" by Patrick Madden

My three-month-old daughter is just beginning to laugh. She is not ticklish; she is not mimicking us. As far as I can tell, she is just delighted by the world. She sees a funny face, sees her brother in a giant witch's hat, sees me with my glasses on upside down, sees her mother dancing to the funky music of a commercial, and she laughs.

I have loved her since she was born—since before she was born, when she was only an idea—and yet I feel I haven't known her until now. Her laughter has become a common ground for us, a mutual realization that the world is an interesting and silly place.

᷍

According to a third-century B.C. Egyptian papyrus, "When [God] burst out laughing there was light . . . When he burst out laughing the second time the waters were born; at the seventh burst of laughter the soul was born." Man as the height of God's laughter: that explains a lot.

᷍

Max Beerbohm, in his essay on laughter, wonders that "of all the countless folk who have lived before our time on this planet not one is known in history or in legend as having died of laughter." But Beerbohm is wrong. Bulwer-Lytton's *Tales of Miletus* speak of Calchas, a soothsayer who was told by a beggar that he would never drink of the fruit of his vineyard. Moreover, the beggar promised that if the prophecy did not come true, he would be Calchas's slave. Later, when the grapes were harvested and the wine made, Calchas celebrated by laughing so hard at the beggar's folly that he died before he took a sip.

᷍

The word *laughter* is like any other word: if you say it enough, it begins to sound strange and wondrous. Listen to the sound as it separates from meaning; feel your tongue jump away from your front teeth, the way you bite your bottom lip slightly—*laf*—the quick strike of the tongue against the teeth again—*ter!* If you say *laughter* fast enough and long enough it will make you laugh.

᷍

Animals that laugh: hyenas, monkeys, the kookaburra or laughing

jackass, an Australian bird whose call is so similar to raucous laughter that early European explorers of that continent were tormented
by it. There is the laughing frog (which is edible), the laughing bird
(or green woodpecker), the laughing crow, the laughing thrush, the
laughing dove (or African dove), the laughing goose (or white-fronted
goose), the laughing gull, the laughing falcon, the laughing owl.

⌐

Democritus (460–357 B.C.), called the Laughing Philosopher, pro-
posed that matter was not infinitely divisible, that there existed a
basic unit of matter, the atom, which was indivisible. It turns out
that atoms can be further broken down into protons, neutrons, and
electrons, which in turn consist of quarks, which name comes from
the James Joyce novel *Finnegans Wake*, because Murray Gell-Mann,
originator of quark theory, loved the line "Three quarks for Muster
Mark!" This makes me laugh.

⌐

In English, laughter as dialogue is often portrayed as *ha ha ha*. Santa
Claus's laugh is *ho ho ho*. The Green Giant's laugh is also *ho ho ho*.
Children are said to laugh *he he he*. The laughter of connivers and old
men is *heh heh heh*. In Spanish, laughter is *ja ja ja*, *jo jo jo*, *ji ji ji*, and
je je je. The same holds true for laughs in Romanian, French, Japa-
nese, and Chinese, and I'd be willing to bet it's the same in most other
languages too. Always a vowel sound introduced by an *h*, the sound
closest to breathing, as if laughter were as basic as respiration.

⌐

Some synonyms for *laughter*: *cackle, chuckle, chortle, giggle, guffaw,
snicker, snigger, titter, twitter*. These words make my children laugh.

⌐

Many things are laughable only later, after everything has turned out
fine and we can reflect on our good fortune or our dumb luck. Such as
my son's many trips to the emergency room for foreign objects in his
nose: raisins, rubber, paper, a toy snake's tail. "See," I once overheard
a nurse telling her coworker when she saw him in the waiting room,
"I *told* you it would be him."

⌐

Laughter heals; it can change the flavor of tears. When our cat died after nineteen years with us, my family was stricken with grief. My brothers dutifully prepared to bury him, digging a grave near the woods where he once romped. The former cat waited in a plastic bag inside a cooler from the vet's office. Everyone was crying silently, speaking in whispers. When the diggers rested for a moment, my father prepared to deposit the body in the hole. But we weren't done, the hole was too shallow, and my brother shouted, *Wait! Don't let the cat out of the bag!*

On a train one afternoon, Fourth of July, hot, tired, my son can't sit still. He can never sit still, but he is extra-can't-sit-still today. He jumps, hangs, clambers, throws his grandfather's hat, drops his crackers, chatters. I plead with him to be still as he wriggles and twists. He laughs, thinking I am trying to tickle him. The woman behind ducks to where he can't see her. He steps on my leg to peer over the edge of the seat. She jumps up and whispers, "Boo!" He falls limp to the seat below, convulsing with laughter. She does it again. He does it again. She does it again. He does it again. His baby sister stares intently at her brother. Her eyes radiate something I want to call admiration. Each time he falls to the seat beside her, she laughs heartily, uncontrollably. Pretty soon the whole train car is laughing. My children's laughter is so bright and clear and pure and unselfconscious that I suddenly understand why a cool mountain brook might be said to laugh.

"And God said unto Abraham," according to the Book of Genesis, "as for [Sarah] thy wife . . . I will bless her, and give thee a son also of her: yea, I will bless her, and she shall be a mother of nations; kings of people shall be of her. Then Abraham fell upon his face, and laughed."

The next passage, you will remember, is Sarah also laughing at the prospect of bearing a child at her age (supposedly ninety). Lesson: God has a sense of humor, a special kind of love. God also chooses the name of their son: Isaac, which means "he laugheth."

We laugh at, with, about: clowns, jokes, funny faces, children, ourselves, contortions, misfortunes, wordplay, irony, other laughs, others' joy, good fortune, madness, sickness, health, debilitation, recovery, things we can't change, things we can change, sports, games, circuses, animals, drunkenness, sobriety, sex, celibacy, errors, equivocations, mistakes, blunders, bloopers, boners, double meanings.

↝

The late Norman Cousins, editor of the *Saturday Review*, when stricken with ankylosing spondylitis, treated himself with Marx Brothers movies. He recovered almost completely. Doctors were not sure why. Cancer and heart patients at Loma Linda University's medical center today are treated with episodes of *I Love Lucy* and *The Honeymooners*. Laughter apparently increases levels of disease-fighting T cells, the very cells killed off by AIDS. Doctors are not sure why.

↝

"Among those whom I like," said the great poet W. H. Auden, "I can find no common denominator, but among those whom I love, I can; all of them make me laugh."

↝

That laughter is sweetest which is unexpected, which takes one unawares. "To that laughter," says Max Beerbohm, "nothing is more propitious than an occasion that demands gravity. To have good reason for not laughing is one of the surest aids." In church, then, in a foreign land, in a foreign language, one might reach such heights of laughter as to lose entirely any semblance of reverence.

A hot Sunday morning in Carrasco, the rich neighborhood of Montevideo. I am one of two gringos among nearly a hundred Uruguayans. The chapel is filled with families in summer dresses and breezy shirts. After a solemn hymn, a member of the congregation approaches the podium to say an opening prayer. "Our kind and gracious Heavenly Father," he begins, and I bow my head, close my eyes, try to keep my mind from wandering as I listen to his invocation. Slowly I become aware of a muffled, tinny music in the air. Appalled, I open my eyes and slyly look around me to find the blasphemer with a Walkman. All other heads are bowed, none with headphones. I close my eyes and try to focus again, but by now the music is clearer; it's the egregiously awful "She's an Easy Lover," by Phil Collins and Phillip Bailey. Then I realize that the speakers in the chapel ceiling are channeling the music along with the prayer.

I slide down the bench away from my friend, so as not to laugh, and I fold over in airplane-emergency-landing position, biting my tongue, casting my mind, feebly, to serious thoughts, solemn thoughts, when I feel the pew start to rumble and shake with my friend's silent convulsions. With that the dam bursts, and no amount of biting our tongues and holding our noses shut can stop the laughter. The tears roll down our faces, we snort profusely. Finally the prayer ends, and as the members of the congregation lift their heads and open their eyes, everyone turns toward us, on every face an expression of dismay.

As I write, I can hear my daughter's laughter behind me. She is lying in bed, sucking on her whole hand, eyes bright with the morning sun through the window, and she is laughing. It is not clear to me what she is laughing about, but her laughter is beautiful. I listen closely, I watch her, and I start to laugh too. Amen.

Patrick Madden's "Laughter" repays the effort to count its (eighteen) sections. It repays the effort to note its sources and types of content: anecdotes, quotes, etymology, lists, and bits of philosophy. It reaches far into history, into ancient texts, into language, as well as telling personal stories. The piece is framed (begins and ends) with a vision of Madden's little daughter. She also comes up somewhere near the center. So the piece has a structure, a beginning and end and a center post to hold it up and add coherence.

Hands On: Writing the Collage

For the creator, forms open doors. Discovering the collage has catalyzed a number of works for me, and this is what happens when you begin working within any specific form. The form itself opens up the subject matter in unique and interesting ways.

Think of a collage as a type of patchwork quilt. The first step may be to begin a literary ragbag—a file for quotes and your own thoughts around a subject. Currently, for example, I am filling such a ragbag with thoughts and quotes on teaching writing. Then the juxtaposing may be a matter of matching or contrasting colors, of likes and opposites, of elaborations and contradictions.

How do you sustain interest? What about closure, since a collage could in principle dribble on forever? (Consider making a frame by matching beginning and end, the way both "Babylon" and "Laughter" do.) How long should individual sections be? Overly long sections will undermine the form. If, while making a quilt, you include as one piece a bedsheet, you have sabotaged your quilt.

Collect your own examples of the form to study and learn from. Brilliant collages that have come under my eyes include C. D. Wright's "69 Hidebound Opinions, Propositions, and Several Asides from a Manila Envelope Concerning the Stuff of Poets," and "Grace Notes" by Brian Doyle (who called this lovely form a mosaic).

8.

The A/B or Two-Strand Structure

You don't really have a workable idea until you
combine two ideas.
—*Twyla Tharp*

The two-strand structure takes two topics and weaves them. Each pulls on the other, stretches the other, pushes against the other. It's a useful way to work your way into a new piece because the technique itself pulls you, the writer, along. Thinking of Thread No. 1 in a certain way forces you to consider Thread No. 2 in that way too. Like so many writing strategies, it is not only a writing plan but also a thinking plan.

Comparing something that interests you to something else that also interests you can open the door to several new pieces. You look at the first through the lens of the second, and then turn it around and look at the second through the lens of the first.

Our first two-strand model is Amit Majmudar's piece comparing poem to novel, poet to novelist. To slow it down, to absorb its qualities, read it out loud.

"The Servant of Two Masters" by Amit Majmudar

The poem makes the self strange. The novel makes strangers familiar.

Both the poem and the novel are tasked with rendering their subjects at once larger-than-life and lifelike. The poem begins with the larger-than-life and narrows it. The novel begins with the lifelike and expands it.

Size matters. In the novel, size is a function of duration. In the poem, size is a function of intensity. A two-line metaphor can weigh as much in the mind as one hundred pages. Collapse those hundred pages into a two-line summary, or expand that couplet to a hundred pages, and everything is lost.

There is nothing poetry can do that the novel cannot do. There is nothing the novel can do that the poem cannot do. (What they do separately now, they once did together in epic and tragedy.) Today it is the novel's audience that grows impatient with purple passages, and the poem's audience that grows impatient with length. A single restriction inheres in all forms even after they are mastered—and that restriction originates in the audience.

The novel allows itself diffuseness so it can tell a story. The poem denies itself diffuseness and restricts itself to the anecdote. A certain amount of *sanctioned diffuseness* made narrative poems possible. (This is one major reason for the decline in the reputations, huge during their lifetimes, of Sir Walter Scott and Henry Wadsworth Longfellow.) To insist on intensity, as the poem does, is to insist on brevity; to insist on brevity is to insist on the image. The novel, by contrast, has all the time in the world. It can afford the slow exposition, the rising action, the climax, the denouement.

The novel, at its best, kills the novelist to give life to a character. The poem can give life to a character, too, but Prufrock will never shake Eliot the way Scrooge has shaken Dickens. The poem makes masks. The novel makes golems.

The novel makes life out of language. The poem makes language come to life. The best of either does the work of both. Joyce's prose is often poetic, Larkin's verse is often novelistic. In life as in language, hybridity breeds vigor.

Goethe, Kipling, and Hardy wrote both, but Victor Hugo is the truest poet-novelist. In his work, the division is taken to its greatest possible extreme. The novels, popular and sentimental, transfer very naturally to the animated film or the musical. The late poems are abstruse, allusive, God-mad. For Hugo, the novel is exoteric art, and the poem is esoteric art. They have a Mahayana-Hinayana dichotomy. In Goethe, Kipling, and Hardy, both the poem and the novel are pursued as exoteric arts. Passing from their novels to their poems, we find no sudden increase in the difficulty of the terrain, no drastic change in climate. Hugo, such a warm host in his novels, froths and goes crosseyed in *La Lengende des Siecles* and *Le Fin de Satan*. He uses the novel as a sitting room where he can entertain readers, and the poem as a dark tower where he can escape them.

Ambidexterity is the least of literary virtues. The truly dual career (as opposed to the occasional prose work) dooms a writer to a two-front war. Energy and time drain from the form you are writing to the form you aren't. To chase one is to stray from the other. But the real concern of the poet-novelist is not logistical. Consider: Hugo's novels rank lower than Stendhal's. At least in the English-speaking world, people revere Goethe but read Rilke. Hardy and Kipling, good writers of both poems and novels, are neither the best of poets nor the best of novelists. How much better to be a Tennyson or a Dickens—to be one thing completely! The novel and the poem may well reserve their highest gifts for the pure at heart. Lancelot wins a reputation; Galahad wins the Grail.

The novel gains its power from inclusion and the broad gaze. The poem gains its power from exclusion and sharp focus. This is not to say a novel "should" not be spare and limit itself to one character's musings, or that a poem "should" not suck up unfiltered the detritus of everyday life. Nor that such work cannot be powerful in its way. But a certain *kind* of power, *specific* to either form, is lost when the principles of one guide the other. The novel becomes poetic but falls short of the poem. The poem becomes novelistic but falls short of the novel.

To call a writer "creative" is to use a hidden metaphor. The metaphor

connects the writer and God. Writers do not create; they recombine.
What they recombine are letters. When we speak of writers "creating"
a character or "creating" a world, we are still speaking of recombina-
tion. Science-fiction worlds and literary characters are actually *recom-
binations of the recognizable.* That is what gives them resonance and
meaning. Inventiveness gives pleasure. Creativity estranges. This is
why we can understand writers but cannot understand God.

Now, what can we observe about Majmudar's piece?

- Both poem and novel are introduced immediately.
- It has eleven sections. The sections are short.
- Each section comprises one and only one paragraph.
- Each section speaks of both poem and novel (the other way of
  doing this form is to alternate sections A [poem] and B [novel]).
- Threads to the big wide world: I count thirteen different
  authors: poets, novelists, or poet/novelists—Scott, Longfellow,
  Eliot, Dickens, Joyce, Larkin, Goethe, Kipling, Hardy, Hugo,
  Stendhal, Rilke, and Tennyson.
- Two other cultural references are to Mahayana-Hinayana
  dichotomy (Buddhist terms meaning something like "lesser
  vehicle" and "greater vehicle") and the knights of Medieval
  English lore, Lancelot and Galahad.
- Majmudar employs many parallel sentences, representing the
  parallel qualities of poems and novels, such as "In the novel, size is
  a function of duration. In the poem, size is a function of intensity."
- That conclusion! It's not just one more iteration of the A/B. It
  takes both to a different level.
- It is fascinating to note that Amit Majmudar, who is both a
  poet and a novelist, mentions neither himself nor his own work
  nor his life in the piece. Yet his deep knowledge of poetry and
  novel, and of the conundrums of serving both, are evident.

Now, what is our assignment? What can we take from this piece?

My assignment is to write an eleven-part piece on two related but different or even opposite things. I am thinking of beauty and ugliness. I am thinking of domestic versus wild. Chastity versus promiscuity. Faith versus secularism. Garden versus wilderness.

Or, to hone more closely to Majmudar's piece, I think I will choose poet versus painter. This is close in subject matter (which is a risk), but I think my experiences and views differ enough from those of Majmudar that I will not unconsciously take word, image, or idea from "Servant of Two Masters." I'm a poet and have an abiding fixation on the visual arts. So let me think of ways painter and poet, or paintings and poems, may be contrasted and compared.

1. Paintings and poems both use images.
2. Both grow out of ancient traditions.
3. They both use color: paint like cadmium red and words like cadmium red.
4. Numbers of painters write poems; numbers of poets paint.
5. Poems about paintings (ekphrastic poems); paintings that incorporate words.
6. The work process: blank canvass, blank page.
7. Deep envy of poets by painters and painters by poets (maybe).
8. Both depend on the visual cortex. Neural aspects. The brain.
9. Painters paint music; poets write music.
10. Performance aspects of each. Preservation aspects of each.
11. Conclusion: something about art?

You see how it works. This is a rough idea. It will change, especially as I do research, exploring paintings and poems and their makers.

Our second model, "Buzzards" by Lee Zacharias, juxtaposes the carrion-feeding vulture with the writer's father. Both threads are introduced promptly. In this case Zacharias introduces the bird (A) in the

first segment and the father (B) in the second. A subtext, introduced in
the first segment, is death.

"Buzzards" by Lee Zacharias

They woof. Though I have photographed them before, I have never
heard them speak, for they are mostly silent birds. Lacking a syrinx,
the avian equivalent of the human larynx, they are incapable of song.
According to field guides the only sounds they make are grunts and
hisses, though the Hawk Conservancy in the United Kingdom reports
that adults may utter a croaking coo and that young black vultures,
when annoyed, emit a kind of immature snarl. But to hear any of
these sounds, you must be quite close. And I am quite close. Crouched
over an unextended tripod at the edge of an empty parking lot in the
Everglades, I am in the middle of a flock of black vultures, a vortex,
maypole for this uneasy circle dance in which they weave and run
at one another, raising their ragged wings and thrusting their gnarly
gray heads. I would not call the sound they make a grunt or a hiss,
nor croaking coo, nor snarl; it is more a low, embryonic woofing, a
sound I know from my dog, who is also a black creature, not a bark
or growl, not the voice itself, but the anticipation of one reverberating
deep inside his throat. And though I keep shooting as they lurch at
one another and dip their heads to peck at bottle caps and flattened
pieces of tin, they creep me out. I have had the same sensation while
snorkeling, an exhilaration in the magic of a world not mine that
manifests itself in the same nauseous thrill of nerve as my dread.
Buzzards. Carrion crows, Jim Crow, Charleston eagle. *Coragyps
atratus*. From the Greek *korax*, meaning "raven," and *gyps*, meaning
"vulture," Latin *atratus*, "clothed in black, as in mourning." The Grim
Reaper's hooded cloak, wing-like sleeves, and protruding skeletal
feet all come to us as a personification of the black vulture; Death's
trademark scythe is the color and shape of the flight feathers, the long
white primaries the bird displays as he hunches and spreads his wings.
The Latin *vulturus* means "tearer." Give voice to the word and you
cannot distinguish it from terror.

To photograph birds requires a great deal of equipment. I paid for

most of mine—the carbon steel tripod and expensive ball head, the
camera bodies lenses, flash, filter, reflectors, and remote—with money
I inherited from my father. He would not have approved. He disap-
proved of most things. Though he could rage, he was a mostly silent
man who had no respect for impractical pursuits. He was not a bad
man, though he was difficult, excitable, hard on others, obsessed
with money. The first time I visited the Everglades he tried to talk me
out of it—it was too far, he said, there was nothing there; instead he
recommended that I visit Silver Springs, a nature theme park boast-
ing glass-bottom boat tours and a narrated Jeep safari. He wasn't
much for nature in the wild. He liked control. He was afraid of the
unknown, not of death, but of life, which had too many variables. It
was the unpredictable and irritating otherness of others that frightened him most.

What frightens me is the otherness of vultures. I am wondering
whether they will tear at my flesh, raise their wings, and run at me. I
should know, but I don't.

To photograph a wild creature, you must learn its habits.

The bible does not differentiate between birds of prey and vultures,
which are rarely predators, living instead as scavengers, consumers
of carrion. One might even call them connoisseurs, for they prefer
their meat fresh and the turkey vulture favors the flesh of herbivores
over that of carnivores. According to the Carolina Raptor Center, in
captivity they won't eat possum, which is greasy, but happily chow
down on rats. The black also feasts on fruit, though it has an unfortunate taste for turtle hatchlings, unlike the palm nut vulture of Africa,
a vegetarian that is surely the strangest of the twenty-three species
that populate the world. But in Biblical wisdom both predator and
scavenger are unclean and hateful birds; if raptors are God's creatures,
according to the Book of Leviticus, they are also an abomination:
"And these are they which ye shall have in abomination among the
fowls . . . the eagle, and the ossifrage, and the osprey, and the vulture.
. . ." Ossifrage, from the Latin *ossifraga*, meaning bone-breaker, is
an archaic name for the bearded vulture, an Old World species once
plentiful in the Alps, Himalayas, and Pyrenees, the only vulture to

consume bone as the primary part of its diet. Ornithologists no longer sanction use of the bird's other names, lamb vulture and *lammergeyer*, since it is incapable of killing lambs, let alone babies, despite myths that have led to its near extinction. While some vultures prey on insects and small amphibians and the black will steal young herons from the nest, they rarely attack live mammals. More than once I have come out my back door to discover a puff of feathers light as dandelion fluff beneath the azaleas, signature of a hawk that has raided the feeder; thrice I have been startled by the sight of a great blue heron advancing across my small city yard toward the pond. Only recently scientists have confirmed that our ancestors, the ape men, were not killed off by ferocious saber-toothed tigers but by eagles, which hunt primates larger than themselves by swooping down and piercing their skulls with their strong back talons. These are predators. "I hate vultures because they only frighten humans," says Mrs. MacKinnon in the Book of Animals, Plants, Trees, Birds, Bugs, and Flowers that informs Craig Nova's novel *The Good Son*. The titmice and chickadees, the thrashers and towhees, chipmunks, squirrels, fantails, koi, and Labrador retriever who share the space of my garden do not fear the vulture.

When Charles Darwin observed the "carrion-feeding hawks" of Uruguay in the summer of 1832, he lamented that although their structure placed them among the eagles, they ill became such a rank. Though Darwin was a self-taught observer rather than a trained scientist, even the most learned scientists of the time mistakenly believed that the New World vultures were related to the eagles. While the Old World vultures that inhabit Africa, Asia, and parts of Europe, did descend from the birds of prey classified as Falconiformes, the seven species that inhabit the Americas are classified as Ciconiiformes, related not to hawks but to storks. The similarities in appearance— the wattled necks, small naked heads, the hooked beaks, weak though fearsome-looking talons, shaggy feathers, and pronounced hunch— are the result of convergent evolution, like but independent physical adaptations.

Yet so inevitable is the vulture's association with death and so staunch our cultural will to deny it, that we persist in the Biblical view

of the vulture even as we tend to perceive those raptors from which
the Old World vultures descended, the hawks and the eagles, as Darwin did: creatures of grace, nobility, and strength, equated with freedom instead of death. Darwin called the turkey buzzard a "disgusting
bird" whose bald scarlet head is "formed to wallow in putridity." He
was right about the formation of the head—bacteria die on the bare
skin of the face, just as the bird's practice of defecating on its legs kills
bacteria. But though their habits may seem repulsive, in fact vultures
are among the cleanest of creatures. Adult condors wipe their heads
and necks on grass or sand after feeding; while other carrion eaters
spread disease, the acids in the vulture's digestive system are so strong
they destroy anthrax, botulin, cholera, and hanta-virus—the birds can
consume the most toxic corpses without passing the germs along.

In *The Vulture* novelist Catherine Heath describes a pet vulture
that preys on its master's thoroughbred dogs as "a huddle of old rags
thrown over a naked body, whose stringy neck and red head stuck
out at the top as if surveying a hostile world from a safe shelter." The
buzzards that perch on the light posts of Arrow Catcher, Mississippi
in Lewis Nordan's *Wolf Whistle* sit "with hunched shoulders and
wattled necks like sad old men in dark coats," and Ernest Hemingway
calls them "huge, filthy birds sunk in hunched feathers." The villain-
ous protagonist of "The Tell-Tale Heart" kills not out of passion or
greed, but because his victim had the eye of a vulture. Pablo Neruda
speaks not of the vulture's appearance but his black habits. It is these
habits that have made "vultures" into a favorite epithet for the media.
We use it for politicians, lawyers, ambulance chasers, talk-show
audiences, corporations, and nosy neighbors. Photographers are often
called vultures. So are writers.

When my father died, his companion of nearly twenty years told me,
"Be sure to take your stories." I found the books I'd signed to both
of them at the back of his closet. Though there were a few books
on their living room shelves, mine had never been among them. My
father was ashamed of my writing. I know because he said as much
to my mother, though they were already divorced. Otherwise I would
not have known he read them, for he never mentioned them to me.

He was ashamed not just of the writing itself but of the fact that I wrote. He didn't see the point. He kept a log of his gas mileage, but he never kept a journal. Skilled at repair, he gave to objects the kind of attention he could not deliver to people; yet I have no recollection of his hands, no memory of the texture of his skin or shape of the nails. He had beautiful handwriting, but no use for words.

Vultures are big birds. The largest bird that ever existed was a vulture of the Pleistocene epoch with a wingspan of sixteen to seventeen feet. Weighing up to thirty-three pounds, with a ten and a half foot wingspan that dwarfs a grand piano, the Andean condor is still the largest and heaviest bird that flies; climbers compare the sound of the wind rushing through its feathers to that of a jet plane. The largest of the Old World species, the Himalayan griffon, is only slightly smaller. Wingtip to wingtip the turkey vulture measures seventy-nine inches, and is larger than the American black, which has the shortest wing-span of all, a mere fifty-four inches. But to crouch in the shadow of the black's scythe-tipped wings and feel the sweep of their breath as they open is to lose all sense of inches. This smallest emissary of death has an embrace of four and a half feet. When they are even partially unfolded, the bird must hunch to keep its wings from dragging on the ground.

In youth my father was a handsome man, tall and broad-shouldered. On the street people sometimes mistook him for the rising film star John Wayne, though by the time I was old enough to remember he was already balding, no longer auburn but gray, with the same har-ried look on his face of other middle-aged men who worked whatever jobs they could find to pay the mortgage and support their families. Perhaps they had wanted children; my father never did. He would have rather sailed on the tankers he loaded with oil before punching a clock and then driving home. I don't think his work gave him plea-sure, but nor do I think he thought it should. For him pleasure was a sign of weak character.

On the ground a group of vultures is called a venue, but a group circling in the air is a kettle, as if they are swirling in a clear cauldron, a school of black fish swimming in a soup of pure air. Ungainly on the ground with their small heads, oversized wings, and heavy bodies, a gait that is at once a lurch and a run, vultures are astonishingly graceful in flight, a glide "in God's fingerprint," according to George Garrett. Darwin marveled at the sight of condors soaring in high, graceful circles. Even the turkey buzzard he found so abhorrent is transformed on the wing "by its lofty, soaring and most elegant flight"; Lewis Nordan's vultures sail "like hopeful prayers." Who has not watched them wheel overhead? Floating high above the landfills that punctuate the flatness of the interstate along the east coast of Florida, they undulate like kites tethered to the earth by invisible strings. In the mountains I thrill to discover how close I am to heaven by the arc of a turkey vulture swooping below. I am too dazzled by the wideness of the sky to connect the dots of the constellations, and I forget the names of all but the most basic forms of clouds; though I know the field markings of many birds, I cannot tell a vireo from a shrike in the air; but even at a distance far too great to note the shorter tail of the black or difference in coloration on the underside of the wings, I can easily distinguish between black and turkey vultures in flight. The turkey rarely beats its wings, holding them raised in a dihedral as it tilts from side to side, rocking as if buoyed by a gentle sea; the black holds its wings flat, beats more often, and does not tilt. Lacking a sense of smell, it flies higher than the turkey, whose olfactory sense is so keen engineers look for circling turkey vultures to locate gas line leaks and NASA used them to find remains of the ill-fated crew of the space shuttle Columbia. The magnifying center of the black vulture's eye is so powerful it can locate food by sight from more than a mile above, though it often follows the turkey to a corpse. Indians of the South American highlands roast and consume condors' eyes in the belief that their own eyesight will be sharpened.

In the tropics the king vulture too flies higher than the turkey; in the dense rainforest both it and the black must depend upon the *Cathartes*, the turkeys and yellow-heads, to locate carrion by smell. With its gaudy orange, red, yellow, purple, and black wattled head, the king is the most flamboyantly colored; in flight its white back and long ebony-tipped wings are spectacular. Rounding a curve of road in the Alajuela Province of Costa Rica one Christmas, our van flushed a king vulture from his roost on the living fence, and I gasped as he spread his wings and slowly swept across the cassava field to the forest canopy beyond, so stunned by the sight that he was gone before I remembered the camera beside me on the seat.

Vultures soar. Unlike most birds, whose breast muscles power the beating of the wings, creating lift and propulsion, a vulture simply opens its wings to the air currents that lift and keep it aloft. Once in a storm so torrential I pulled to the side of the interstate, I watched a small bird flying in place, flapping its wings frenetically in an effort to battle the wind, which finally blew it backward, as if it were no more than a bit of ash. The vulture's flight is so beautiful because it appears effortless. And in fact it nearly is, for a vulture uses scarcely more energy in flight than it would in standing still. It's not surprising that the Wright brothers should have designed their first plane with the curved wingtips of the turkey vulture in mind. According to Michael Alford Andrews, Andean condors spread their wingtip primaries "like fingers feeling for life as they turn." David Houston explains that once a vulture has gained altitude by circling inside a thermal, it can "glide away into still air, where it will slowly lose altitude" until it nears the ground, finds another thermal, and climbs again. They travel at remarkably high altitudes, as great as 15,000 feet for the vultures of Africa and the Andean condor; Houston reports a Ruppell's griffon alleged to have collided with a commercial aircraft at 37,000 feet. Imagine the alarm of passengers looking out a plane's window to see a vulture cruising just off the wing like a seagull following a boat's wake.

It is said that vultures circled above Romulus and Remus. Over and over they appear in literature and film as a dark omen. In Alain Robbe-Grillet's *Jealousy* the vulture pictured atop a mast on a calendar seems to confirm in the husband's mind his wife's infidelity. The hero of Ernest Hemingway's "The Snows of Kilimanjaro" knows that he is going to die when the buzzards move in, three "squatting obscenely" on the ground while a dozen swirl overhead "making quick-moving shadows." In Zora Neale Hurston's *Their Eyes Were Watching God* a thousand buzzards precede the deadly hurricane. In William Faulkner's *As I Lay Dying* it is the sight of vultures in the distance that tell Darl his mother has died. And whenever we see them in a cartoon or Hollywood western, we know another outlaw is expiring just over the next hill.

My father died shortly after noon. He shot himself in the treeless backyard of the Florida house he shared with his companion, which backed on the open fairway of the community golf course, though he did not play. She had gone to the beauty parlor. When she returned a few hours later, she went through the house calling his name. She saw him through the window. I don't know if she stepped outside. In any case I'm sure she wouldn't have looked up.

Though from the vulture's point of view it would hardly seem to matter which side prevails, many nations have used vultures as symbols of victory. Wayne Grady's eclectic and fascinating *Vulture: Nature's Ghastly Gourmet* lists several ancient monuments decorated with gruesome depictions of vultures devouring or hovering over the slain enemy. Grady also recalls Samuel Johnson's fable "The Vulture," in which a female is overheard instructing her young in the arts of a vulture's life—the easiest way to find food, she tells them, is to look for the place where enemies wage war. In the first scene of *Patton*, which opens with the image of an African white-backed vulture sitting on the mountain above the film's title, soldiers shoot two vultures to keep them from the battlefield corpses, denying them the cherished memories of Lewis Nordan's ancient Mississippi buzzards, who endure the lean twentieth century of roadkill by feasting on their recollection of "the glorious Festival of Dead Rebels."

But as the turkey vulture has extended its range northward, some see the bird not as the harbinger of death but the harbinger of spring. Bruce Ehresman, a biologist with the Iowa Department of Natural Resources, calls turkey vultures "much more reliable than robins," and Scott Weidensaul, whose observations contest the notion that turkey vultures are nonmigratory, maintains that they are the real sign of spring in the central Appalachians, reappearing "most often around the first week of February," followed by common grackles, then the red-winged blackbirds, until finally the robin returns at the end of February or early March, though only if the snow has melted. Here, on the Piedmont Plateau of North Carolina, I see no such sign, and so I wait for the Bradford pears and poke around the ivy for crocus.

My father was from Wisconsin. He grew tired of waiting for spring, and when he retired he moved to Florida. He might have moved to El Paso, but he didn't like the radio station. In Florida, he reported proudly, it was summer nearly all year round, which is why the black vulture, which does not tolerate cooler temperatures as well as the turkey, is so common there. Vultures used to drink from the bucket beneath his downspout.

I have often observed black vultures at Florida's Myakka River State Park. There they flock in great numbers, trolling the air above the lake, roosting on railings and roofs as if they are basking—and perhaps they are—the russet winter afternoon sun warming their dull black feathers and lending a subtle lavender to the wrinkled gray skin of their heads. One year when they seemed particularly active, I spotted half a dozen standing on a car parked beside the lake, where they appeared to be gorging on bloody bits of flesh, though the grisly morsels turned out to be only shreds of the car's red upholstery. The windows were closed, and in my ignorance, assuming their olfactory organ to be as keen as a bear's, I supposed the owner had left cold cuts in a cooler and was astonished to think they could have pecked through the roof as easily as a chick liberates itself from the egg. On the lake a boat was gliding toward shore, and as I watched, the occupant leapt to his feet, screaming, "My car! My car! Get off my car, you damn buzzards!" and promptly fell in the lake.

Yet in my photographs the unbroken shell of blue-gray metal reflects the vultures' silvery talons like still water. A few years later a chatty ranger at the Everglades Anhinga Trail told me that Ford had used fish oil in the sealants on the 1999 Taurus. The occasion for our conversation was the unusual number of black vultures on the trail, brought to the ground by the cool weather. He had just come from the parking lot, where on such days he had seen flocks of black vultures attack the sealant so vigorously that tourists returned to their cars to find the windshields popped out; he had been checking the lot for damage. True, the black, which prefers coastal areas, often dines on fish. At the Wild Bird Center on Key Largo I have watched it eat its sardine more delicately than my dog eats his meat and kibble. Once at the Anhinga Trail my husband, son, and I all observed a black vulture attending a great blue heron that had caught a fish too large for it to swallow. The heron tried it headfirst, then tailfirst, and sideways, dropping the fish to the ground after each attempt and walking a few steps away as if to consider another approach, but the vulture moved in to feed only after the heron gave up and departed. Perhaps its patience was only caution, for the same ranger regaled me with the tale of a researcher who got too close to a great blue, which drove its beak into the man's skull and killed him. "Most aggressive bird there is," he remarked of the heron. Who can say whether a vulture is fearful or forbearing? In Darwin's era vultures liked to tear the leather from ship's rigging, though the leather would have borne no more visual resemblance to a cow than Ford's sealant to a gar. They may be prudent, but if it's true that the blacks have no sense of smell they are not just scavengers but vandals.

My father loved cars, though he never drove anything fancier than a Ford Crown Victoria. Mechanical though he was, a noise beneath the hood sent him into a panic. A dent or a scratch drove him wild. In the empty parking lot where the single driving lesson he gave me took place, he was so afraid I would hit something that I didn't learn to drive for another ten years. Many years after that, when I had failed to sell a new novel and had to buy a used car instead of a new one, I asked my father's advice. To my astonishment he sent me a check for five thousand dollars. I think all he ever really wanted was for me to ask his opinion on something that mattered to him. He didn't care if I told him I loved him, but he wanted that token of respect.

Properly speaking, we should not call them buzzards, buzzard being a

British designation for a large hawk. The word comes from the French *busard*, which means hawk, and in the Old World *busard* refers to the genus of soaring hawks called *Buteo*, the most common of which in North America is the familiar red-tailed hawk; in Australia the bird called a black-breasted buzzard is a hawk of the genus *Hamirostra*. But we do not speak properly; in common American usage a buzzard is the same thing as a vulture; it is a contemptible, cantankerous old person; it is a greedy and ruthless person who preys upon others. As an adjective in the past it was used to mean senseless or stupid. A search of books on Amazon brings up 342 results for vultures and 363 for buzzards, including one titled *The Old Buzzard Had It Coming*.

Once I came across a lone black vulture feeding at the side of the road from Florida City to Key Biscayne. When I slowed the car to watch, it paused and looked up, standing over the carcass and watching me until I drove on. An hour or so later, when I drove back the same way, there was no evidence that it had ever been there. Perhaps it dragged the skeleton into the brush the moment I was out of sight. I imagine it glancing back as it carries the corpse in its mouth like my dog bearing a stick he knows I plan to confiscate. It could not carry its prize off through the air like an eagle, for though its talons are as fearsome in appearance as the eagle's, their grasp is weak. Only the bearded vulture uses its talons to grip.

At the table my parents, my brother, and I often sat with our heads bowed. It was not to pray. We were trying not to talk. My parents didn't seem to remember how to have a conversation, though once, surely, they had been able to talk without erupting, had been able to speak without a fight. My father had so many allergies he didn't enjoy eating anyway. We picked at our food and waited for the meal to be over.

Generally the black is a communal feeder. In the rainforest the turkey vulture is most likely to locate a kill, but at a larger carcass it yields to the black, and both yield to the king. Even among its own ranks the turkey is a hierarchical diner, but feeding is less a competition than collaboration, with each species dining on a different part of the animal. When larger vultures tear into mammals the size of horses or cows, they make the flesh available to the turkey, which has the weakest beak and on its own must content itself with animals the size of chipmunks and squirrels. The long necks of the largest vultures allow them to reach into the organs, while others feast on skin, tendons, and the tougher meat; the turkey, black, and hooded species take the scraps and pick the bones clean. In its habitat the bearded, the only vulture to have a feathered head, is the last to feed, for its specialty is bones, which it picks up with its feet, swooping down to crack them against a rock. It is reputed to prepare tortoises the same way, and the ancient Greeks blamed it for the death of Aeschylus. As the story goes, a bearded vulture with a tortoise in its talons mistook his bald head for a rock and dropped the tortoise, cracking the poet's skull. I like the irony, but the image that enchants me is that of the feeding chimango, the caracara that Darwin observed to be the last to leave the table, lingering at the carcass so long that it might often be "seen within the ribs of a cow or a horse like a bird in a cage." I picture the cathedral arch of those bleached white ribs, inside a dark canary without song.

The turkey vulture is more solitary and less aggressive than the black. While the black defends itself by vomiting, as a friend who shot one with an air rifle as a child learned firsthand, the turkey more often plays dead. At the Carolina Raptor Center, which stages a photo shoot every spring, I have been close enough to touch it, though I would not. The bird's very solitariness precludes it.

To see a turkey vulture up close is to know the bird's tragic beauty, for there is a majesty to the crimson head, bare save for a sparse black stubble; the bird looks less bald than vulnerable and shorn, a Nazi collaborator exposed before a French village. The raised nostrils have no internal division; they are like the space left by a handle, the eye of a bloody needle of bone. All the vilification and fear the vulture inspires seem contained in the sidelong wary sadness of the eye, not the sharp black stare of an eagle or a heron's mean pupil in its fixed yellow ring, but a doleful attention that is the same soft shade of brown as my dog's. The bird's muteness sits upon its shoulders. It knows what death tastes like, but cannot speak of the flavor. To see a turkey vulture up close is to be reminded of death not as portent but as the weight of an unbearable witness. His dirge has no throat, his wisdom no voice. Two million years of silence haunt his expression. To see a turkey vulture up close is to know what loneliness looks like.

When my father was young he did some hunting. When I was young he liked to fish. But he was not the kind of man who took up hobbies. He had friends, but no close ones. I don't think he ever had a pet. He filled his time by fixing things, so many things it seems now as if he must have thought everything we owned was broken.

In the United States it is illegal not only to shoot a vulture but also to keep one as a pet. I would think few people want one, though the sister of a former president of Ecuador kept a condor, and wildlife rehabilitators report that vultures are intelligent, more so than other raptors, as well as mischievous and inquisitive. Darwin claimed that they stole a pocket compass in a red morocco case and carried off a big black hat. At the Carolina Raptor Center one developed a habit of untying the staff members' shoestrings; when they tried to trick it by wearing shoes with Velcro tabs, the bird learned to undo those too. I think of George the Goose, who used to unlace my boots at the train station in Princeton Junction the year I lived in New Jersey. Or my dog, who loved to steal socks and make us chase him through the house when he was a pup, who greets me every morning by dropping a tennis ball on my face. Like crows, which I have often observed skating across the frozen surface of my backyard pond, vultures frolic. Young blacks toss rocks like balls. They play tag and follow-the-leader. According to the Turkey Vulture Society, some of the soaring and circling they do may be for fun, just as Darwin suspected. Their lives seemed so pleasurable to Edward Abbey—"floating among the clouds all day, seldom stirring a feather"—that he insisted he wanted to be reincarnated as one. They're not just personable birds, they're sweet, insists the Society's president. Vultures raised by humans love and trust them; even after rejoining their natural communities they continue to respond to human attention. One is reported to have followed a boy to his school bus each day, flying off to forage only after the bus was gone, and returning in the afternoon to accompany the boy home. Only my dog comes close to being that loyal.

My father was a misogynist, a deeply conservative man who felt women should be seen and not heard. He detested women drivers and did not see the point of sending me to college. The whole problem with his marriage, as he saw it, was that my mother didn't want to follow; a marriage, he said, can't have two leaders. Still he always claimed that he would not be there for her if she ever got sick—in that case, he seemed to believe, it was everyone for herself.

Though we think of the Grim Reaper as male, in most vultures it is not possible to tell the difference between male and female by appearance, and in Federico Garcia Lorca's *Blood Wedding*, the figure of death is not a vulture itself but a beggar woman in a vulture costume. The ancient Egyptians believed that only female vultures existed; they were able to perpetuate the species because they were impregnated by the south and southeastern winds. The Egyptian goddesses Nekhbet and Mut wore vulture headdresses. Nekhbet, goddess of Upper Egypt, often portrayed as a vulture hovering at the Pharaoh's head, was also the goddess of childbirth; the hieroglyph for Mut, whom the Greeks associated with Hera, meant mother. The crown of Upper Egypt bore the image of a vulture, and the gold face mask of King Tut has a vulture over the right eye and a cobra, symbol of Lower Egypt, over the left. So sacred was the bird to the Egyptians that "Pharaoh's chicken" is the first wild animal known to have been given legal protection.

In some versions of Mayan legend the vulture is the mother and protector of the Serpent Priestess, who lived among jaguars, though in other versions the bird is male, perhaps in reference to the king vulture, whose scientific name, *Sarcorhamphus papa*, means the Pope's fleshy beak and refers to the bulb of bright orange skin above the orange and black beak. The common name predates the Spanish conquest of South America. A royal tomb dating from 450 AD in

the pre-Columbian city of La Milpa in Belize contains the remains
of a ruler known as Bird Jaguar whose adornments include a large
pendant of a king vulture's head carved from jade. In Mayan legend
humans descended from jaguars; the vulture, who was personified as
a lord or king, was the messenger who mediated between humans and
the gods, "the conduit to the gods and the afterworld . . . deified and
venerated as an ancestor and god after his death."

Some Indian villages in Peru have annual ceremonies involving the
condor. One re-enacts the Spanish conquest and Quechua myth by
pairing a bull, introduced to Peru by the Spanish, with a native condor, whose feet are sewn to the back of the bull with strips of leather.
In frenzy the two creatures buck, pitch, and lurch around the plaza
together. If the condor survives it is released, a victory that symbolizes
successful Indian resistance, though I can't help wondering how the
Indians overcome the resistance of bird and beast to the process of the
sewing.

The Andean condor, which appeared on the pottery and textiles
of cultures that predate the Incas, is still a symbol of strength and
endurance in South America, figuring on the national crests of Bolivia,
Chile, Columbia, and Ecuador. In Chile the condor is a coin featuring
the bird's image. The name of Chile's capital province, Cundinamarca,
comes from the native word for condor, and in Bolivia the Order of
the Condor is the highest award of merit.

In North America we know the California condor as the Thunder-
bird through the legends of the Tlingit, who believed the flapping of
its wings to cause thunder and lightning to flash from its eyes. In many
West Coast native communities shamans were believed to receive their
powers from the condor. The Costanoans raised raptors to be sacrificed
at funerals, eagles to Venus and condors to Mars. In Iroquois legend the
Golden Eagle, Head Chief of all the birds, chose vultures as his faithful
servants, for it was his law that the earth be kept clean.

In African folklore the bird's ability to show up wherever there is a
carcass is a sign of extrasensory powers, though not all myths vener-
ate vultures. In Hindu belief, vultures are carriers of the human spirit
but also the gatekeepers of hell. In European folklore the bearded
vulture has a reputation as predatory as that of the wolf, though its

otherworldliness makes it more frightening. In North American Tsimshian legends the condor abducts young women and destroys its rivals with a great wind. And in ancient Greek myth, it was not two eagles, but two bearded vultures that flew down to tear out Prometheus's liver every day. Whether they were male or female legend does not say.

My father was not a religious man. As a child he was sent to Catholic schools, where a nun rapped his hand with a metal-edged ruler and split his knuckles. Did he look up, I wonder, when he felt the chill of her shadow, or did he just hear the sweeping wing of the nun's black habit as she brought the blade of the ruler down? I don't know if he had any faith before. He never did after. His view of death was practical, his view of life dark. He threatened to die so often it was a shock when he did.

Both Tibetans and the Parsees of India dispose of their dead by feeding them to vultures. According to myth Sakyamuni Buddha gave himself to feed a hungry tiger; in another version he fed his own flesh to a hawk in order to spare a pigeon—thus sky burial is regarded as a final act of charity in which the deceased provides food to sustain living things, and the Tibetan name for the practice, *jhator*, means giving alms to the birds. Interference with *jhator* is a serious breach of Tibetan religion, in which the vultures, sacred messengers called *Dakinis*, the Tibetan equivalent of angels, are believed to carry the soul up to heaven, where it will wait reincarnation; Tibetans fear they will not return if driven away. In Xue Xinran's nonfiction account of a Chinese woman's search for her soldier husband in Tibet, the Tibetans were so angry at the Chinese solder, who accidentally disrupted a wartime sky burial by shooting one of the vultures, he could placate them only by killing himself, allowing the Tibetans to call back the sacred birds by feeding them his flesh.

Although *jhator* is embedded in Tibetan Buddhism, its origins predate the religion in Tibet. The kings of the Yalung dynasty were entombed and the remains of Dalai Lamas and other high Buddhist figures are preserved in stupas or encased in gold, but neither burial nor cremation is practical in a country with so little fuel and such hard ground. Until Buddhism was introduced in the ninth century water burial was the most common method of disposal—poor people simply dropped the bodies of their dead into a river, though in more elaborate forms of water burial the corpse was cut into small pieces to be consumed by fish, just as it is dismembered and hacked into pieces for the vultures in *jhator*, which is now chosen by more than three-quarters of Tibetans; those who cannot afford the *o-yogin* butcher simply place their dead on high rocks for the birds and wild dogs.

At the Drigung Monastery in Central Tibet, the best known of the three major sites, as many as ten sky burials are conducted a day. Here the vultures are so sated they must be coaxed to eat, but at many of the more remote sites the birds are so ravenous they must be fended off with sticks while the body is prepared. Though it is considered a bad omen if they do not consume the entire corpse, a sign that demons have taken over the spirit, some remote sites are strewn with tufts of hair and bones, as well as scraps of clothing, beer bottles, broken axe handles, and rusty blades. At Langmusi on the Sichuan border, where tickets to the *jhator* illustrated with a flock of vultures devouring a human body are sold despite the efforts of the Chinese to restrict attendance, one witness reports seeing a headless, armless skeleton.

At such remote sites the ceremony may be no more than a prayer uttered by the single butcher, but at Drigung preparations begin the day before, when the body is washed, shaved, placed in a fetal position, and wrapped in a white shroud. Lamas chanting prayers to release the soul from purgatory lead the procession to the charnel ground, a large fenced meadow with a circle of stones surrounded by prayer flags. At dawn the sky burial master blows a horn and lights a fire of juniper or mulberry branches to summon the vultures to roll out a five-colored road between heaven and earth, though surely the incense also helps purify the foul air. While the mourners watch, the *o-yogin* butcher or *tomden* rips off the shroud and begins the dismemberment, cajoling the vultures as he hacks off limbs, removes the flesh and smashes the bones. Often he and his assistants laugh and chat as they work, mixing the pulverized bones with a *tsampa* of roasted barley flour, yak butter, and tea to make them more palatable to the birds. All the while they speak to the vultures, coaxing, inviting.

"Eat, eat," they say in Tibetan, "*Shey, shey*." "Birdies," they call in a language that seems less their own than the birds'.

In India, where the actual consumption of the body is hidden from view, sky burials are required by orthodox Parsee doctrine, which holds that corpses contaminate anything they touch and therefore cannot be buried, cremated, or thrown in the river. Here the body is placed in a closed granite structure with one-hundred foot towers known as the *dakhma*. Once all clothing and adornment have been removed with hooked rods and the body has been washed, perfumed with myrrh, and blessed by the officiating priest, it is placed on one of the three-tiered stones atop the towers, open at the top to the vultures. When the body is ready, a signal is given, and male mourners in a nearby prayer pavilion begin praying. It is the voice of their prayers that summons the birds.

There was no service for my father; he wanted none. No prayers, no eulogies. He would have liked a brief notice of his death in the news-letter put out by Texaco, the company for which he had worked for forty years, but his companion was afraid for strangers to know she was alone, and so he had no obituary either. Only a death certificate marked his passing. His body was cremated, his ashes scattered from a plane over the Gulf of Mexico.

Years later, in a restaurant where I had taken her to lunch, my mother said, out of the blue, "I think it's good what your father did. Potassium for the fish."

I was so upset—we were *eating*; we hadn't been talking about my father, except for the running conversation in her head—I dropped my fork and went to the ladies' room and wept. When she came in a few minutes later it was to rinse her partial plate.

"You don't know how lucky you are," she said. "You still have all your teeth. You can eat whatever you want."

My father was who he was. He died how he died. But because he was my father I loved him.

Though it seems as if the symbol of death ought to be eternal, vultures, slow breeders who eat at the top of the food chain, are particularly vulnerable to environmental threats. What will we fear if the buzzard is gone? In the United States though populations of black and turkey vultures are increasing thanks to our bounty of roadkill, a captive breeding program was necessary to save the California condor, which came so close to extinction that by 1987 there were only three birds left in the wild. It will take more than that to save the Old World vultures of South Asia, the Old World long-billed griffon, slender-billed, and Indian white-backed vultures, all listed as Critically Endangered, the highest level of risk for extinction, by the World Conservation Union.

So radically has the vulture population of South Asia declined that in 2001 the Parsee Council of India installed solar reflectors to speed decomposition in the *dakhma*, where more than a hundred vultures are needed to keep up with the three or four corpses a day. It is not just the Parsees who are affected by their disappearance. We may loathe vultures, but we need them.

Carcasses of animals that the vultures are no longer numerous enough to consume have created public health problems in Pakistan, India, and Nepal. Besides the diseases spread by the carcasses themselves, rotting carrion has resulted in a booming population of feral dogs and outbreaks of rabies. In Europe the vulture population is one percent of what it was in the nineteenth century. We may have learned the lesson of DDT, but only recently has the decline of the vulture population in Asia been traced to Diclofenac. An anti-inflammatory used to treat sick cattle, it causes renal failure in vultures and is so lethal that contamination of less than one percent of livestock carcasses created the most rapid population decline ever recorded for a wild bird. Perhaps the recent ban will save them, though it's too soon to know whether anything can keep them from going the way of the dinosaurs and woolly mammoths.

My father left no note, of course. I wouldn't have expected one, though I looked.

When vultures woo they seem to summon all the voice their
unequipped throats can muster. The New World black spreads his
wings, lowers his head and emits a puffing sound; the turkey groans.
It is as close to a serenade as these creatures without song can come.
When they warn they grunt or hiss; they may even snarl. But what
I hear does not sound like a grunt or a hiss, neither snarl nor groan,
not a puffing or even a croaking coo; it is more a low, embryonic
woofing, not the voice itself but the anticipation of one reverberating
deep inside the throat. I cannot tell whether they are warning me or
wooing, though here in their midst, surrounded by a flock of them
at the edge of an empty parking lot in the Everglades, it would seem
important to know.

In the end they ignore me. They wander off; I pack up my camera
and tripod and go. I will learn their habits and more, but I will never
speak their language.

Yet some of the happiest hours of my life have been spent in the
open air of a salt marsh in the company of birds. It is an acquired
taste, for I grew up in the Midwest, where farmland falls away from
the road like a low tide and the highway seems an endless bridge
over nothing, the horizon so treeless and vast that if someone beside
a farmhouse a mile away lifted a hand to wave I would see it. The
Midwest affords everyone a vulture's view. Perhaps that is why it has
always seemed such a lonely place to me. Even in the safety of my car
I feel dwarfed and exposed.

If I ever saw vultures wheeling in the sky over the Midwestern
cornfields I don't remember. The first time I saw one on the ground
was at Merritt Island National Wildlife Refuge in Florida. My father
had died less than two months before, and I was on my way home
from his house, the house that I now owned, where I had spent the
past week working on his estate. I knew of the Refuge only from a
picture on a calendar; it was not a place I had always longed to see,
but a place that was on my way home. Stopping was an attempt to
give that dark errand some small facet of pleasure.

Driving the highway through the Everglades to Flamingo, I always
feel on the edge of openness in the way I am on the edge of it as I

pass over the Midwestern farmland, a traveler, an observer, a person apart. It is different at Merritt Island, where an unpaved road winds along dikes once used for mosquito control, a sandy seven-mile lane through one hundred forty thousand acres of saltwater estuaries, brackish marsh, and freshwater lagoons. I rarely saw another car in the two days I spent cruising the wildlife drive and paved back road, the radio off, windows and sunroof open, eating peanut butter crackers for lunch and peeing in a Dixie cup I dumped out the window. In the afternoon I walked the trails through the hammocks of oak and palm, listening to the drill of a pileated woodpecker whose bright red crest I could just spot through the trees. At dawn I parked beside the small swales where egrets, ibises, and wood storks fed and squabbled. Each time I opened my door they flushed upward with a great whooshing of wings, then settled again like parachutes, pecking and squawking. On the ponds there were great black formations of coots, and in the distance a streamer of dazzling white pelicans. In the clarity of the weak winter light the mudflats glittered, quivering with sandpipers and tiny crustaceans, while an osprey sailed the far sky. A rail skittered into the brush at the start of the Cruickshank Trail, the five-mile loop I hiked around a shallow lagoon and through the marsh while a balmy breeze wisped at my collar and fingered my hair. The only sound was the whistling kik-kik-kik of the terns that swooped and dipped and flashed their forked white origami tails against the bright blue heaven. I had not spoken a word for two days. The landscape was as wide, as exposed and dwarfing as the Midwest, but I had disappeared inside it. When I got back to my car, four turkey vultures blocked the narrow road. They were huge, rough feathered, dark, a color I would describe as more a dirty chocolate than black; the sun shone off the red heads and ivory hooks of their beaks. Though I confess to superstition, they did not strike me as an omen. Despite the recentness of grief they did not remind me of death or its tedious business. They were simply there, as I was, in a kind of matter-of-factness so profound we can know it only in nature. It may have been a minute or ten that we regarded one another. Then they waddled to the side and let me pass. That evening, driving the back road, I came upon a vulture tree. It was dusk, and the hunkering vultures and bare black bones of the branches were silhouetted against the faded dust-blue sky in a way that seemed incredibly beautiful to me. It is in such confrontations with the eternal shape of death that we know most fully we're alive.

In "The Snows of Kilimanjaro" the dying writer dreams that he is saved, carried by a small silver plane up over the wildebeest and zebras, the forests and bamboo slopes, only to understand that where he is going is into the unbelievable whiteness of death. He is borne on the buzzard's wing, like a Buddhist carried up to heaven by the *dakhini*.

I do not dream of vultures. I have never dreamed of flying, though as a child, lying in the dark, voiceless, awake, listening to my parents fight, I used to dream of escape. Perhaps that's why I grew up to be a writer. In bed at night now my dog nests against my thigh. Sometimes in his sleep he twitches and yips, chasing squirrels, tasting the hunt. Africans believe that vultures dream the location of their food. But who really knows where the dog and vulture soar while they sleep? Why would we dream never to leave the domain of our waking world? I don't know where I go as I sink into the blackness of that temporary death, only that in the morning I wake with a low woofing in my throat that, if I'm lucky, will turn into song.

What can we learn from Zacharias's monumental reflection on death, on that old buzzard her father, and on the vultures she photographs and studies? Do we think it earns its word count (almost nine thousand words)? As previously noted, "Buzzards" appeared in *Southern Humanities Review* and was reprinted in *The Best American Essays 2008*. The vulture, seen as a "death bird" (because it is a scavenger) in so many cultures, seems a powerful matrix in which to embed a painful family story.

In using "Buzzards" as a model, should we take our own piece to its length, knowing how difficult it is to publish such a long piece? We might, given a weighty subject matter. But we can also profitably study the qualities of Zacharias's piece to write a shorter piece of our own.

First, let's look at the piece literally. That is the way to begin. Count the sections (twenty-eight), one of them one line only, some rather short, some considerably longer. How long? The longest section, the last, comes to 1,112 words. The shortest section comes to fifteen words. Most sections come to between 200 and 400 words. Yes I did count the words in each section. What is fascinating is that the family story is told in the shortest sections.

What glues the vulture sections to the father sections are the subject-matter links between them. The piece goes from photographing vultures to the writer purchasing photography equipment with money inherited from her father; from the father's fear of others to the writer's fear of otherness in vultures; from the epithet "vulture" used against writers to the father's dislike of this writer's writing; from physical attributes of vultures to the father's physical appearance; from vultures as an emblem of death to the father's suicide; from vultures as a harbinger of spring to the father's move to Florida since he was tired of waiting for spring; from vultures eating cars to the father's love of cars; from vultures dining on road kill to the family gathered for dinner; from a vulture's look of loneliness to the father's lack of close friends; from the loyalty of the vulture to the disloyalty of the father; from the ritual feeding of corpses to vultures in Tibetan Buddhist culture to the feeding of the father to the fish ("potassium for the fish," according to the mother). And there are others.

Things to consider when using "Buzzards" as our teacher in thinking about a piece of our own: What is out there in the larger world that would mirror or serve as a matrix for a personal story? This something-or-other is not causally tacked on but rather deeply researched. It is notable that the vulture matrix Zacharias uses to elegize her father comes from the natural world, a world entirely external to the family. I might think of writing about my sister Susanne's mental illness within a matrix of rivers flooding and exceeding their bounds, or I might think of a piece on addiction and compulsivity within a matrix of gravity.

Hands On: Writing the Piece

The two-strand form invites many sorts of pieces and you will want to explore its riches by adding it to your repertoire of structures.

- Begin your own collection of models. Among those I admire is T. Coraghessan Boyle's "Chicxulub," which alternates between a teenage daughter and the danger she is in, and the danger of a meteor hitting the earth. Jane Kramer's "The Reporter's Kitchen" mixes writing and cooking (this reporter cannot write without cooking and her account of this difficulty is both hilarious and breathtaking in its virtuosity).
- Again list out the key subjects that interest you, that would repay research and reflection. Make a list of ten subjects. Which of these might be compared? Which contain analogous requirements and attributes? Which contain opposite requirements and attributes? Are there persons who stand for these attributes?
- Now, begin a piece in your writer's notebook. Write the piece. Make it the first of a series.

9.

Dramatic Story Structure

> Most short stories focus on a main character. . . .
> We expect the character's experiences will change him /
> her, because change is the way we perceive that something
> has happened. . . . Readers are also very much interested
> in the struggle toward that change.
> —*Charles Brashear*

The last structure offered here, illustrated by Steve Almond's "A Dream of Sleep," is the dramatic story structure. ("Story" refers to both nonfiction and fiction.) This structure has a complication or problem in the beginning, an escalating series of actions, a climax, and a resolution.

The complication or problem at the beginning belongs to a protagonist with a passionate goal or else with a need to surmount the complication. There are a series of rising actions, most typically involving the protagonist's attempts to overcome the complication or to achieve his or her goal. They are rising in that each new one is more serious or consequential than the previous one. An antagonist—a person or nature or a series of related events—challenge the protagonist and block or impede his or her efforts to gain the goal. The dramatic story structure has a climax, which is the final battle or struggle. It ends with a resolution—the protagonist either succeeds or fails. Preceding this resolution, often, an intruder enters, a helper or its opposite. In any story, the entrance of an intruder is a significant structural moment.

In Almond's story, the antagonist comes in the form of the events of urban change. It's the changing urban environment and its agents that escalate the action. The protagonist is impinged upon and his efforts to protect his position are entirely defensive until the big turn at the end.

The classical dramatic structure is what Aristotle was talking about in *Poetics*, which he composed in 350 BCE. For him, plot was "an imitation of an action that is complete, and whole, and of a certain magnitude; for there may be a whole that is wanting in magnitude. A whole is that which has a beginning, a middle, and an end." *

The dramatic story structure is old, reliable, faithful, and remains the structure of choice for any number of short stories, articles, and essays. There are writers who think it's the only way to write a piece. Two instruction books that I would not be without elaborate this dramatic structure for fiction and nonfiction. They are Janet Burroway's *Writing Fiction* and Jon Franklin's *Writing for Story*. It's important for writers to command dramatic story structure if only to comprehend how nondramatic structures must rely on something *else* to drive them forward. Or to comprehend how, in some cases, a piece constructed in a seemingly different form, such as a collage, can be powered by an underlying dramatic structure.

Note two key strategies that inform successful dramatic stories. First, the story's problem or complication, the thing that sets it off, should be *important* (not "wanting in magnitude," as Aristotle put it). A trivial complication will give you a trivial story. Second, the complication should be something that the protagonist attempts to solve (whether successfully or not) *by his or her own efforts*. Passive protagonists don't make good stories because it is the protagonist's actions to solve the problem that move the story forward. Often, before the protagonist resolves the complication, he or she must arrive at a new understanding of what the complication is.

Now let's read Steve Almond's story, out loud.

"A Dream of Sleep" by Steve Almond
The caretaker's name was Wolf Pinkas. He lived with his two cats in a

---

* Aristotle, *Poetics*, http://classics.mit.edu/Aristotle/poetics.html.

stone cottage at the rear of the cemetery. The building, a square structure six feet high, had been erected as a family crypt. But the wealthy Prussian immigrant who commissioned it disappeared without a trace before the First World War. Unable to sell the vault, the owners of the cemetery, a family named Gardner, converted it to a caretaker's shed.

In the decade following World War II, when Wolf assumed the position of caretaker, the yard was a thriving concern. Its high walls shimmered with ivy; dainty wood benches lined its paths. The graves were in the eastern European fashion, aboveground, great slabs of marble or slate etched with names and dates and inlaid with small circular photos of the deceased. On weekends and holidays, relatives came to set out flowers, votive candles, wreaths of hazelnut. They carried picnic lunches and sat on the benches and ate and laughed with the dead.

But the yard had fallen from prosperity. The elder Gardner died, leaving management to his son, a young man with slicked-back hair who informed Wolf he no longer had the funds to pay for both caretaking services and security.

Wolf was a shy man, unaccustomed to speech. His face reddened and his hands, unusually large for a man who stood barely five feet, began to tremble. "Them visitors," he said slowly, hoping to undo the effects of his heavy accent, "what will they do?"

"No one's buying plots," the young Gardner murmured. "I'm sorry, Mr. Pinkas."

The implication was clear: Wolf would have to find work elsewhere. The thought sent dread scouring through him. After some hesitation, he declared he would take a pay reduction in exchange for permission to move into the shed.

Gardner glanced at the crypt and broke into a grin. "But you're still a young man, Pinkas. You might want . . . company."

Wolf's throat constricted. He knew Gardner found his proposal morbid, but Gardner was an American. He understood the body as an object of desire. He had been spared a true accounting of the world, its rancid plains and oceans of tormented flesh. Only the dead were safe.

"It will not be a problem," Wolf said.

Gardner pursed his thin lips. "You'd have to double as security," he said at last.

Wolf, who was frightened of weapons and their use, quietly assented.

The young man removed a small whisk brush from his coat pocket and dusted his wing tips. "Nothing but ghosts in this place anyway, right?"

"I hope," Wolf said.

The shed had never been intended as a domicile and Wolf spent an entire autumn making it habitable. He purchased a potbellied stove from an estate sale, placed a tin basin beside it for bathing, drilled holes in the roof for ventilation, built a privy out back, and conveyed the few furnishings from his nearby apartment. The architect of the crypt had been thoughtful enough to include several arched window slots, intended for stained glass, and Wolf constructed wooden shutters for them. On cold nights he bolted the shutters and unplugged his tiny refrigerator from the portable generator and attached a heater. In the warm months he left the shutters open and breezes stirred the room's air.

Wolf spent his days as he always had, clearing vines from footpaths, hacking at the weeds that encroached upon remote plots. Waxed paper bags and wrappers drifted in from the street out front, where there was a trolley stop, and found their way into corners of the yard. Wolf made a round before sundown, jabbing them with a wooden spear he had fashioned for this purpose. He worked methodically to preserve the rightful peace accorded the dead.

At night he listened to classical music, Chopin mostly, Mozart and Bach, played on an ancient crank phonograph. It was his lone concession to the past, for his father, Dr. Pinkas, had loved Chopin, the fragile nocturnes, the rousing mazurkas. These were the songs he would hum to Wolf and his older sisters at night and, later, in the dim chaos of the boxcars and roads. Wolf lay on his cot and closed his eyes. The nocturnes made him weep, quietly and with some relief.

He ate lightly. Tea and toast in the mornings, fruit at lunch, a sandwich with soup for supper. He treated his cats to a bit of meat each day. He had not intended to keep pets. No, the cats had come to him. Dempsey was a large orange tom with frayed ears and a left eye that had been battered into a rakish wink. Coal, a skeletal black kitten, had arrived on a frosty morning and immediately, to the distress of all involved parties, attempted to suckle Dempsey.

Each month a small check signed by young Gardner was slipped into the mailbox outside the gate. The next morning Wolf walked the half mile to his bank, where he cashed his check and then continued on to the barber and grocer.

When the bank and barber closed, he climbed onto a trolley to do his errands. Then the city's trolley service ceased, its tracks ripped from the ground and piled about. Asphalt and pavement seemed to wash outward from the roads, welcoming a greater flow of cars. Tar fouled the air. Wires snarled overhead. In the near distance, cranes pieced together the skeletons of skyscrapers. No matter how neatly men striped the center of the streets, no matter how bright the billboard promises, disorder hurtled on. Wolf ventured out less and then less.

Frail figures still appeared in the cemetery, occasionally seeking Wolf out to praise the upkeep of the yard and the garden he had coaxed from the sandy soil around his cottage. Wolf nodded at these comments and smiled and disappeared from view as courteously as possible.

But these older visitors, who understood the importance of spending a few hours each week in the company of the dead, died off themselves. Though there were still unfilled plots for sale, their younger relatives buried them closer to their own neighborhoods, in suburban cemeteries that looked to Wolf like a species of park, acres of grass smoothed of unsightly wrinkles. Small stone tablets marked the graves, or discreet plaques of the sort used elsewhere to announce historical sites. A road wound through the indistinguishable rows, for those who sought a whiff of the dead as they drove past.

The decline in visitors increased Wolf's workload, as the care of individual plots, which had once been the assumed duty of relatives, now passed to him. It was he who ensured that headstones were kept free of rubbish, the photos polished, the dead flowers cleared away. He enjoyed these tasks, which seemed to him the logical completion of a cycle to which he had given his life over contentedly.

Wolf was not a man prone to fancy. But sometimes, as he hunched
to clean a sheet of marble or set a bouquet of wildflowers at the foot
of a favorite grave, he heard a faint voice on the breeze. Once in a
great while, these apparitions materialized outside his cottage and
hovered in the moonlight. When he played Mozart, they waltzed with
cautious grace. The cats perched on the sill and watched.

After a lengthy period of construction, the road fronting the
cemetery became a four-lane highway, and thereafter the surrounding
neighborhood declined precipitously. Private homes were demolished
and large, drab public-housing projects built. During the cold months,
after supper, Wolf lay on his cot and read, the cats flung atop him
like pelts. But when the nights turned warm, Wolf could hear young
blacks in the park next door, laughter and shouts, bottles shattering
against the cemetery's brick walls, the snap of firecrackers, which
frightened the cats. Graffiti surfaced on the walls near the front gate.
Wolf considered apprising Gardner of the problem, but decided to
purchase additional paint instead.

Gardner was a busy man and his annual visits lasted barely long
enough for Wolf to count the buttons shining on his coat. "Sales
have been a bit off," he observed. "Orders will come up by winter." With a sour expression, he would then inquire if anything was
needed, to which Wolf would respond, with a slight bow, in the
negative.

One evening, after closing, a tall figure in a sagging suit presented
himself at the gate. He let himself in with a key and tromped about
the place with a tape measure in one hand and a notepad in the other,
so engrossed that he failed to notice Wolf's approach and nearly
walked over him. The man leaped backward, his suit seeming to follow a second later.

Wolf apologized.

"Quite all right," the man said. "Yes, Gardner mentioned you.
Mr. Pinks, correct?"

"Pinkas, yes."

"You live on the premises, correct?"

Wolf pointed to his cottage.

"Yes. Well. I didn't mean to startle you. Ham Tallaway." He

extended a hand. "Development commission. Just a routine inspection."

Wolf said, "How did you get a key?"

"Why, Bob Gardner gave it to me. I'd have rung the bell, but you don't seem to have one." Tallaway laughed. "I'll just look around and be out of your way." While the two men stood talking, Dempsey hobbled out of the cottage and nudged against Wolf's shin. "What a nice kitty." Tallaway bent to pat him. "This retaining wall—you know if it's furrow-grounded, or overlaid?"

Wolf shrugged. "It was here when I arrive."

"I see. Well. Don't let me interrupt you. I'll be done in a few minutes."

When Wolf returned to the cottage, Dempsey was gone. A week later he found the body sprawled beneath a gorse bush just beyond the rear gate. Coal glanced at the frozen eyes and matted fur, then scampered back to the cottage.

With his garden and the new varieties of dehydrated foods, Wolf no longer left the yard more than a few times a year, and then only to cash his checks. His hair grew wild. At rush hour, cars chuffed past, exhaling smog. Ambulances flashed and shrieked, planes roared overhead, black boys loped by on foot, carrying plastic boxes that pumped out cruel imitations of music. Even the quietest moments resounded with electronic beeps and metallic sighs, a faint persistent ringing.

Against these, Wolf placed his wooden shutters and the chirping of tinder in his stove, the music from his phonograph. He allowed ivy to overrun the front gate and found comfort in the gradual vanishing of highway and streetlight and wire. He removed the mailbox and, excepting his monthly stipend, fed to his stove the envelopes dropped near the yard's entrance. He surrendered his battle against the graffiti. Then, without so much as a letter to young Gardner, he bolted the yard shut with a large padlock.

He had hoped to make the ruin outside his kingdom disappear. But rather than feeling reassured, he felt oddly besieged. His sleep grew restless with dreams.

Wolf had never before remembered his dreams. He might awaken with a strange sense of elation, or dread, even expectation. But as he swung his legs over the edge of his cot, as he sipped his morning tea and surveyed the yard, the turbulent rhythm of these feelings dissipated. He simply immersed himself in the day's routine. As if by a gentleman's agreement, all was forgotten.

Now he woke with distinct memories: a vulture swooping down on Coal while Wolf watched from the doorway of his cottage, unable to wrestle himself into motion. Other nights, Wolf found himself cast out, stumbling through a featureless landscape: the stink of diesel and dead horses, eyes peering at him from dank basements, blue-black air.

Most disturbing was his dream of sleep. He could see himself in this dream. He slept on his mother's deathbed. Yet he could also see images from his childhood: families marched down muddy roads, his father heaped on a wet road, his sisters crying out for potatoes. Bombs dropped from the sky and turned gardens to violent dirt. The dry pop of machine guns shoved bodies into pits. Ashes settled onto his skin. Wolf saw and heard and smelled all of it. Yet he slept. Even as he rose to fire the stove, fifty years on, he could see himself curled peacefully. He looked dead, but he was dreaming.

One day, in the midst of mending a fissured tombstone, Wolf heard the strokes of a hacksaw. He found Ham Tallaway on the other side of the gate. Next to him stood a black man in a work shirt beginning to sweat through.

Tallaway stared at Wolf. "If you wouldn't mind opening the gate, Mr. Pinkas."

"Of course."

"You mean this son of a bitch had the key all along?" The black man scowled. "I been coming out here for how many months, Mr. Tallaway?"

With a strained smile, Tallaway instructed his workman to return to the truck. Wolf swung the gate open and Tallaway proceeded to the nearest shaded bench and sat. "We need to speak, Mr. Pinkas. I am sorry about my colleague, but you can understand his frustration. I myself have grown . . . frustrated. Mr. Gardner has sent a number of letters informing you of the situation, as has the city." He gestured with his chin toward the beheaded mailbox post and paused. "I understand that you have grown quite attached to your home. I see by your care of the premises that you have been diligent in the exercise of your duties. But the city owns this land now. Do you understand?"

"Yes," Wolf said. "I understand." He felt eager to return to his repair, fearful the grout would dry improperly.

Tallaway pulled a handkerchief from his pocket and dabbed his forehead. "And the situation calls for me, you see, to inform you that the city, as it should arise, no longer requires your services."

"Services?"

"It's nothing personal, Mr. Pinkas. We appreciate your dedication," Tallaway said. "This has nothing to do with job performance."

"What will you do? Hire another man?" His tongue flustered at the words.

"No. You see, this property, the city plans to build an arena here. For sports, music concerts, *cultural* events."

"But this is a graveyard. You can't move graves."

"The interred and all existing markers will be relocated," Tallaway said. He folded his handkerchief and tucked it back into his pocket. "Construction won't start until after Christmas, so you have several months to wind up your affairs here. I've discussed the possibility of your obtaining employment with one of our municipal cemeteries. That's a decision for you to make on your own, of course." Tallaway stood and walked to the gate. "I'm sorry," he said without slowing.

That night, Wolf heard a commotion behind his cottage. He felt certain the dead had been agitated by Tallaway's visit. But the voices were young. They licked the night with laughter. Wolf rose from the cot and fetched his trash stick and his lantern and stepped into the night. Summer, with its languid breath, was gone, but autumn had yet to arrive. A fragment of moon hung in the sky.

The giggling came from the north corner of the yard. Wolf walked past the privy and the brass monument honoring the yard's wealthiest family, past the small clearing where Dempsey had hunted mice, and toward a low wooden gate. Inside, weeds obscured two rows of waist-high headstones. When he first took the job, Wolf tended to the children's graveyard. But these visits became more than he could bear: to be stared at by the mounted photos, forced to consider the bodies below.

Gooseflesh prickled his arms. He heard a cry and stepped inside the gate and made his way toward the back, where two figures were intertwined beneath a stand of cedar. They seemed to be wrestling. He stepped closer and lifted his lantern. For a long moment he watched the boy's muscled back, watched him struggle with the pleasures of congress, arching and thrusting, grunting in satisfaction while the second figure breathed extravagantly and dug her plump ankles into the ropy muscles of her lover's calves. Against the crisp white of the cedar trunks they composed a tableau of brutal desire.

Wolf stepped backward, but in so doing stumbled on a root. The girl lifted her head and looked at him and shrieked. The boy continued his exertions. But she shrieked again and he tumbled from her and they both lay stunned on the blanket they had set down. Bits of dried leaves clung to the girl's braided hair. She ducked behind the boy, who raised his arms as a boxer might and peered into the dull nimbus of Wolf's lantern. "Who the fuck out there?"

Wolf could smell what they had been doing, the slightly putrid scent of bodies opened in this way. The girl reached to cover herself.

"I am the caretaker here," Wolf announced unhappily.

"He's crazy," the girl said. "Look at him, D. Keep him away from me."

The boy reached past her, for his clothes. "Come any closer and I'll kill your ass." He showed his teeth. "I got a gun."

They spoke too fast for Wolf to understand every word. But he saw their fright. "I do not want to hurt you," he said.

"Ain't nobody scared," the boy said. "You the one should be scared."

"This is private property," Wolf said. "A graveyard is here. This is not a place for what you do."

"Look at his face," the girl cried. "*Do* something, D." She squirmed into her T-shirt.

"You have no rights to be here," Wolf said.

The boy seemed to consider this. He took note of the steel-tipped stick in Wolf's hand.

"This ain't no private property," the girl said suddenly. "City own it. We got the same right here as you."

As she spoke, the boy snatched up a pint bottle and dashed away. The girl scrambled after him. They retreated quick and sleek, as if they belonged to the night. Wolf hurried back to his cottage and lay down to calm himself. Wind whistled thinly through the graves. His cottage moaned.

Toward dawn there was a faint knock at the door. Coal lifted his head. Wolf stoked the fire and pulled on his trousers. He rubbed his eyes. As he set the kettle for tea, a second, more distinct knock sounded.

Wolf opened the door. The girl fell to the floor like a swimmer frozen in mid-stroke. Scratches raked the length of her forearms and blood from a gash at the knee ribboned her calf. Her T-shirt rode up around her hips, revealing the muddied seat of her panties. She looked at Wolf and began at once to sob. Wolf thought, for just a moment, of the dying girl he had come upon in a field so many years ago, and of her final wish, at which he shuddered.

"What's happened to you?" Wolf asked. "Was it the boy who did this?"

"Your damn wall too high."

Wolf flew into a brief panic. He wanted the girl gone, out of his home. "There is a place here for washing," he said. "You may clean up. Then you return home. The front gate is open."

The girl nodded drowsily.

When Wolf returned at lunch, he found her on his cot, wearing one of his undershirts, her dirty T-shirt folded and set in a corner. Coal was draped on the prominent swell of her belly. With no great interest, she was inspecting one of his records.

"Young lady," he said.

"You ain't got to tell me," she said. "I was just waiting around to say thanks."

"Yes. I appreciate."

"I'm going," she said. And yet she did not move from the cot.

Wolf looked at her face. Her small features lacked sharpness. She was young. Thirteen? Fourteen?

"I could sue you," she said. "For reckless abuse and some other shit."

Wolf thought about his cache of twenty-dollar bills. Would she have had the ingenuity to check the tin hidden behind his phonograph? "Young lady."

She stood. Coal tumbled and hit the floor with a squeak. Wolf held the door open. But rather than leaving, she ambled around the cottage, inspecting his domestic arrangements, as if he were the interloper and his presence an inconvenience she had chosen, for the moment, to tolerate. "Where you from?" she said.

"What do you mean?"

"You got a accent," she said.

Wolf shook his head. "What does this matter?"

"It don't. I'm just asking."

"You must leave."

"I *am* leaving." She smiled flirtatiously. "You from Mexico?"

"Poland," Wolf said softly.

"You don't look Polish. Them Polish are *big*. Where's your wife, anyway? You old enough to have a wife."

"You must leave," Wolf repeated. "Your mother will worry."

"If you had a wife she'd make you cut that hair, I tell you that right now. Hoo boy, you like one of them flower children. How old are you? You sixty?" She walked over to the stove and peeked inside. "Why you live here? It's *spooky* round here."

Wolf cleared a strand of hair from his face and noted, with some distress, that she was the same height as him. "The front gate is open. Go home. Your mother will worry."

"I live with my auntie. You got any Coke?"

"Young lady—"

"Any kind of *soda*?"

"Young lady," Wolf repeated, as firmly as his manner allowed. "This is my home. I am a busy man."

"Taking care of dead folks. Real busy."

Wolf's cheeks reddened.

"All right, all right. I'm going. Don't get all crazy on me." She looked him up and down, a girl staring out from the body of a woman. Then she began undoing the buttons on her shirtfront.

For a moment Wolf could only watch in astonishment. "That is not necessary. No, please. Stop that, young lady. You may keep that. As, as payment. For your fall."

The girl looked down at the shirt, then over to her T-shirt in the corner. "Fine. You can keep mine, then." She made her way slowly to the door, looking about distractedly. "Your cat's pregnant," she said, before stepping outside.

"What?"

"Your kitty. She pregnant."

"No," Wolf said. "Coal is a boy cat."

"Look at her. She fat. She *pregnant*."

Wolf sighed. "If you need bus fare—"

"Nah." She breezed out. "I don't want nothing from you."

"Do not come back," Wolf called to her. "I am warning."

That night Wolf smelled her everywhere, on his clothes and on Coal and especially on his cot, a smell like the oil applied to babies. He settled down and cranked his phonograph and attempted to clear his mind for sleep. But the odor interfered. He felt a longing that was not lust, but something less easily dispelled. He wanted to cry out. Coal, lying on the foot of the cot, regarded him quizzically. Wolf rushed outside in his bed shirt. He stumbled this way and that, peering at nothing, at the heavy ink of night, at his garden, at what might have been her footsteps in the dust.

A week later she was back, her voice circling the treetops, then a deeper tone, that of a boy. Wolf selected a record from his collection, an obscure chorale by Emanuel Bach, and cranked his phonograph and listened to Moses sing in German. The cottage swelled with his somber promises, an end to the desert, the milk of Canaan. Wolf closed his eyes and saw her body, bent to its awful purposes.

The next morning he marched to the children's graveyard and stood between the two rows of headstones. The couple had left behind their thin quilt. He burned it in his stove. He drank his tea and struggled to forget these interruptions. But she made this impossible, for she returned to the yard, routinely, on the very night he managed to convince himself he was free of her.

Only in October, with the rains now steady, did her visits cease. As if to compensate, surveyors sent by Tallaway arrived and spent the

afternoons pacing the yard's perimeter. A helicopter hovered overhead
one morning. Wolf surrendered the pleasures of peaceful sleep. The
snows began. He lost track of the days. A notice arrived informing
him of the yard's closure. He had thirty days to vacate. Wolf began
harboring the conscious wish that he were no longer alive.

On a frigid night deep into December, the girl's voice roused him.
He took her screams to be those of ecstasy. Then they lengthened and
rose and timbre.

He burrowed under his blankets, for a moment unable to determine if he was awake or asleep, if he lay in the garden of his boyhood
or the graveyard that had been his home for thirty years. Then Coal
purred thickly, and the phonograph crackled as its needle dipped into
the empty grooves at the end of a record. He had been dreaming. A
dream.

The girl's next cry drowned out everything. It was like a siren. Wolf
threw his coat on over his nightshirt and pulled on his boots. The
spirits jeered him. They turned themselves into black veils and twirled
indignantly.

He found her in the children's cemetery, on the ground, her legs
thrown open. Her monstrous belly heaved under a glaze of sweat.
Steam puffed from between her legs. Her arms lay to each side, like
sticks propped in the pegs of her shoulders. Every few seconds her
fists pounded the frozen earth. "Oh God," Wolf said. "Young lady.
No. No. God, we got to get you to a hospital." He wondered if he
might be able to lift her into his wheelbarrow. But she grew panicky
when he tried to move her. She wasn't going anywhere.

Wolf felt an instant revulsion at the prospect of having to play a
part in the delivery. He told the girl he was going to find help, and
started toward the gate. Surely someone had a phone, which would
lead to an ambulance, a doctor. But he could hear her pleadings.
"Don't leave me! I'm gonna die!" Wolf made it as far as his cottage,
then turned back with an armful of blankets. He laid these under
her and over her torso. He shucked his coat to make a pillow for her
head. There was no choice now—he lowered himself between her legs.
The smell of blood and waste punched into the air. Her genitals were
red and grotesquely swollen. He reared back and pressed tentatively

at her stomach and told her to push. The girl thrashed. She clamped his wrist until the bone ached.

"Push," Wolf said. "You must push." The girl cursed him. "Push," Wolf commanded. "Young lady, please." Wolf could feel the muscles inside her clenching. The baby dropped down into the birth canal. The girl's stomach hardened and her hips bucked and the flesh at her center, engorged with blood, prepared to rend. Snow began to fall. The flakes melted on her legs and Wolf's own reddened hands. "Please," he said. "Young lady, *please*." The girl seized up, let out a wheeze, then ceased moving. Her muscles went slack.

Wolf took off his nightshirt and held it out, as if its presence might coax the child. Naked but for his boots, he entreated the girl. The tears on his cheeks had begun to freeze. Then the idea stuck him that the child was asleep. Wolf himself had slept through the trauma of his own birth according to his father. "Your own mother dying and you slept, Wolfie. Peaceful. Asleep."

But if the baby was asleep, and the mother as well, how was the birth to occur? He jostled the girl, to no effect. He kneaded her stomach. Finally his hand came forward and probed unsteadily. It was not like touching earth, the wet rubber of her, the slick hairs, the muck. His fingers slipped inside and immediately felt the baby's head. Her flesh held to it like the seal on a jar of preserves. He pushed in farther and felt something hard against the baby. One of its shoulders was lodged behind the pelvic bone. With a sharp jab Wolf wedged two fingers between the mother and child and tried to pry the child free. Blood and fluid spurted onto his hands. The girl convulsed. He lost purchase.

For a moment, the situation appeared almost comical: he, a naked old hermit crouched in the cold, reaching into a young girl, trying to deliver life into a world he wished mostly to leave. Again he worked his fingers in and searched for the point of contact. He dug at the child's soft shoulder, his fingers cramped. The girl convulsed again and Wolf felt something give, collapse downward.

The baby's head emerged, a dark crescent, then a bit more, a forehead and nose smashed nearly flat. A second dark blotch eased into view, a shoulder, and in a single precarious moment the baby slid out, as if sprung from a trap. Wolf held the steaming body in his huge hands. It dripped and pawed the air, the umbilical cord dangling. He smacked its bottom twice, then a third time, until he heard a sputter. Next, he swaddled the baby in his nightshirt and set it on the mother's chest, nestled beneath the blankets. "Hold," he said, placing her hands on the baby. He shoved one arm under the girl's back and the other under her knees. But she was dead weight now, half-conscious if that. Using his nightshirt as a sling, he tied the baby to his chest and dragged its mother, yard by yard, away from the cedars. The snow fell harder. His knees ached. Blood rushed to the surface of his skin.

Back at the cottage Wolf placed mother and baby on the mattress removed from his cot. He moved the heater close and fed the stove the last of the kindling. With a jackknife he cut through the umbilical cord and moved the baby, a boy, onto his mother's breast. His delicate lips rooted for a nipple, found it, suckled. Wolf boiled water and cleaned the baby as best he could with a towel, then the girl, too. He placed tea bags between her legs to ease the swelling. Coal wandered over and licked at the blood on the stone floor.

Wolf pulled on his trousers and coat and ran outside to fetch wood. He was gone less than a minute. When he returned, he found the baby sprawled beside his mother on the mattress. Coal had retreated to the corner, his tail puffed. Wolf lifted the child and pressed him again to his mother's breast. The child fell away, limp. His eyes were open but clouded. Wolf touched two fingers to his neck and felt a flickering pulse.

He looked at the girl. "What happened here?"

She smiled the glassy smile of delirium. "You killed my baby."

Wolf shook his head. "Something happened to this child."

"You killed him. You a killer."

"No," he whispered. He picked up the child and cradled him against his chest. "I tried to save. Do you understand? I am doing what I can."

She stared blankly at the space where he stood; her eyelids slid down.

"What else must I do? You should have gone to a hospital. Why did you come here? *Why?* I did not ask for you. Why did you bring this trouble into my home?" He looked down at the baby and trembled. "I will not take blame for this, young lady." He knelt and whispered into the girl's ear. "I am trying to save both of you."

But the girl couldn't hear him.

Wolf turned away and struck his head against the stone wall. The baby was still against him, a tiny pulsing thing, and the girl was there, her feverish body tossing. He sank to his knees, remembering the sting of death, how it left its imprint on even the simplest human gestures. His father set flowers on the dark soil of a grave mound. His sisters—in pinafores and terrified smiles—sang him to sleep. And later, when the war was over and the killing had stopped, he staggered alone into a field and came upon a naked girl, perhaps thirteen, who stared at him from the place where she would perish, whispering her terrible wish. She wanted to be held.

Death did this. It transmuted each act of love into something unbearable. Was it any wonder he had buried himself?

Light seeped through the shutters. Wolf rose from the floor with the baby. He hurried to the door of his cottage and, in one curiously exuberant motion, burst outside. He moved with the child through the cemetery on an old man's legs, aching but stubbornly alive, not seeing the graves he had tended, the headstones touched with dew, the spirits in their tattered gowns, only hurtling himself toward the gate, the city beyond, a hospital, a doctor, the pink thread of dawn.

Now let's take a look at this structure.

First, the status quo is established. Who is this, when is this, where is this? Wolf Pinkas assumed his position of caretaker of the graveyard (caring for the dead) in the decade after World War II. The context of World War II in Eastern Europe (and, by implication, the genocidal atrocities that occurred) is immediately established.

First challenge to status quo or first statement of the complication. Owner can no longer pay for caretaking services.

Reaction: Wolf moves into a crypt and takes a pay reduction. Life and death are juxtaposed. Life: the owner's idea that Wolf might "want company." Death: Wolf's knowledge of "oceans of tormented flesh." Wolf is aligned with death. He even moves into a crypt. He moves in with death. He stays with the deaths of the past, which, we discover, include his entire family.

New status quo. Wolf fixes up the crypt. He picks up trash with a "wooden spear"—an antique weapon wholly inadequate to the battles he must fight. Here his backstory of trauma and the war is told in the line "dim chaos of the boxcars and roads." He gets his check, walks to bank and barber and grocer.

Second escalation of complication. The bank closes, so Wolf begins to take the trolley but then the trolley shuts down. Further, the frail elderly who come to tend the graves begin to die off. Plus, their children don't use this old traditional graveyard to bury their dead.
  Reaction: Wolf has an increased workload but rather enjoys it. He has given his life to the care of the dead. The apparitions appear. Now he is dancing with the dead. He withdraws, goes out less and less.

Third escalation of complication. A four-lane highway replaces the street; public housing replaces the old houses. Young blacks who shatter bottles and write graffiti arrive.
  Reaction: Wolf buys more paint.

Fourth escalation of complication. The development commissioner comes in to measure the graveyard. Dempsey, one of his two cats dies. (Note that in this story the big themes are life and death and the two cats mirror life and death. Think about setting up mirrors within a story.)
  Reaction: Now Wolf retreats even further. Seldom leaves. Bolts the graveyard gate shut. Ignores graffiti rather than repainting it. The horrors of his past in Eastern Europe begin to return in his dreams: the

dream of the stink of diesel and dead horses, his father heaped on a wet road, his sisters crying for potatoes, machine guns, bodies in pits, and the "dream of sleep" of the title—in his dream he is sleeping on his mother's deathbed.

Fifth escalation of complication. Developer gets in with a hacksaw, informs that the city is going to build an arena on site and Wolf is going to lose his job.

Intruders complicate the complication. Long scene in which Wolf interrupts teenagers having sex in the children's graveyard. The graveyard he can't bear to maintain. Again, life (sex) and death (the dead children) juxtaposed. Then the girl arrives at his crypt-home. She is the story's main intruder. He takes care of her despite their hostile conversation. He freaks out when she starts to unbutton his undershirt to return it to him. She notes that the second cat, Coal, is pregnant (pregnant = life). Indeed, the girl is pregnant. She keeps returning. She represents life.

Sixth escalation of original complication. The takeover of the graveyard commences with surveyors and the thirty-day notice that he must leave. Wolf now reaches his lowest point, wishing consciously for death (despite that a force for life, the girl, has now entered the scene).

Rise in dramatic action, to resolution. The lengthy crisis of the birth scene. Birth in the children's graveyard. Wolf actually reaches into the girl's birth canal and helps the baby be born. Then drags mother and child to his crypt. Then runs out of the gate to find a doctor, a hospital. So he has made a total turnaround, now standing for birth, for life, for the living child, now running out of the place of death to save a life. Wolf's goal has mutated from a wish to stay with the dead to the wish to save a life, to save the infant from the graveyard for dead children in which it was born.

What else can we learn from Almond's story? The complication and its escalations are really a stepped escalation of one complication or

challenge (to Wolf), the new urban ways having no more use for this
old way of honoring the dead. And honoring the dead (and staying
with the dead) is the only way Wolf wants to be. So the series of complications can be boiled down to two: the escalating encroachment of
the city and the entrance of the black teens and sex. The black teens
and the girl seem to escalate Wolf's crisis but in the end this intrusion
ejects Wolf back to the side of life. I find it instructive to see how
Almond lays in the backstory of the Holocaust, not in scene but in
flashes of memory.

Hands On: Writing the Piece

What is the significant complication? What are the big forces in oppo-
sition? Who is the character with enough grit to fight to resolve it?
These are the two key ingredients required for dramatic narrations.
Take any volume of *The Best American Short Stories* put out by
Houghton Mifflin or of *The O'Henry Prize Stories* and go through
and reread the stories. Which stories clearly follow this dramatic structure? Can you name the complication? Is it a significant complication?
Can you show how the protagonist fights to resolve it? (Whether or
not the complication is resolved successfully is not at issue.) If a story
seems obscure in terms of this structure, just pass it by. This is not the
only structure in existence. To learn dramatic structure, look for stories that plainly use it.

Now turn to a story of your own, whether fiction or nonfiction.
What significant complication engages you? Do you have a character
with enough grit to fight toward resolution? Or to react clearly and
strongly to each provocation? Keep in mind that trivial complications
do not give good story.

Beyond that you can proceed to structure just about any dramatic
narrative using three or five attempts to overcome the difficulty or
achieve the desired object. Who or what is opposed to the success of
the protagonist? Add an antagonist. (Writers Jack Remick and Robert J. Ray ask the writers in their classes, Who is the antagonist? The

implication is, no antagonist, no story.) And who is the helper? And does the resolution come about in part due to the fact that the protagonist comes to understand the complication differently? Wolf Pinkas's original complication is how to preserve his way of life with the dead. In the end, the complication has reversed: it is how to keep this infant within the realm of life.

Is the protagonist forced to his or her resolution by a helper, the way Wolf Pinkas is helped toward loving life by the girl in Steve Almond's marvelous story?

10.

How to Open

When in doubt, or wherever possible,
tell the whole story of the novel in the first sentence.
—*John Irving*

A great opening works like a Baked Alaska: the server lights a match and it bursts into flame. It's mesmerizing, and when the flame dies down, you are ready to eat.

Open with the most important thing you have to say. Spend your capital—fast. Open with a swift, well-placed whack:

> Once a guy stood all day shaking bugs from his hair.
> (Philip K. Dick, *A Scanner Darkly*, 3)

> "You must not tell anyone," my mother said, "what I am about to tell you. In China your father had a sister who killed herself. She jumped into the family well."
> (Maxine Hong Kingston, *The Woman Warrior*, 3)

For five years I was on the team of short-fiction readers for *The Seattle Review*. What an enlightening experience. Above all, I learned—again and again—how a weak opening can kill a piece. Nice writing does not do the job. A nice description does not do the job. A windup explanatory sentence, typically begun with a dependent clause, does not do the job.

Take up one or more anthologies of short masterworks, fiction or nonfiction. Page through. Look at each opening. What can you learn?

- Often a good opening consists of a small sentence that concentrates into its short little self the essence (sometimes the central dramatic conflict) of what follows.

> When had she begun to suspect that her second-floor tenant, Mr. Han, was building a bomb?
> (Julie Orringer, "Neighbors," 147)

> I am haunted by waters.
> (Olivia Laing, *To the River*, 3)

> I woke to a downpour the March morning in 1989 when I had to identify my mother's body at the New York City morgue.
> (Kim Dana Kupperman, "Relief," 96)

> After my boyfriend left me, I went a little crazy for a while.
> (Katha Pollitt, "Webstalker," 21)

- Begin with an aphorism. An aphorism is a pithy truth that the rest of the chapter or piece or book then proceeds to prove out or defend. Or begin with your conclusion.

> Research is formalized curiosity.
> (Zora Neale Hurston, *Dust Tracks on a Road*, 127)

> The universe has its secrets.
> (Lisa Randall, *Warped Passages: Unraveling the Mysteries of the Universe's Hidden Dimensions*, 1)

> Music has soul.
> (Rick Moody, "On Celestial Music," 163)

- What is the central question of the piece? Ask the question in the first sentence.

  Is winemaking an art?
  > (Jim Harrison, "Is Winemaking an Art?," 28)

  Is there a richer and stranger idea in the world than grace?
  > (Brian Doyle, "Grace Notes," 41)

  What is the charm of necklaces?
  > (Emily R. Grosholz, "On Necklaces," 75)

- An elegant and simple way to begin is to state directly and immediately what a piece (whether short or book-length) is about.

  This book is intended to be an informal and friendly guide for writers.
  > (Richard Marius, *A Writer's Companion*, 3)

  This book is about the steps you can take and the choices you can make to combat global warming.
  > (Seth Shulman et al., *Cooler Smarter*, 3)

  God on Trial tells the stories of recent conflicts over religion in six American communities: towns and cities that have become battlefields in America's growing religious wars.
  > (Peter Irons, *God on Trial*, xi)

- Immediately establish your own or the protagonist's connection to the subject matter at hand.

  Today it is January, midmonth, midday, and mid-New

Hampshire. I sit in my blue armchair looking out the window. I am eighty-three. I teeter when I walk, I no longer drive, I look out the window.

(Donald Hall, "Out the Window," 40)

When I walk into a bookstore, any bookstore, first thing in the morning, I'm flooded with a sense of hushed excitement.

(Lewis Buzbee, *The Yellow-Lighted Bookshop*, 3)

I love houses, all the things they tell me, so that's one reason I don't mind working as a cleaning woman. It's just like reading a book.

(Lucia Berlin, "Mourning," 236)

I was born and raised in rural upstate New York, but who I am began with a younger brother's death in a hunting accident when I was twelve and he was eight. I held the gun that killed him. But if my life began at twelve with my brother's sudden, violent death, then my end, determined by the trajectory of that harsh beginning, could easily have taken place a scant six years later, when, in June 1965, I was kidnapped at gunpoint by vigilantes near the small town of Hayneville, Alabama.

(Gregory Orr, "Return to Hayneville," 125)

- Begin with a telling anecdote or quote. Remember that the reader must be completely oriented as to what the essay is about by the end of the second paragraph, at latest.

Once, in the Ecuadorian Amazon, I was obliged to lighten my baggage prior to boarding a seemingly lighter-than-air plane. I wouldn't have minded giving up my waterproof poncho, my hiking boots, and my chloroquine tablets, but when the pilot asked me to leave behind *Waterton's*

Travels in South America and Alec Waugh's *Hot Countries*, I became rather upset. What if I were laid up in some remote jungle hut? I wasn't worried about dying, but I was worried about dying without a book to read.

Of all the maladies capable of striking down a traveler in a foreign land—malaria, blackwater fever, typhoid, sleeping sickness, and so on—the one I fear the most is being caught with nothing to read. Let the monsoons play havoc with my itinerary, the national airline go on strike, and the foreign land itself prove unabashedly dull: a good book or indeed a bad book will always save the day. Nor do I even need to open this book. Simply the knowledge that it's there, waiting to be opened, is enough.

(Lawrence Millman, "Bookless in Biak," 169–70)

- Rely on the reliable What? When? Where? Why? Who? It is remarkable how many works, both fiction and nonfiction, begin by stating the time, the place, and who is in that place at that time.

At half past six on the twenty-first of June 1922, when Count Alexander Ilyich Rostov was escorted through the gates of the Kremlin onto Red Square, it was glorious and cool.

(Amor Towles, *A Gentleman in Moscow*, 9)

We always had a gas stove in the kitchen, in our house in Piedmont, West Virginia, where I grew up.

(Henry Louis Gates, Jr., "In the Kitchen," 117)

It was in the early seventies, a time of violence in Northern Ireland. Our front room was a rectangle with white walls, hardly any furniture and a small television chanting deaths and statistics at teatime.

(Eavan Boland, "Subject Matters," 175).

My mother once had a boyfriend named Glen Baxter. This
was in 1961. We—my mother and I—were living in the
little house my father had left her up the Sun River, near
Victory, Montana, west of Great Falls.

(Richard Ford, "Communist," 394)

A sunny, windy day on the lower East Side of New York.
The year is 1942. Sean, aged six, is being more or less
pulled along the sidewalk by his father, who has shown up
from nowhere to take him home from school.

(Frank Conroy, *Midair*, 3)

- Begin with a good title. A good title says what the book or the
  piece is about:

  The Sea Around Us (Rachel Carson)
  "Consider the Lobster" (David Foster Wallace)
  "Grace Notes" (Brian Doyle)
  A History of Reading (Alberto Manguel)
  "This Old Man" (Roger Angell)
  I Know Why the Caged Bird Sings (Maya Angelou)

These titles, and all of these beginnings, give readers a good idea
of what's behind the door they are about to walk through. They shun
lyrical flourishes and anecdotes with delayed points. They are direct.
They are plain and simple. They put the reader in a time and place,
or they say what the problem is, or they flatly state what the piece is
about. They make instantly clear what the relationship of the *I* is to
the matter at hand.

The temptation is to begin fancy. The practice is to condense what
is offered into its shortest, most accurate, most telling form. Often, in
the process of composing, beginnings do not clarify themselves until
endings arrive. "Good leads often show up late," writes many-book
author Ralph Keyes in *The Courage to Write*. "In my own writing

and that of students, I generally find the best opening deep within the narrative. This opening only makes itself known as I read drafts, see what catches my eye, something that sets a tone, that gets the piece up and running. Knowing this I don't concern myself with beginnings till the end."[*]

Hands On: Openings

As with all the exercises, do this one in relation to work you have in progress.

- Take five of your works that have yet to be published. Lay them out on the table or on the floor. Choose one type of opening, say Rick Moody's "Music has soul." For each of your chosen works, make an opening that is syntactically identical to Moody's opening, that is, it is an equation using the "to be" verb—X is Y or X has Y. This sentence holds the essence of what you want to say in the piece.
- Take the piece that pleases you most or that you most want to finish. *Do not go into it and begin flailing about.* Rather, copy out into your writing-practice notebook or type out the present opening. This is your "before" paragraph. Now, below it, make your new opening, beginning with your new "X is Y" sentence. Work on the paragraph to make it fit the new opening and in any other way you see fit. Here's an example of a Before/After from a piece I wrote called "Solitude." This is the opening paragraph:

  Before
  When I was five years old, we moved to a farm in Maryland called Ravenswood. We lived there for a year before

---

[*] Keyes, *Courage to Write*, 154.

moving to Comegys Bight Farm a few miles down the road. At Ravenswood, I got a room of my own—an attic room with steep gables and a square casement window made of wood on the vertical end wall. To me at the time—I'm a twin and have a brother ten months older—it was pure happiness to possess this sunny, silent kingdom at the top of the house.

After
Solitude is delicious. It can be delicious even to a five-year-old. The year we turned five—I have a twin sister and a brother ten months older—our family moved to a farm in Maryland called Ravenswood. At Ravenswood, I got a room of my own, an attic room with steep gables and a square wooden window that opened sideways like a book. This was my own silent kingdom at the top of the house.

That is a great improvement, or so it seems to me.

Do the Before/After exercise with each type of opening offered here. You can do the Before/After exercise again and again. In the years of assigning it and actually doing it myself, I cannot remember a case in which the "after" paragraph did not turn out better; often it is much better. The exercise works almost like magic, partly because you are focusing on a single paragraph in your notebook.

The act of removing the paragraph from your piece before starting to work on it is essential. This makes the job finite, one you can entertain yourself with for an hour or so before returning the paragraph to its appointed place. Doing this exercise on the *first* paragraph of any given piece will repay your efforts many times.

- Begin your own collection of virtuoso openings written by others. Write them in your sentence book (see page 173). Study them. What can you learn from them?

PART III

The Art of the Sentence and the Art of the Paragraph

As a beginning novelist long ago, I learned to write
dialogue not in a fiction workshop ruled by a
sophisticated "mentor," but by reading Graham Greene's
The Heart of the Matter over and over again. . . .
The perfected work was the mentor.
—*Cynthia Ozick*

11.

Sentence Craft

A good sentence alters the world.
—*Jonathan Raban*

Superb writers write superb sentences. Writers like Cormac Mc-Carthy and Eavan Boland and Don DeLillo and Susan Sontag and James Baldwin and William H. Gass and Maya Angelou have taken on the sentence as its own project. The project is: How does this sentence structure carry this content? To begin with, superb writers have taught themselves the basic sentence structures and know how to use each one fluently. And why not? Is there such a thing as a good carpenter who does not know the types of woods and nails?

First-rate writers do not use sentence forms out of tired habit or conventional but mistaken notions of correctness. All really good writers use fragments. They repeat words and phrases as a saxophonist repeats notes and phrases. They use parallel structures to express parallel thoughts. They write very short sentences and they write very long sentences. They write list sentences, that is, sentences that contain a list. Here's one about Charles Darwin:

> He suffered from anxiety, boils, dizziness, eczema, flatulence, gout, headaches, insomnia, and nausea.
> (Jonathan Weiner, *The Beak of the Finch*, 30)

The most gratifying way to work with the sentence is to make the form of a sentence perform its own meaning. Make the sentence do what it says. A sentence about a long slow quietly flowing river should be a long slow quietly flowing sentence. A sentence about something sharp and hard-hitting should crack, bite, kick, or slap. Sentences describing soft pillowlike afternoons or persons should puff and billow with hazy, willowy, pillowlike words. A sentence that brings a car screeching to a halt should itself screech to a halt. A sentence describing something going on and on should itself go on and on. There might be a clean, empty sentence or again a sentence crowded as a shoe-clotted closet. Here's a sentence that holds the ever-recurring menu of an ancient people:

> They ate corn, beans, squash, corn, beans, squash, corn,
> beans, squash, corn, beans, squash and once in a while a
> wild green onion.
> (Anne Carson, Plainwater, 220)

Virginia Tufte's eye-opening book on the sentence, *Artful Sentences: Syntax as Style*, offers this sentence written by Stewart Alsop to show how diction (word choice) can intensify meaning. Of the American political system Alsop writes:

> That system, for all its elephantine cumbersomeness, is also,
> in the long run, wonderfully adaptable and flexible.
> (Stewart Alsop, *The Center* quoted in *Artful Sentences*, 254)

Here the diction is cumbersome just as the American system is cumbersome. The signifier (the sentence) enacts or performs that which it signifies (the American system).

Tufte's marvelous museum of sentences includes one from James Agee's *A Death in the Family*, about the death of a father in a car wreck, written from the point of view of the son, a small boy. In this scene the family has spread quilts on the grass in the back yard and mother, father, aunt, uncle, and the child are lying on the quilts. The grownups are talking.

> They are not talking much, and the talk is quiet, of nothing
> in particular, of nothing at all in particular, of nothing at all.
>
> (James Agee, *A Death in the Family*, 7)

The talk is about nothing; the word *nothing* is chimed three times. The sentence about talking about nothing has nothing in it, no concrete word that refers to any visible concrete object (perceivable by eyes, ears, nose, skin, taste buds). The sentence talking about talking about nothing sounds like a child's perception of adults murmuring. Think of sound as an element to work with when you are making sentences that both say what they mean and do what they say.

Here Jack Kerouac lengthens a sentence about a long valley:

> The valley was long and long and long.
>
> (Jack Kerouac, *The Dharma Bums*, 79)

Can sentences express silence? What is silence? Is there such a thing as absolute silence? Or is silence, rather, a pause in human cacophony, a moment when the clock ticks, the rain rains, a branch taps the kitchen window:

> Camille did not answer. The clock ticked. Zackery turned
> from the cookstove to look at her. The rain grew louder. A
> branch tap-tap-tapped the kitchen window.

Whenever you write a physical action, a movement, try making the sentences move that same way in order to intensify the motion being described. Here, in Jean Toomer's *Cane*, a boxing match between dwarfs is rendered in short fragments, short sentences, short fast hits— like boxing:

> The gong rings. No fooling this time. The dwarfs set to. They
> clinch. The referee parts them. One swings a cruel upper-cut

and knocks the other down. A huge head hits the floor. Pop!
The house roars.

(Jean Toomer, Cane, 67)

The Pop! the head makes as it hits the floor and the Pop! the sentence
makes as the head hits the floor are perfect echoes of each other.

Here Kathleen Dean Moore renders a thunderstorm in which thunderclap follows thunderclap:

> Thunder slams from one side of the canyon to the other.
> Thunder on thunder on thunder.
> (Kathleen Dean Moore, "The Little Stoney River," 50)

A sentence can be as junky and overstuffed as a junky overstuffed
apartment. Here's the apartment of an impecunious, worn-down,
working-class woman, Sarah Cole, with her "dumpy, off-center wreck
of a body" as seen by her handsome, upscale lover. Sarah Cole's apartment could stand for Sarah Cole:

> The apartment is dark and cluttered with old, oversized
> furniture, yard sale and second-hand stuff bought originally
> for a large house in the country or a spacious apartment
> on a boulevard forty or fifty years ago, passed down from
> antique dealer to used furniture store to yard sale to thrift
> shop, where it finally gets purchased by Sarah Cole and gets
> lugged over to Perley Street and shoved up the narrow stairs,
> she and her children grunting and sweating in the darkness
> of the hallway—overstuffed armchairs and couch, huge,
> ungainly dressers, upholstered rocking chairs, and in the
> kitchen, an old maple desk for a table, a half dozen heavy
> oak diningroom chairs, a high, glass-fronted cabinet, all peel-
> ing, stained, chipped and squatting heavily on a dark green
> linoleum floor.
> (Russell Banks, "Sarah Cole: A Type of Love Story," 14)

A sentence can move the way its action moves. In Charles Frazier's sentence below, the protagonist flips his wrist. As the wrist completes its motion, there is a pause (a comma). Then the hat sails forth in a curved motion without hesitation or pause. Just so, the sentence:

> He flipped his wrist, and the hat skimmed out the window
> and caught an updraft and soared.
>
> (Charles Frazier, *Cold Mountain*, 5)

Frazier forms the sentence to perform its meaning, to move the way the hat moves. In contrast, a less skilled writer might write, out of convention: He flipped his wrist and the hat skimmed out the window, catching an updraft and soaring.

Here's a scene from Jack Kerouac's *The Dharma Bums*. As the two men leap and fall down the mountain, so the sentence leaps and falls:

> Then suddenly everything was just like jazz: it happened in one insane second or so: I looked up and saw Japhy *running down the mountain* in huge twenty-foot leaps, running, leaping, landing with a great drive of his booted heels, bouncing five feet or so, running, then taking another long crazy yelling yodelaying sail down the sides of the world and in that flash I realized *it's impossible to fall off mountains you fool* and with a yodel of my own I suddenly got up and began running down the mountain after him doing exactly the same huge leaps, the same fantastic runs and jumps, and in the space of about five minutes I'd guess Japhy Ryder and I (in my sneakers, driving the heels of my sneakers right into sand, rock, boulders, I didn't care any more I was so anxious to get down out of there) came leaping and yelling like mountain goats or I'd say like Chinese lunatics of a thousand years ago, enough to raise the hair on the head of the meditating Morley by the lake, who said he looked up and saw us flying down and couldn't believe it.
>
> (Jack Kerouac, *The Dharma Bums*, 85)

In contrast, here is a slow passage, a dream, the dream of John Grady, the protagonist in Cormac McCarthy's *All the Pretty Horses*. The dreamer is in danger. Exhausted. John Grady's dream is visual and unpunctuated just as most dreams are visual and unpunctuated:

> That night he dreamt of horses in a field on a high plain
> where the spring rains had brought up the grass and the
> wildflowers out of the ground and the flowers ran all blue
> and yellow far as the eye could see and in the dream he
> was among the horses running and in the dream he himself
> could run with the horses and they coursed the young mares
> and fillies over the plain where their rich bay and their rich
> chestnut colors shone in the sun and the young colts ran
> with their dams and trampled down the flowers in a haze of
> pollen that hung in the sun like powdered gold and they ran
> he and the horses out along the high mesas where the ground
> resounded under their running hooves and they flowed and
> changed and ran and their manes and tails blew off of them
> like spume and there was nothing else at all in that high
> world and they moved all of them in a resonance that was
> like a music among them and they were none of them afraid
> horse nor colt nor mare and they ran in that resonance
> which is the world itself and which cannot be spoken but
> only praised.
>   (Cormac McCarthy, *All the Pretty Horses*, 161–62)

Here is Joe Wilkins, in his memoir of childhood. The child is entering his parents' bedroom at the dusk of dawn, preparing to crawl in between his sleeping parents. They are breathing the breath of sleep and so does the sentence breathe:

> And the two of them: they are mountains of cream sheets, of
> musky warmth, of slow breath, slow breath, slow breath.
>   (Joe Wilkins, "Eleven Kinds of Sky," 32)

Once you get the idea of forming sentences to perform what they are saying, you can begin experimenting with syntax to make it intensify its load of meaning.

Hands On: Working on Sentencing

How do you embark on the project of becoming more skilled at sentencing? First, obtain a nicely bound, rather commodious blank book in which to collect exquisite sentences (and paragraphs and passages) written by others. This is the way to begin. I possess an ample and ever-growing treasury of beautiful sentences. The more I study them, the more they teach me.

Second, sentence work requires a decent reference work, a grammar-and-usage handbook. Numbers of how-to-write books provide useful advice but do not explicate the simple, compound, and complex sentence. You want a handbook that has a chapter or chapters on sentence forms. A good one is Karen Elizabeth Gordon's *The Deluxe Transitive Vampire*. Another one—particularly enlightening for writers and delicious despite its deplorably tiny print—is the *Writer's Digest Grammar Desk Reference* by Gary Lutz and Diane Stevenson. And there are others. Without such a reference work, you will at some point get lost. We all do.

Let me be clear: Different forms of the sentence produce very different effects. In order to render these effects, it is necessary to command these forms. To struggle along on instinct will take you only so far.

And what are these forms? The fragment. The simple sentence. The compound sentence. The complex sentence.

I suggest two initial moves. First, learn the prepositional phrase and learn it cold. (See chapter 17, on the phrase.) Second, learn to distinguish a clause (which has a subject and a verb) from a phrase. Learning these two forms will save you years of trouble. Now proceed.

Experiment. Try writing a scene of constricted emotion with constricted sentences. Begin with diction—word choice. Pick sharp short words like tick, whack, or poke to express a tight, tense, tough situation.

Pick words like voluminous, mellifluous, or mellow to express softer scenes, scenes that languish or meander or drift like smoke. Try writing a scene of lazy happiness with lazy happy sentences. Try making sentences that dream along, sentences that race. Master the basic sentence forms: simple, compound, complex, compound-complex. Take a look at the particular uses first-rate writers make of fragments. Now begin using fragments.

There are great pleasures in sentencing. Don't set out trying to learn everything at once. Rather, take pleasure in copying down a sentence you like, word for word. Then, in your writer's notebook (different from your sentence book, which contains only sentences composed by other writers), try making your own sentence using that form. Make certain moves—the list sentence, the fragment—habitual. Take a paragraph and write it several ways. Note the effects. Savor your growing skill.

You will want at your fingertips all the forms of the sentence. First-rate writers, unlike the vast majority of writers, use them all. They are driving with a full tank of gas.

Hands On: Imitating Great Sentences

This is an old exercise. Jack London did it. Other writers have done it. It is thought of as a beginner's exercise and certainly, beginners benefit from it. But I suggest that very experienced writers can learn from it as well. Imitation acts as an aid to close, writerly reading and can carry you into strategies, styles, and forms different from your accustomed ones. Imitation can help you expand your range.

First, copy out a piece of superlative writing done by someone else. It can be a sentence or a paragraph.

Don't skip the physical act of copying out the passage. Copying it out slows it down, puts you almost physically inside it. Always, when I am copying out a paragraph, whether by hand or on the keyboard, I see moves and turns that I entirely missed when I merely read it. Consider the passage to be your master-teacher for this moment. When an interviewer asked Gina Berriault how she taught herself to write, she responded:

> One thing I'd do was put a great writer's book beside the typewriter and then I'd type out a beautiful and moving paragraph or page and see those sentences rising up before my eyes from my own typewriter, and I would think, "Someday maybe I can write like that.". . . The someone whose words were rising from that typewriter became like a mentor for me. And when I went on with my own work, I'd strive to attain the same qualities I loved in that other person's work. Reading and writing are collaborations.*

Go to any great art museum and you will see artists copying paintings. Artists have always trained themselves by copying masterworks. And composers copy. Beethoven so admired Handel's work, the curator of an exhibition of his music manuscripts wrote, "that he wrote it out so as to get the 'feeling of its intricacies' and 'to unravel its complexities.'"†

After you've copied out your model paragraph, imitate it by making a sentence or sentences of your own, using different words, but the same syntax, the same level of diction, the same parts of speech, the same sound strategies (if two words alliterate, make your own two words alliterate). In doing this exercise it is of paramount importance to use your own material. It is fairly easy—and quite useless—to make up nonsensical or irrelevant sentences. The sentence achieved through the imitation must be a good sentence and it must mean what it says. We find that this exercise, done properly, is quite time consuming. As you are working, consider the following strategies.

---

* Berriault, "Don't I Know You?," 62–63.

† Karpeles Manuscript Museum website accessed November 28, 2003, http://www.rain.org/~karpeles/taqfrm.html (web page discontinued).

- Pay attention to diction (word choice). Replace low diction (*Shit*!) with low diction (*Drat*!), not *Goodness me*! Replace latinate words with latinate words, body parts with body parts, colors with colors, verbs with verbs, nouns with nouns. For any repeated word in the model, repeat your substitute word.
- Pay attention to concrete words (*salmon, coal, sweat, salt*) versus abstract words (*anxious, love, dream, notorious, silly, bad, gentle*). Keep in mind that there are degrees of concretion: soft is concrete but feather-soft and mud-soft are more concrete.
- Replace verbs with similar kinds of verbs. Example: "Her eyes rent the air and left phosphorescent streaks" (Anaïs Nin, *Ladders to Fire*, 9). Replace *rent* with *cut* or *slash*, not *decompose*.
- Look at the sentences in a piece you admire, and repeat that structure in what you write. Choose a passage written by a superb writer that carries the very emotion—the joy or misery or boredom or fear—of the piece you are writing. How does the sentence structure carry the emotion?

12.

Fragments

Indian summer. Montana. Rivers. You get the picture.
—*Annick Smith*

We begin with a form that is a nonsentence. Most great writers use fragments. Why then, have so many of us been taught that to use a fragment is an error? (What *is* an error is writing a fragment when you mean to write a sentence.)

Once you begin to appreciate fragments in your reading, and once you decide to use them in your own writing, the question becomes, What makes a good fragment? A fragment, stripped as it is of connectors, can hold a pure image, a critical moment, the point, or the pivot. Because it is isolated, it is emphatic. A fragment can add detail, minus words that add nothing. Here's a passage from a Lucia Berlin story:

> We came to the bridge and the smell of Mexico. **Smoke and chili and beer. Carnations and candles and kerosene. Oranges and Delicados and urine.**
>
> (Lucia Berlin, "Tiger Bites," 75)

Judith Kitchen was a master of the fragment. It is tempting to think that for her it stood for memory, for the way memory arrives in bits and scraps.

> Everything's gone. **Childhood washed away. The rabbits in their little hutch. The maple closest to the house, cut down in its prime, a jungle of branches. The flowering quince.**

> Hopscotch chalked on the sidewalk. Roller-skate keys. The
> voices of our playmates, ceded to time.
>
> (Judith Kitchen, "Requiem," 173)

Shocking, traumatic moments can be held in shattered language—fragments. Here, a boy, Lotto, in boarding school, is sneaking around in the boathouse. It is dark at night, no lights. He bumps into something.

> His hands flailed, touched cloth. **Cloth over wood, no, not
> wood, foam with a steel core, no, not foam, pudding with
> a tough skin? Felt down. Felt leather. Laces? Shoe?** He was
> dabbed in the teeth.
>   He crabwalked backward, a high-pitched keening noise
> coming from somewhere, and moved wildly down the walls,
> and after an eternity found the light switch, and in the
> horrible bright found himself looking at the boat suspended
> from the ceiling, tipped down on one side, dangling the
> worst Christmas ornament ever. **A boy. Dead boy. Blue-faced.
> Tongue out. Glasses cocked.** In a moment came the recog-
> nition: oh, poor Jelly Roll, hanging from the bow ball of a
> sweep eight. He'd climbed up, tied the noose. **Leapt. Mint
> brownie from dinner all over his shirt.** The sound died out of
> Lotto's chest. He ran.
>
> (Lauren Groff, *Fates and Furies*, 28)

Very commonly, too, fragments serve a more mundane purpose: to show the view from a protagonist's eyes, whether this person is a character or the "I" of memoir or nonfiction. Here is Gwendolyn Brooks's Maud Martha, a teenager now, looking at her family's living room through the eyes of an impending visitor, who, unlike any previous visitor, is white.

> Maud Martha looked the living room over. **Nicked old
> upright piano. Sag-seat leather armchair. Three or four**

straight chairs that had long ago given up the ghost of whatever shallow dignity they may have had in the beginning and
looked completely disgusted with themselves and with the
Brown family. Mantel with scroll decorations that usually
seemed rather elegant but which since morning had become
unspeakably vulgar, impossible.

(Gwendolyn Brooks, *Maud Martha*, 158)

Use fragments to saturate the prose with sensory detail. Fragments
made of concrete words like *blue* or *hot* are vivid and immediate. Here
is John Edgar Wideman:

Returning to the day now, I don't need to invent to make it
perfect. **Blue sky, hot sun, whitecaps breaking on miles of
gloriously vacant beach.**

(John Edgar Wideman, "Fanon," 124)

And here is Colum McCann:

Corrigan liked those places where light was drained. **The
docklands. The flophouses. The corners where cobbles were
broken.**

(Colum McCann, *Let the Great World Spin*, 15)

Fragments can bring a place vividly to the page. Here is Mexico
City, the Mexico City of Ana Castillo's mother, who was a street
urchin in the 1930s:

My mother's México was the brutal urban reality of
Luis Buñuel's *Los Olvidados*. **Children scamming and
hustling, fire-eaters, hubcap stealers, Chiclet sellers, minia-
ture accordion players with small, dirty hands stretched out
before passersby for a coin, a piece of bread:** "Please señor,
for my mother who is very sick." This was the Mexico City

of my family. This was the México from which my mother
spared me.

(Ana Castillo, Black Dove, 11)

Hands On: Working with Fragments

If you've never used fragments before, begin by studying the models to
determine what makes a good fragment. I urge you to bypass a common move made by writers who've just discovered to their joy that
fragments are "legal" and begin lopping off the subjects of rather long
sentences. Keep in mind that most fragments are quite short and that
they hold the vivid, the crucial, and the hot. Gray ordinary language,
noncritical moments—these do not belong in fragments.

Take a passage from something you are working on. Can you use a
fragment or two in imitation of one of the models? Try it. Then read it
aloud. This way you will develop your ear. Keep trying a fragment or
two in various passages and see how they sound to you. You will soon
develop a knack for it.

13.

The Simple Sentence

I write three hours every morning.
—*Walter Mosley*

The simple sentence—a sentence with one subject and one predicate (the verb and words connected with the verb)—can be made quite long by piling on phrases. (But add a clause and you've made a compound sentence or a complex sentence.) Simple sentences can be long but often they are short. A short simple sentence can deliver a good punch.

> People are not dopes.
> (Howard Zinn, *Failure to Quit*, 77)

> Writing engenders more writing.
> (John Dufresne, "Holdalls," 113)

> Exile is not simple.
> (Eavan Boland, "A Fragment of Exile," 37)

A short simple sentence is emphatic. It calls attention to itself. Upon opening, it can make a key statement. At the end, it can slam the point home.

> The sentence is a vessel.
> (Gary Young and Christopher Buckley, *One for the Money: The Sentence as a Poetic Form*, 1)

Here the seasons are rain and no rain.

> (Leslie Marmon Silko, *The Turquoise Ledge*, 112)

Piety is a nasty little virtue.

> (William H. Gass, "Lust," 293)

Happiness is available.

> (Thich Nhat Hanh, *Being Peace*, 40)

I couldn't explain it. I loved this little girl.

> (Jamaica Kincaid, *Lucy*, 53)

A simple sentence has one clause. It is an independent clause. A clause must have a subject and it must have a verb. A simple sentence with one subject can have multiple verbs. A simple sentence with one verb can have multiple subjects. But as soon as you add a second *clause*, which has *both* a subject and a verb, you have either a compound sentence (two or more linked independent clauses) or a complex sentence (one independent clause and one or more dependent clauses).

Here are four simple sentences with multiple verbs:

Mama **died** at sundown and **changed** a world.

> (Zora Neale Hurston, *Dust Tracks on a Road*, 65)

Nenna **made** the tea and **lit** the wood stove.

> (Penelope Fitzgerald, *Offshore*, 48)

She **stopped** and **took out** her handkerchief and **dried** her eyes and **looked** at me.

> (James Baldwin, "Sonny's Blues," 118)

We **sat** in the presence of death and **did not mention** it.

> (Janisse Ray, "Whither Thou Goest," 209)

Here are two simple sentences with multiple subjects:

Both poet and painter want to reach the silence behind the
language, the silence within the language.

> (Howard Nemerov, "On Poetry and Painting, with a
> Thought on Music," 178)

Reading and writing are collaborations.

> (Gina Berriault, "Don't I Know You?," 63)

A simple sentence can be long, short, or somewhere in between. A
very short sentence (or a short fragment) within a paragraph of longer
sentences can focus the matter, punctuate it, drive it home:

For two hours, a heron stood at the side of a field, by
the hedge, facing the furrowed stubble. He was hunched,
slumped, and drooping, on the long stilts of his legs. He
shammed dead. His bill moved only once. He was waiting
for mice to come and be killed. **None came.**

> (J. A. Baker, *The Peregrine*, 45)

A series of short simple sentences can carry a series of discrete
events. Here's a run of five short events before a longer sentence kicks
in. ("The aunt" is not the writer's aunt but that of his guide):

**The aunt smiled at me. The thunder crashed. A donkey
brayed. The imam ranted. The rain poured. A drill thumped
like gunfire.** Somewhere higher up the valley, the wadi
started to run with water, and the old path we had walked
became a new river.

> (Robert Macfarlane, "Limestone," 226)

Hands On: Working the Simple Sentence

Again, take out a piece you are working on. Using it and its subject matter, practice making simple sentences that mimic and attain the weight and effectiveness of the models offered here. Each model offered, and certainly each *type* of model offered, will repay a work session or two to integrate into your skills. Do not rush. Keep reading your new sentences out loud to develop your ear.

- Take one of your pieces to work on. Does it have any sentence that resembles "The sentence is a vessel" or "Piety is a nasty little virtue"? Big statements compressed into small nuggets? Try a few. These sorts of sentences invariably give you clichés at first. Be aware and revise against. Strive for extreme accuracy.
- Try making a simple sentence with multiple verbs.
- Try writing a Very Long simple sentence by multiplying a prepositional phrase (see pags 210–11).
- Take a paragraph you've written—this is your "before" paragraph. Now make one of the sentences extremely short (or make a short fragment). Make the short sentence capture the main point or the most burning moment.

14.

The Compound Sentence

> Writing is not a matter of obeying rules; it is a matter of
> observation and imagination.
> —*Richard Marius*

Think equality. Think of two racehorses, neck on neck. Think an eye for an eye. Think seesaw, one end balancing the other. Or one end completing the other.

> This place is violent, and it is raw.
>> (Mark Spragg, "Wind," 208)

> You're a writer now, and a writer writes.
>> (John Dufresne, "Holdalls," 119)

> The years flowed away, and no one counted them.
>> (Hermann Hesse, *Siddhartha*, 96)

> Then they all gathered around Sonny and Sonny played.
>> (James Baldwin, "Sonny's Blues," 140)

The compound sentence has two or more independent clauses connected by a coordinating conjunction, or by a colon or a semicolon. A clause has both a subject and a verb. This sentence—*I got up and washed my face and poured coffee and sat down to write*—is a simple sentence with multiple verbs. Why? Because there is only one subject, the *I*. To make it compound you would write: *I got up and I washed my face.* A compound sentence has two or more independent clauses. A clause has a subject and a verb, so any compound sentence must have at least two subjects.

The independent clauses in a compound sentence can stand alone and still make perfect sense.

> This place is violent.
> It is raw.
> (This place is violent, and it is raw.)

> The years flowed away.
> No one counted them.
> (The years flowed away, and no one counted them.)

Conjunctions are connectors. Coordinating conjunctions connect sentence elements of equal grammatical rank. Use them to hook together two independent clauses to make a compound sentence.

for	and	nor	but
or	yet	so	

The parts are parallel or they are begging to be parallel. Often, in a two-clause compound sentence, the second clause loops back to the first or speaks to the first:

> Dreaming is beautiful but dreaming is not enough.
> (Danelle Morton, "Setting Achievable
> Goals and Meeting Them," 185)

> He didn't care for women and he couldn't care for men.
> (Joy Williams, "Winter Chemistry," 94)

This sentence by Sandra Cisneros opens a chapter titled "Born Bad":

Most likely I will go to hell and most likely I deserve to be there.

> (Sandra Cisneros, *The House on Mango Street*, 58)

Think of lifting dumbbells, one in each hand, high over your head. That image of strength—equally distributed weight—is the image of the compound sentence. No part hangs off any other part.

Gauguin's art dazzles, but it cannot be trusted.

> (Peter Schjeldahl, "Runaway: Paul Gauguin," 32)

But we still have books, and they give our day-dreams countless dwelling-places.

> (Gaston Bachelard, *The Poetics of Space*, 25)

A compound sentence can have two clauses, three clauses, four clauses, or many clauses. Still, the clauses are equal to one another. Each independent clause has its subject and verb, and they are connected with a conjunction, or with a colon or a comma or semicolon. Don't confuse a phrase with a clause. Don't confuse a dependent clause (*When you come . . .*) with an independent clause that makes sense all by itself.

I have wrestled with the angel and I am stained with light and I have no shame.

> (Mary Oliver, "Of Power and Time," 7)

It could be done; it would be done; it had to be done.

> (Ben Fountain, "Near-Extinct Birds
> of the Central Cordillera," 2)

Nonvirtuoso writers seldom use the compound sentence. I don't know why. I've often wondered if it's because compound sentences—*I pat the goat and the goat bleats*—seem like baby sentences. But why not express equal actions or equal conditions or equal directives in equal independent clauses—in a compound sentence?

> The script of *Macbeth* does not need to be bloodstained and spattered with tears; it needs to be legible.
> (Robert Bringhurst, *The Elements of Typographic Style*, 83)

To write such elegant sentences requires a technical grasp of the simple, compound, and complex sentence. These sorts of sentences do not flow from the pens of writers oblivious to the differences among them. It has never happened. At least I have never witnessed a lovely compound sentence extruded from the pen of a writer who couldn't tell a compound sentence from a complex sentence.

A compound sentence can express an action-reaction or an action-consequence.

> She held out her hands and snowflakes landed on her open palms.
> (Eowyn Ivey, *The Snow Child*, 86)

> He asked a series of questions and we made earnest notes.
> (Don DeLillo, "Midnight in Dostoevsky," 131)

A compound sentence can state a situation and something that emerges from or depends upon the situation. In the first model sentence the novelist is speaking of Napoleon:

> He was in love with himself and France joined in.
> (Jeanette Winterson, *The Passion*, 13)

> For he only ever mentions two pleasures and he does not call them pleasures.
> (Anne Carson, *Plainwater*, 13)

A compound sentence can express two or more sequential actions that have equal weight or value:

> She made cocoa and we ate and watched the day come.
> (Marilynne Robinson, *Housekeeping*, 55)

A compound sentence can shift equal small actions from one person to another. In this scene the two had been playing chess:

> Carlos had entered with a tea tray and he set it on the table and she pushed aside the board and pulled the tray forward and set out the cups and saucers.
> (Cormac McCarthy, *All the Pretty Horses*, 134)

The compound sentence can exude authority, even grandeur, and we often find it in sacred texts. Its steady feel has to do with its structurally equal clauses. No clause is hanging dippy-dependent off another clause. It is a steady marching thing, one foot after the other. Solid on the ground, nothing dragging. Consider:

> I have cried to the Lord with my voice, and he has answered me from his holy mountain.
> (Psalms 3:4)

> Our lives are made of days and hours, and each hour is precious.
> (Thich Nhat Hanh, *Being Peace*, 40)

Hands On: Working the Compound Sentence

I have taught the compound sentence over and over, to classes consisting mostly of advanced writers. Still, I've yet to teach a class in which some of these advanced writers did not confuse the compound sentence with the complex sentence, even after we've devoted an entire class to the compound sentence. (Don't despair: Mastering syntax requires time, attention, practice, and a good reference work. Be patient with yourself.) The compound sentence delivers its own feel, which differs within different contexts and for different writers. The idea is to master the form and then begin experimenting. If you mistakenly include complex sentences in your compound-sentence experiments, you will confuse your ear. The compound taps like a hammer; the complex skips, jumps, falls, and runs. You can hear the difference.

A compound sentence has no *dependent* clause. As soon as you put a dependent clause in a sentence, what you have is a complex sentence. Mastering the compound sentence requires mastering the complex sentence.

- To get a feel for the form, sit with yourself or with your writing buddies with your notebook and a timer. Set the timer for a full fifteen minutes. Describe your day in minute detail up to the present moment. Make every sentence a compound sentence. Now read this out loud to get the rhythm of this form into your ear.
- Again, take out a piece of your writing. Using the material of the piece, make a list of ten *really good* compound sentences. Use the equal-weightedness of the form to express two or more things that have equal weight. Then integrate this work back into the piece.
- Make a compound sentence with three clauses, four clauses, seven clauses. Keep experimenting. Ingest the form, masticate it, make it your own.

15.

The Complex
(and Compound-Complex) Sentence

I want to touch my blameless dreams, even if to date it is
all paper and mistakes.
—C. D. Wright

The complex sentence, which has one independent clause and one or more dependent clauses, can be a comely thing. But, alas, it can easily overrun a writer's skill level and become chaotic, tangled, and terribly untidy. There are two ways out of this unfortunate mess. The first is to practice making very short complex sentences: *Wherever you go, there you are.* The second is to practice multiplying one and only one *type* of dependent clause in a longer complex sentence. Here's one using a *that* clause:

> For my part, I wish to live in a community **that is peaceful,**
> **that cares for the weak and the poor, that welcomes the**
> **immense variety of humankind, that fosters the health and**
> **happiness and full development of all its members, young**
> **and old, male and female.**
>
> (Scott Russell Sanders, *Hunting for Hope*, 70)

In the complex sentence, the dependent clause is hitched to the main clause with a subordinating conjunction—*which, because, when,* et cetera. Now let's step through the types of dependent clauses. Remember that a clause has both a subject and a verb. The types are:

what, why, and *how* clauses
who (or *whoever, whomever*) clauses
that and *which* clauses
adverbial clauses (nine types, see ahead)

Here are complex sentences with *what* and *how* clauses:

What makes our lives worth living is love.
(Karsten Harries, The Ethical Function of
Architecture, 263)

In my book poetry is a necessity of life, **what they used to
call nontaxable matter.**
(C. D. Wright, Cooling Time, 4)

He knows **how much I need to write.**
(Hope Jahren, Lab Girl, 276)

Here are complex sentences with *who* clauses:

I am with Mayela, **who is dancing with another man.**
(Dagoberto Gilb, "Mayela One Day in 1989," 23)

My father was **who he was.**
(Lee Zacharias, Buzzards, 208)

Here are complex sentences with *that* clauses. Note that in the James Baldwin sentence the word *that* is omitted. Although the subordinating conjunction *that* is implied rather than articulated, the sentence remains complex. *That* clauses are restrictive: they supply information essential to the meaning of the sentence. Thus, no comma.

All this was carrying me some place **I didn't want to go.**
(James Baldwin, "Sonny's Blues," 107)

I feel **that I want to paint my own century.**

(Eugène Delacroix, *Painter of Passion*, 34)

Mariah did not know **that Lewis was not in love with her anymore.**

(Jamaica Kincaid, *Lucy*, 81)

Here are complex sentences with *which* clauses. Most *which* clauses are nonrestrictive: they add extra information, information not strictly necessary to get the meaning of the sentence. The nonrestrictive *which* clause must be set off by a comma.

They had arrived at the wharf, **which was exceedingly ill-lit.**

(Penelope Fitzgerald, *Offshore*, 18)

A movement describes a mass of people collectively moving towards a definite goal, **which they either achieve or fail to achieve.**

(John Berger, "Wanting Now," 8)

There's also such a thing as a restrictive *which* clause, which, like the *that* clause, is necessary to the meaning. The restrictive *which* clause comes with no comma:

This vampire **which is my talent** does not suffer other suitors.

(Gloria Anzaldúa, *Borderlands/La Frontera*, 97)

Now we come to the adverbial clauses. Most of us use adverbial clauses without much thinking about it, and a common writing fault is to write rangy loose sentences that unconsciously employ several different types of adverbial clauses. Using them consciously is a different matter entirely. We begin by mastering the nine types. Does this require struggling to memorize them as if we were miserable eighth-graders

facing an English test? Not at all. Instead, we study them, we play with
them, we try them. And yes, we do master them.

1. **The adverbial clause of manner.** Modifies the independent
   clause by answering the question *how*. The subordinating
   conjunctions are *as if* and *as though*. Adverbial clauses of
   manner are not overused. When apt, they work in any kind
   of writing, but are most often found in literary writing.

   > Rosenberg was frowning, holding out that grammar
   > toward the master **as if it had the clap.**
   > (Alix Christie, *Gutenberg's Apprentice*, 81)

   > Her hair had been pulled back tightly that morning, **as if**
   > **she were about to perform for the Bolshoi.**
   > (Joshua Ferris, *To Rise Again at a Decent Hour*, 87)

   > He absorbed this slowly, frowning **as though he was trans-**
   > **lating it from another language.**
   > (Octavia E. Butler, *Kindred*, 135)

Note: *Fowler* instructs: "In the great majority of *as if* clauses, when
the choice of verb is between were or was, the subjunctive form *were*
is preferred. It indicates that something is hypothetical, uncertain, or
not factually true."* However, in excellent writing you see *was* used all
the time too, even when uncertainty rules, perhaps because in our own
time *were* is beginning to sound a bit formal. So let the writer decide.

2. **The adverbial clause of comparison.** Compares one action to
   a different action. The subordinating conjunction is *as*.

---

* Fowler, *Modern English Usage*, 70.

As artists have sketchbooks, writers have notebooks.
(Diana M. Raab, *Writers and Their Notebooks*, ix)

As a dog returneth to his vomit, so a fool returneth to his folly.
(Proverbs 26:11)

The hawk had filled the house with wildness as a bowl of lilies fills a house with scent.
(Helen Macdonald, *H Is for Hawk*, 65)

3. **The adverbial clause of place.** Modifies the independent clause by answering the question *where*. The subordinating conjunctions are *where* and *wherever*.

No one yet has made a list of places where the extraordinary may happen and where it may not.
(Mary Oliver, "Of Power and Time," 5)

Shadrack rose and returned to the cot, where he fell into the first sleep of his new life.
(Toni Morrison, *Sula*, 13–14)

4. **The adverbial clause of time.** Places the independent clause into a framework of time. Subordinating conjunctions are *when, as, after, as soon as, before, since, till, until, whenever,* and *while*.

Until I was five, I spoke only Yiddish.
(Leonard Michaels, "My Yiddish," 188)

I sang as I made the coffee.
(Olivia Laing, *To the River*, 15)

When my father died recently, I did several drawings of him in his coffin.

>(John Berger, "Drawn to the Moment," 419)

5. **The adverbial clause of cause.** Modifies the independent clause by explaining why it happened. The subordinating conjunctions are *because, for, since, now that, that.*

I wrote *Colored People* **because I was grieving for my mother.**

>(Henry Louis Gates, Jr., "Lifting the Veil," 103)

Great poetry is not obvious or easy to grasp **because it means so much.**

>(Robert L. Bergman, "Blue Notes:
>Poetry and Psychoanalysis," 189)

Because we were quiet we were considered docile, and **because our work was not exceptionally good or bad** we were left alone.

>(Marilynne Robinson, *Housekeeping*, 76)

Here Cary Tennis illustrates the effective strategy of repeating the same adverbial clause. In a small space he uses the adverbial clause of cause six times.

Because we fear death, we deny death. **Because we deny death,** we pretend time is limitless. **Because we pretend time is limitless,** we feel we can always get around to our project later. **Because we feel we can get around to our project later,** we never do it. **Because we never do it,** we lose our shot at immortality, and we become unhappy and don't know why we can't do it, and we begin to hate ourselves and seek psychotherapy.

>(Cary Tennis, "The Winchester Mystery Novel," 89–90)

6. **The adverbial clause of condition.** Begins with the following subordinating conjunctions: *if, even if, provided that, unless,* and *in case.*

> **If you give me five dollars** I will be your friend forever.
> (Sandra Cisneros, *The House on Mango Street,* 14)

> **If there is magic on this planet,** it is contained in water.
> (Loren Eiseley, *The Immense Journey,* 15)

> **If there is a support group for Christmas depressives,** I will be your leader.
> (Leonard Michaels, "My Yiddish," 192)

7. **The adverbial clause of concession.** Presents a fact that is in contrast to the fact presented in the independent clause. The conjunctions are *although* and *though.*

> The winter air was crystalline, **though snow had yet to fall.**
> (Alix Christie, *Gutenberg's Apprentice,* 76)

> **Although I mostly kept myself in check,** I did do one or two questionable things.
> (Joshua Ferris, *To Rise Again at a Decent Hour,* 114)

8. **The adverbial clause of purpose.** Tells the intention, the reason why. Subordinating conjunctions are *in order that, so, so that, that.*

> Jack tried to quiet his breathing **so he could see and hear.**
> (Eowyn Ivey, *The Snow Child,* 13)

> I was wild to get settled as soon as possible, **so that I**

could begin living in the house at last.
>   (May Sarton, *Plant Dreaming Deep*, 54)

9. **The adverbial clause of result.** Explains what happens as a result of something else. The subordinating conjunctions are *so* and *that*.

> The limbs we drag back to camp are **so green with sap or rotten with rainwater they will not burn.**
>   (Joe Wilkins, "Eleven Kinds of Sky," 34)

> This January the sycamores, barren of leaves, showed themselves **so white and heavy with hundreds of branches that they looked like ivory carvings.**
>   (Craig Childs, *The Secret Knowledge of Water*, 126)

> The slopes and peaks were **so heavily wooded with dark pines that from a distance the mountains actually looked black.**
>   (Luther Standing Bear, "From *Land of the Spotted Eagle*," 176)

COMPOUND-COMPLEX SENTENCES

Finally, of course, there is the compound-complex sentence. These too can be beautiful sentences. Now you should be able to see what makes them compound and what makes them complex.

> Joey felt that his romance with Daisy might ruin his life, but that didn't stop him.
>   (Mary Gaitskill, "Daisy's Valentine," 10)

> Long, dark, and lovely she had been, in those days before her mind broke and the parts scattered and she let them go.
>   (Daniel Woodrell, *Winter's Bone*, 6)

Just as we reached the bright lights of the neighborhood
liquor store, a car pulled up and the enraged boyfriend
jumped out.

(Ana Castillo, Black Dove, 64)

We had been seduced into thinking that we were immortal
and suddenly the affair is over.

(Anne Carson, Plainwater, 15)

Finally, here is Nenna, the single mother in Penelope Fitzgerald's
novel *Offshore*. She lives on an old boat with her two children, and
one night confesses:

> "I can't do the things that women can't do," she said. "I can't
> turn over *The Times* so that the pages lie flat, I can't fold up
> a map in the right creases, I can't draw corks, I can't drive in
> nails straight, I can't go into a bar and order a drink without
> wondering what everyone's thinking about it, and I can't
> strike matches towards myself."

(Penelope Fitzgerald, Offshore, 12)

Hands On: Working the Complex Sentence

As you have discerned, there is a method to this madness. From one
of your works in progress, separate an average sentence from its paragraph. Return it to your writer's notebook. Now make it into a beautiful sentence. In the case of the complex sentence, I suggest forego-
ing for the moment complex sentences that use two or more *types* of
dependent clauses. This will bring to a halt any tendency to write those
rangy, out-of-control, chaotic complex sentences.

- Make a list of ten very short complex sentences. Use one and
  only one kind of dependent clause.
- Make a complex sentence that is at least a half-page long and
  that repeats one and only one type of dependent clause.

- Using a piece of writing you are working on, make two stunning complex sentences of each of the nine types.
- Make sentences using the adverbial clause of manner (as if . . .) and work on them until the metaphor seems apt and natural.
- Take one of the model compound-complex sentences in this chapter and imitate it with a new sentence of your own.
- Always, after you've worked on individual sentences, reintegrate them back into your paragraphs.

16.

The List Sentence

> He [Barthes] speaks of the quiver, thrill, or shudder
> of meaning, of meanings that themselves vibrate, gather,
> loosen, disperse, quicken, shine, fold, mutate, delay,
> slide, separate, that exert pressure, crack, rupture,
> fissure, are pulverized.
> —*Susan Sontag*

A sentence containing a list is a list sentence. It is a compression technique, like a well-packed suitcase. At some point many years into my apprenticeship, I began to notice list sentences in the work of superb, first-rate, virtuoso writers. And, really, I saw them nowhere else. Certainly not in my own work. So I began to fiddle with them and compose them. I began to love lists for their sounds and rhythms. Here is a specific craft technique that will repay the writer in pleasurable hours of wordplay and in striking effects.

Listen to the sounds in Gretel Ehrlich's sentences (well, fragments) upon waking up to her first solo morning of sheepherding. We are deep in the desolate hills of Wyoming:

> Morning. Sagesmell, sunsquint, birdsong, cool wind.
> (Gretel Ehrlich, *The Solace of Open Spaces*, 54)

The beauty of this passage happens, I think, because of the sibilance but also because of the repeated two-beat rhythm. The first four words go stressed/unstressed (a pattern called a trochee). *Cool wind* is a spondee: stressed/stressed.

Especially good for a list sentence are lists of nouns. A good trick is to count the number of items in another writer's list and put that same number in your own—one or two more if you are feeling a bit competitive. Here Melissa Fay Greene makes a list composed of eight items. Each item comprises no more than two words. She is on the southern coast of Georgia:

> I studied the correct names for the layers upon layers of foliage and the delicate life of the salt marsh: great egrets, fiddler crabs, ghost crabs, ant lions, cabbage palms, bald cypresses, sea oats, and pennywort.
>
> (Melissa Fay Greene, "On Writing Nonfiction," 230)

I mentioned—didn't I?—that the items in a list sentence should consist of no more than one or two words. This is a list of nouns or adjectives or verbs. It is not a string of phrases. Of the editor Bob Boehme, Brian Doyle writes:

> He was a past master of the exotica of bindings, glue, papers, inks, imprints, frontispieces, tissue sheets, stitching, dingbats, doohickeys, and bookplates.
>
> (Brian Doyle, "A Sturdy Man," 138)

A list can clarify a concept cogently and quickly. How does one arrive at creative insight? Here William H. Gass speaks of Poincaré, the moment when the mathematician, thinking of something else, steps on a tour bus and receives in a flash of insight the solution to a mathematical problem he'd been struggling with for months or years:

> In each stage of Poincaré's amazing discovery, there are the same factors: initial talent, life preparation, focus, failure, distraction, revelation.
>
> (William H. Gass, *Reading Rilke*, 99)

Environmentalist Janisse Ray is studying wildlife on Wild Horse Island in Montana's Flathead Lake:

> The coyotes had two camps, one to the east and one to the west, and their songs passed back and forth: bays, trills, howls, barks.
>
>   (Janisse Ray, "Whither Thou Goest," 203)

A list can hold a world. Here is Zora Neale Hurston:

> They did not know of the way an average Southern child, white or black, is raised on simile and invective. They know how to call names. It is an everyday affair to hear somebody called a mullet-headed, mule-eared, wall-eyed, hog-nosed, 'gator-faced, shad-mouthed, screw-necked, goat-bellied, puzzle-gutted, camel-backed, butt-sprung, battle-hammed, knock-kneed, razor-legged, box-ankled, shovel-footed, unmated so-and-so!
>
>   (Zora Neale Hurston, *Dust Tracks on a Road*, 98)

A list can hold a way of life. Here Barry Lopez speaks of his hands:

> I had stripped them in those years of manure, paint, axle grease, animal gore, plaster, soap suds, and machine oil; I had cleaned them of sap and tar and putty, of pond scum and potting soil, of fish scales and grass stains.
>
>   (Barry Lopez, "A Passage of the Hands," 216)

Everywhere you look among first-rate writing you find the list sentence. Annie Proulx's character Diamond is five feet, three inches tall:

> All his life he had heard himself called Half-Pint, Baby Boy, Shorty, Kid, Tiny, Little Guy, Sawed-Off.
>
>   (Annie Proulx, "The Mud Below," 48)

The list sentence is a prime place to work sound. In his *New Yorker* profile of James Brown, Philip Gourevitch details the qualifications of talent scout Ralph Bass to recognize greatness when he heard it:

> So Ralph Bass knew the repertoire; he'd heard more gravel-voiced shouters, high-pitched keeners, hopped-up rockers, churchy belters, burlesque barkers, doo-wop crooners, and sweet, soft moaners—more lovers, leavers, losers, loners, lady-killers, lambasters, lounge lizards, lemme-show-you men, and lawdy-be boys—than any dozen jukeboxes could contain.
>
> (Philip Gourevitch, "Mr. Brown," 46, 48)

Kathleen Dean Moore must rattle stones in a pan to shoo away bears as she hikes through high brush near Alaska's Maclaren River. Look at how she also rattles vowels and consonants:

> I was a leper shuffling along the streets of a medieval town, ringing his bell *clang clang* as required by law, warning the townspeople that he is poisonous, contagious, covered with sores, seeping, dangerous and ashamed.
>
> (Kathleen Dean Moore, "The Maclaren River," 191–92)

Maya Angelou relates the "dishware, silverware and servants' bells" she was required to memorize in her new job as apprentice servant to a white lady. She continues:

> There were goblets, sherbet glasses, ice-cream glasses, wine glasses, green glass coffee cups with matching saucers, and water glasses.
>
> (Maya Angelou, *I Know Why the Caged Bird Sings*, 106)

Viet Thanh Nguyen opens his novel:

I am a spy, a sleeper, a spook, a man of two faces.
                        (Viet Thanh Nguyen, *The Sympathizer*, 1)

Finally, here is the filmmaker, painter, and writer Derek Jarman, listing the possible side effects of a drug, DHPG, he's agreed to take in an attempt to combat the AIDS he is dying of. (The list continues beyond this passage, and yes he did sign the paper saying he understood.) Jarman died in 1994.

> The side effects of DHPG, the drug for which I have to come into hospital to be dripped twice a day, are: low white blood cell count, increased risk of infection, low platelet count which may increase the risk of bleeding, low red blood cell count (anaemia), fever, rash, abnormal liver function, chills, swelling of the body (oedema), infections, malaise, irregular heart beat, high blood pressure (hypertension), low blood pressure (hypotension), abnormal thoughts or dreams, loss of balance (ataxia), coma, confusion, dizziness, headache, nervousness, damage to nerves (paraesthesia), psychosis, sleepiness (somnolence), shaking, nausea, vomiting, loss of appetite (anorexia), diarrhoea, bleeding from the stomach or intestine (intestinal haemorrhage), abdominal pain, increased number of one type of white blood cell, low blood sugar, shortness of breath, hair loss (alopecia), itching (pruritus), hives, blood in the urine, abnormal kidney function, increased blood urea, redness (inflammation), pain or irritation (phlebitis).
>
>   (Derek Jarman, "Into the Blue," 117)

Hands On: Making List Sentences

- Begin making lists in your writer's notebook. Begin putting lists in sentences. Put words together that sound good together.
- Make a list to make a setting.

- Make a list to put a person on the page.
- Make a list to make a philosophical statement.

Begin with a simple list of nouns. Or a simple list of verbs. Don't get tangled up in one complicated phrase following another. Stretch those lists out. Can you make a five-item list? A ten-item list?

17.

The Phrase

To paint is to love again.
—*Henry Miller*

Phrases are not clauses and do not a complex sentence make. It's handy to be able to easily recognize the types of phrases. The chief types are infinitive phrases, participial phrases (verbs used as adjectives), gerunds (verbs used as nouns), and the prepositional phrase.

These two sentences use the infinitive phrase:

> But isn't life a struggle **to gather the funds to cover one's vices?**
>> (Jim Harrison, "My Problems with White Wine," 32)

> It is easy **to become besotted with a willow.**
>> (Hope Jahren, *Lab Girl*, 90)

Here are three simple sentences, each containing a participial phrase (present participle):

> I spent most of my childhood and adolescence **messing with my hair.**
>> (Henry Louis Gates, Jr., "In the Kitchen," 120)

> In the morning we packed and left, **walking east.**
>> (Craig Childs, *The Secret Knowledge of Water*, 57)

Flies buzz around me, their green bodies **shining in the sunlight.**

(John Haines, "Spring," 80)

Here are three simple sentences, each containing a participial phrase (past participle):

Sleeping bags with their inbuilt hoods hang cadaverous and larval from pegs on the walls, **surrounded by a tangible aura of dried sweat.**

(Simon Armitage, *Walking Home*, 76)

The goats shat and left their smells in the air, **unmoved by the wind.**

(Ben Okri, *The Famished Road*, 175)

The days sloughed past **uncounted and uncalendared.**

(Cormac McCarthy, *The Road*, 273)

Here are sentences containing a gerund—a verb acting as a noun. In the first model sentence the gerund *knowing* is the subject of the dependent *that* clause.

I would say that **knowing is a road.**

(Anne Carson, *Plainwater*, 165)

Mourning is my theme, and a stack of recently published volumes on "grief work," as the counseling industry now calls bereavement, accumulates on my desk.

(Francine Du Plessix Gray, "The Work of Mourning," 60)

It is clarifying to grasp that gerunds and participles do not function as verbs. Therefore they cannot make a clause. They make phrases. For this reason, the model sentences we've just read are simple sentences, with the exception of the Francine Du Plessix Gray sentence, which is compound-complex.

THE PREPOSITIONAL PHRASE

The prepositional phrase is as common as bugs and dust. Learning it cold clarifies so many things about sentences. Sentences, you come to see, are not about individual words prancing and mincing along; instead they are constructed of units, rather like a freight train. The units consist of various types of clauses and phrases. Once you easily recognize the prepositional phrase you begin to see it everywhere.

It is ubiquitous and also highly mobile. Mastering it enables the writer to start moving it around as a unit, with varying effects. Writers who haven't mastered the prepositional phrase frequently divorce the preposition from its complement, creating misery all around. Writers who haven't locked onto the notion that the end of the sentence is the most conspicuous location are constantly putting this prime location to use as a prepositional-phrase dump as if the prepositional phrase was the most important thing. Sometimes, of course, the prepositional phrase is the most important thing:

She gained the recognition she deserved—**after her death.**

A preposition expresses the relation between two entities. The entity that resides within the prepositional phrase is the prepositional complement. Often, but not always, the relationship will be one of time or space: where something is, or when it happens.

In the morning I sent the big boys a message.
(James Ellroy, *The Black Dahlia*, 184)

People who poke around have seeds **in their socks** and rocks **in their pockets.**
(Kathleen Dean Moore, "Winter Creek," 31)

We live **in an age of rising seas**.
                              (Rachel Carson, *The Sea Around Us*, 97)

In Ellroy's sentence, *in* is the preposition and *the morning* is the complement of the preposition. In Moore's sentence *in* is the preposition in both prepositional phrases. The complements of the preposition are *their socks* and *their pockets*. In Rachel Carson's sentence (published in 1950) *in* and *of* are the prepositions and *an age* and *rising seas* are the complements.

A preposition and its complement make a prepositional phrase. A prepositional phrase often acts as a transition and thus may sit happily at the beginning of the sentence:

> **In those tender mornings** the Store was full of laughing, joking, boasting and bragging.
> (Maya Angelou, *I Know Why the Caged Bird Sings*, 8)

> **In 1990**, Pop died; he was ninety-four.
> (Oliver Sacks, *On the Move*, 316)

You can make an elegant sentence by multiplying a single type of phrase. Here is Zora Neale Hurston saying goodbye to a place she had no fondness for. She repeats the prepositional phrase eight times (using the prepositional form of *to*).

> I shall never forget the exaltation of my hurried packing. When I got on the train, I said goodbye—not **to anybody in particular,** but **to the town, to loneliness, to defeat and frustration, to shabby living, to sterile houses and numbed pangs, to the kind of people I had no wish to know; to an era.** I waved it goodbye and sank back into the cushions of the seat.
> (Zora Neale Hurston, *Dust Tracks on a Road*, 93)

And here is Violette Leduc.

> I missed the private jargon of our street and was homesick
> for it. To be separated **from my mother, from our big bed,
> from my basket, from the gardens** I plundered, **from the
> sawdust in the bar, from the tobacco juice, from Caramel's
> spitting, from the love songs, from the red heat of our iron
> stove, from the stew** spread on bread, **from the nocturnal
> visits of our smuggler** gave me a fever. I learned nothing.
>
> (Violette Leduc, *La Bâtarde*, 26)

Subtract all but one of the prepositional phrases and the long sentence
reads *To be separated **from my mother** gave me a fever.* The subject is
To be separated, an infinitive phrase.

I like the way Leduc's long sentence performs its meaning by cling-
ing to all that is longed for. And then *I learned nothing* also performs
its meaning by being a little nothing.

Here are common prepositions shown with complements:

for your efforts
at the store
to the store
during the summer
in 1874
after the deluge
before the deluge
under the bridge
between a rock and a hard place
until tomorrow
over the river and **through** the woods
despite the cold
out of the frying pan
into the fire

Prepositions can consist of more than one word:

> **According to** my mother, beggars can't be choosers.
> **Because of** your kindness, we have survived.
> **In addition to** the plum pudding, we served plum ice cream.
> **Thanks to** the dry weather, the garden withered.

When a prepositional phrase does occur at the end of a sentence, it can be made even more conspicuous by being set off with a dash:

> For two decades I wrote and wrote—**without teachers.**

Learn the prepositional phrase cold. Then you will never separate a preposition **from its complement.** You will have fun moving it around **as a unit.** You will be the happiest writer **in the world.** Never again will you wander **from the path of righteousness into the pit of confusion and darkness.**

Hands on: Working with Phrases

- Take a page of your writing and circle all the prepositional phrases. Make "before" and "after" sentences in your notebook to gauge the effects of moving them around.
- Write a Very Long sentence by multiplying one type of prepositional phrase.
- Take something you are working on and make five sentences using the infinitive phrase. If you haven't done so already, incorporate this type of phrase into your repertoire.

18.

Passive Voice

Art is made by ordinary people.
—*David Bayles and Ted Orland*

The passive voice turns sentences wordy, flabby, and flatulent. Except when it turns them forceful and eloquent.

Art is practiced by the artist and the audience.
(Muriel Rukeyser, *The Life of Poetry*, 26)

In the active voice, the actor—the he, she, or it that performs the action—forms the subject of the sentence. (The girl throws the ball.) In the passive voice, the thing acted *upon*—the *receiver* of the action— forms the subject of the sentence. (The ball is thrown.) In the passive voice, the actor, the one who did it, is omitted or is tacked on following the word *by*. (The ball is thrown *by the girl*.) The passive voice is appropriate when the actor needs to be concealed or is unknown:

Mistakes were made. (by?)
Jay's car was stolen. (by?)

Of necessity, a sentence in the active voice supplies the actor:

Jonathan made mistakes.
A teenager stole Jay's car.

In some situations the actor is entirely unimportant:

> The food was brought in and covered in a corner.
> (Ben Okri, *The Famished Road*, 42)

The following sentences are *not* in the passive voice:

> There is no tulip festival in Wyoming.
> (Mark Spragg, "Wind," 209)

> In the West, in the Blue Mountains, there are creeks of grey water.
> (Barry Lopez, *Desert Notes; River Notes*, 29)

Some English-usage experts call the *there* a dummy subject, delaying the real subject. Here, *there* is a pronoun. *There* can also serve as an adverb, indicating place: *There I found my keys.*

In the following passage, the second sentence is in the passive voice. Can you see why it could hardly be otherwise?

> The peregrine is devoted to tradition. The same nesting cliffs are occupied for hundreds of years.
> (J. A. Baker, *The Peregrine*, 22)

Use passive voice consciously. Awareness is the key. When we fall into the passive voice all unawares (because, usually, we are focusing on the thing acted upon), it often begs to be converted. Editors of nuts-and-bolts writing spend a good deal of their time converting passive voice constructions to active voice, and rightly so.

Still, there are no hard rules. Only strategies toward effects.

Hands On: Employing Passive Voice Actively

- Take a piece you are working on. Look through it and identify any passive voice constructions. Would the sentence read better in active voice?
- Using one of your current projects, make a list of ten passive-voiced sentences. Make them earn the passive voice. Make them sentences you would not, on second thought, revise to active voice.

The Art of the Paragraph

Every paragraph should develop a central idea.
—*Richard Marius*

No one has read all the world's paragraphs. Whatever the qualities of many paragraphs, there may be other paragraphs with different qualities. Principles commonly taught such as "a paragraph is about one thing" may not be true of some paragraphs. But, often a paragraph *is* about one thing, and often the topic sentence says what that thing is.

Let's consider four different types of paragraphs.

TYPE I. THE DIRECT PARAGRAPH

The direct paragraph begins with a topic sentence that says what the paragraph is about. It is a generalization, a statement of the paragraph's controlling idea. Following the topic sentence comes a list of *at least three* specific examples illustrating the general statement. First-rate writers give many examples (three, four, five, even ten). Average writers skim. They tend to illustrate a topic statement with only one example or maybe two before moving on. Writing is partly about taking the time to thoroughly articulate a thing, to think it through. Spelling out specific concrete examples to illustrate your controlling idea is one way to do this.

> No pain, no death, is more terrible to a wild creature than
> its fear of man. A red-throated diver, sodden and obscene

with oil, able to move only its head, will push itself out
from the sea-wall with its bill if you reach down to it as it
floats like a log in the tide. A poisoned crow, gaping and
helplessly floundering in the grass, bright yellow foam bub-
bling from its throat, will dash itself up again and again on
to the descending wall of air, if you try to catch it. A rabbit,
inflated and foul with myxomatosis, just a twitching pulse
beating in a bladder of bones and fur, will feel the vibration of your footstep and will look for you with bulging,
sightless eyes. Then it will drag itself away into a bush,
trembling with fear.

(J. A. Baker, The Peregrine, 121)

The controlling idea is that wild creatures fear us. Then Baker gives
us three specific instances: the red-throated diver, the poisoned crow,
and the dying rabbit.

This direct paragraph on the Affordable Care Act appears in a *New
Yorker* article by Atul Gawande:

> But Obamacare, it turns out, has done a lot of good. It guar-
> antees that people with preëxisting health conditions cannot
> be rejected by insurers or charged more than others. It has
> reduced the number of uninsured people by twenty mil-
> lion. It has increased access to primary care, specialty care,
> surgery, medicines, and treatment for chronic conditions.
> Patients are less likely to skip needed care because of the
> cost. As a result, according to studies conducted at Harvard,
> the A.C.A. is saving tens of thousands of lives each year.
>
> (Atul Gawande, "Trumpcare vs. Obamacare," 21)

Gawande gives four specific instances of the good the Affordable
Care Act achieved and then a summary result—"saving tens of thousands of lives."

TYPE 2. THE CLIMACTIC PARAGRAPH

The climactic paragraph is the exact reverse of the direct paragraph. It begins with a list of specific illustrations that build to the controlling idea at the end.

Here's a climactic paragraph I wrote:

> Genetics ties me to my ancestors, which, I discovered, include the Neanderthals. It's a personal connection I have with the Neanderthals—I carry some of their genes in my body. Botany, too, is personal. Plants give us oxygen to breathe and food to eat. This morning for breakfast I had blueberries with granola (grain and nuts and seeds) and milk from cows, which live on grain and grass. And astronomy is personal—the tilt of the earth gives us seasons, gives me this slow hot summertime. Science is not distant, not remote, not the exclusive bailiwick of the scientists we learn it from. Science is personal, and we writers could do worse than to include a thread of it in our stories, poems, memoirs, and novels.

Since the beginning of a climactic paragraph doesn't summarize or generalize anything or make a broader point (which comes at the end), it can begin rather dully. Don't let it.

TYPE 3. THE TURNABOUT PARAGRAPH

The turnabout starts in one place and ends up in the opposite place. It begins with an observation or suggestion, not a controlling idea. It begins with an idea that opposes an idea you are going to argue for: *Some people think* . . . It has a turn in the middle that reverses the direction—often signaled by words like *and yet, but, neverthe-less,* or *however.* Turnabouts are fitting when you want to argue for something or when you are of two minds about something or when a feeling or perception has another side.

Here's a turnabout paragraph from Margo Livesey's novel *Eva Moves the Furniture*:

> Working in the operating theatre was part of every nurse's training and I had duly put in my time there before I met Samuel, but I never did grow comfortable with this aspect of nursing; my job was to tend the body and I hated to watch someone take a knife to the flesh I had bathed and bandaged and fed. **Samuel's feelings, however, were the exact opposite.** Ordinary doctoring struck him as vague, almost mystical. The patient has a pain; the doctor makes an informed guess and prescribes medicine which may or may not help. But in surgery you could see the problem—a tumour, a broken bone, a malfunctioning joint or organ—and, hopefully, you could fix it.
>
> (Margot Livesey, *Eva Moves the Furniture*, 63)

And here's a turnabout paragraph I wrote for a class I was teaching. The exercise reminded me how writing works as an aid to thinking. Often the turnabout paragraph requires you to express, in the sentences before the turn, a point of view opposite your own. A good writer will express this opposing viewpoint as fully and fairly as possible.

> Some writers believe that writing every day is a bad idea. The poet Louise Glück writes only when inspired, believing it a mistake to write as if forced. And Glück is a fine poet. There's a how-to-write book, *A Writer's Time* by Kenneth Atchity, which suggests sitting on a park bench *not* writing until you have something definite to say. The brilliant novelist Robert Olen Butler has devised an elaborate system of dreaming scenes on 3 × 5 cards for ten or twelve weeks before actually beginning to write a novel. Believers in not

writing wonder, What is the good of bad writing, aimless writing, writing going nowhere? **But** I've found writing every day to be a benison. Writing every day, even if only for fifteen minutes, makes you a writer. It renders moot the whole aimless discussion of "writer's block." It terminates any question of whether or not you are really a writer. You write to find out what you have to say and that in turn opens out the next thing you have to say. You write to observe, to record your day, to work on stories or essays or poems. You write to think and you write to play. Writers who write every day have the chance to improve, to become good writers and even great writers. Writers who write every day can open out all that is given to them to write. They always have material to work on, to shape, to craft. They forever subtract themselves from that huge population of would-be writers who "want to write," who "would write if they had time," who "will write a novel once they retire," who "could write a really great memoir."

I must admit that here I failed in my goal—in what should be our goal—to make both sides of the argument equal in length.

TYPE 4. THE OTHER ONE

We began this chapter by stating that there are four types of paragraphs. What is the fourth type? Simply a paragraph that begins with a statement, not a topic sentence but just a statement, followed by a sentence that closely follows the first sentence, followed by a third that elaborates the second, and so on. This paragraph doesn't have a topic sentence but it does have a controlling idea. You can say what that controlling idea is. Here's one such paragraph from Gay Talese's classic piece on New York:

Each afternoon in New York a rather seedy saxophone

player, his cheeks blown out like a spinnaker, stands on the sidewalk playing Danny Boy in such a sad, sensitive way that he soon has half the neighborhood peeking out of windows tossing nickels, dimes, and quarters at his feet. Some of the coins roll under parked cars, but most of them are caught in his outstretched hand. The saxophone player is a street musician named Joe Gabler; for the past thirty years he has serenaded every block in New York and has sometimes been tossed as much as $100 a day in coins. He is also hit with buckets of water, empty beer cans and eggs, and chased by wild dogs. He is believed to be the last of New York's ancient street musicians.

(Gay Talese, "New York," 396)

Hands On: Composing Paragraphs

As always, do your assignments using your own real works-in-progress.

- Write out a "before" paragraph from something you are working on. For your "after" paragraph, make a strict and lovely direct paragraph. This paragraph is about one thing. It has a general statement about that thing at the top (or right after the transition). It provides three or more specific concrete instances of the generalization expressed in the topic sentence. In doing this exercise, I often find that my "before" paragraph contains only two concrete examples, whereas it ought to have three or six. Often, too, I must purge a digression. As usual, the writing exercise is also a thinking exercise, forcing you to articulate the thought more completely.
- Write a classic turnabout paragraph either from scratch or as an "after" paragraph. Once you have mastered this lovely form, look around among your pieces. Where would such a paragraph fit? Make the turnabout paragraph one of your specialties.

- Write a classic climactic paragraph. Work especially on the beginning of the paragraph.
- Plan out a new piece by making a list of eight or ten topic sentences. This is, essentially, your list of paragraphs. Work on your list, making sure it captures all you want this piece to include. Now write the ten paragraphs. You will have a piece of about one thousand words. After all, what is prose but a series of paragraphs?

20.

Transitions

Meaning is not in things but in between; in the
iridescence, the interplay; in the interconnections; at the
intersections, at the crossroads. Meaning is transitional as
it is transitory; in the puns or bridges, the correspondence.
—*Norman O. Brown*

Meanings move from one paragraph to the next. Transitions are the bridges. They are the way across. They get you from here to there. They connect what was not before connected. They hold two things together: what has been said and what is to come. Transitions are two-faced, like Janus, the Roman god of gates and doorways. They look backward and forward at the same time.

Consider a few simple transitions:

The next afternoon, . . .
Also, . . .
After that, . . .
Besides which, . . .

As a young writer I had a terrible time with transitions. I blame my utter lack of mobility in getting from one paragraph to the next on the fact that I had no teacher—and neither did I seek one out. (I don't think I realized there were teachers who could teach you to write.) Relief arrived in the form of three lucid pages on transitions in the late Richard Marius's lovely little book, *A Writer's Companion*. That book (and I mean the first edition, the one published in 1985 during the author's lifetime), *was* my companion for a few years, and I'm grateful for it.

Marius allows that *however, moreover, furthermore,* and *therefore* make clunky transitions, to be avoided whenever possible. We seldom see such clinkers in first-rate writing found in such publications as *The New Yorker* or *The American Scholar* or *Time* or *The Smithsonian.*

Instead, try these transition techniques.

TRANSITION BY REPETITION

A transition is like a switch in a railroad track—it connects the track you're exiting to the track you're entering. An excellent switching mechanism is to repeat a word or phrase from the previous paragraph at the beginning of the new paragraph:

Repeated Verb
"Goddamn it, **get into bed**," Rachael said.
  He got into bed.
(Philip K. Dick, *Do Androids Dream of Electric Sheep?*, 195)

Repeated Noun
May Sarton wrote of her adopted town, Nelson, New Hampshire:

> Passions there are bound to be in every small community. I sometimes think people have to have a **grudge** to keep them warm in winter!
>
>   But these **grudges** tend to unknot themselves as the warm weather comes, and by the time the next gathering of the whole town takes place, Old Home Day, on the second Saturday of August, they have slipped away with the snow and the bitter winter winds, and we are in harmony again, a community that for over two hundred years has evoked deep love in its members.
>
>   (May Sarton, *Plant Dreaming Deep*, 168)

Repeated Adjective

The Swiss writer Robert Walser wrote:

> This painting portrays something like a **moral** dilapidation.
> But are not loosenings of **moral** strictures at times
> elegant?
>> (Robert Walser, "A Discussion of a Picture," 133)

TRANSITION BY SYNONYM OR PRONOUN

He, she, they—pronouns always link to what has gone before while propelling the action forward. Simon Armitage records this snack break taken on a weeks-long hike on the Pennine Way, Britain's renowned 260-mile trail:

> There's more cake, which **Claire** cuts with her pocket knife.
> "It's not going to be full of toenail clippings, is it?" I ask,
> when **she** passes me a slice.
> "No, this is the blade I use for dissecting birds," **she** says,
> with a mouthful of crumbs.
>> (Simon Armitage, *Walking Home*, 27)

Like repeated words, synonyms link back to what has just transpired while also carrying a thought forward. Here's a passage from Tobias Wolff's *This Boy's Life*:

> Sometimes I just sat on a railing somewhere and looked up
> at the mountains. They were always in **shadow**. The sun
> didn't make it up over the peaks before classes started in the
> morning, and it was gone behind the western rim by the time
> school let out. I lived in **perpetual dusk**.
> The **absence of light** became oppressive to me. It took on
> the weight of **other absences** I could not admit to or even
> define but still felt sharply, on my own in this new place. My

father and my brother. Friends. Most of all my mother.

(Tobias Wolff, *This Boy's Life*, 98–99)

FROM THIS TIME TO THE NEXT TIME

Grounding the reader in time by using phrases such as "The next day . . ." or "That night . . ." at the beginning of a new paragraph or section is a simple way to drive a story forward while keeping the reader oriented. In most cases such phrases should go at the beginning of a sentence, not in the middle, not at the end. Tim Gautreaux uses such transitions a number of times in his short story "Idols":

> He went outside, out of the late June heat . . .
> The next day . . .
> For the next three weeks, Julian swept down the rooms . . .
> Every day, he walked through his rooms . . .
> The following Monday . . .
> That day Obie mixed mortar . . .
> The work went on through September . . .
> On Wednesday, he drove to Chance Poxley's store . . .
> He drove into Memphis the next day . . .
> Two weeks later . . .
> In late October, the money finally ran out . . .
> The next morning he got out of bed and fried a ham steak . . .
> In the middle of November, a freakish weather pattern set in . . .

FROM THIS PLACE TO THE NEXT PLACE

Moving the reader from place to place works the same way. These paragraph beginnings are from Andrea Wulf's account of the naturalist/explorer Alexander von Humboldt in *The Invention of Nature*. The year is 1801. Humboldt is making his way across South America.

> On 6 April, they left Cartagena to reach the Río Magdalena . . .
> Then, just as they were preparing to leave Bogotá . . .

From Bogotá they crossed the first mountain chain along the
Quindío Pass . . .
Their progress towards Quito was slow . . .

FROM FACTS TO MEANING

Writing can march in regular fashion from one place to another or it
can leap like the jump cut in a film. One type of leap is from a literal
presentation of some activity or process, the facts of the matter, to
what these facts stand for—to their meanings whether emotional or
personal or philosophical:

> I've had the bug to sleep in the woods ever since I was a
> child. My brothers and sisters and I—five of us—rarely slept
> in the house during the summer. We would gather at bed-
> time and traipse off to the woods, trailing our sleeping bags
> and dragging our pillows in the dirt. Out beneath the trees
> in the Breeds Woods forty, we'd lie on our backs and pick
> out stars, and speculate on the nature of the satellites that
> moved through the branches on their slow, straight line. I
> don't remember ever being caught in the rain, or worrying
> about bears or hydrophobic skunks. I also don't recall the
> mornings . . . whether or not we trooped home *en masse*, or
> just straggled home as we woke. We didn't always sleep in
> the forest. I can remember sleeping in the yard, although not
> often. . . . I recall sleeping in the smooth concrete mangers of
> the cow barn. . . .
>
> But back to the woods. To sleep in the presence of trees
> and in the proximity of the earth is to get a sense of what it
> is to be holy. They say when Christ needed to get his head
> together, he did forty days in the wilderness. I stop at forty
> winks, but I believe I get a taste of what he was after. When
> I sleep on the forest floor, I never feel as if I'm simply taking
> a nap. I feel as if I'm performing some sort of embryonic
> ritual. When I awaken, I feel as if some important work

has been done. This is not rest—this is ablution. By placing
myself on the altar of the earth and retiring all my defenses,
I am receding within myself, plucking a little transcendence
from the perpetually gnashing jaws of time.

(Michael Perry, "The Big Nap," 322–23)

MOVING WITH THE MIND

Writing does not always proceed in logical order, as if words were
soldiers and paragraphs were troops in an army. Some types of reflec-
tive writing can drift and dream just as the mind does. Addressing
art students, the art-weaver Anni Albers said, "You can go anywhere
from anywhere."* And so it is in narration. (Still, you need transitions.) Here, Jericho Parms uses a red door to leapfrog from a lover's
apartment to a childhood memory:

> When I did slip away, the air a little pink as it turned heav-
> ily to day, the metal door to his walkup that shut forcefully
> behind me—a **door** that still floats like a buoy in the shad-
> owy sea of the Bowery—was solid and padlocked and **red**.
>
> While on the subject of **doors**, let this serve as an entry-
> way into my memory of the **red-doored** church in the old
> neighborhood—landmark of my greatest curiosities, my
> greatest shame—that I used to circle as a girl, trying to learn
> something, waiting for its sober advice.
>
> (Jericho Parms, "A Chapter on Red," 93–94)

FROM REAL TO MAGIC OR MYTHIC REAL

Moving from real to magic or mythic real can capture a worldview in
which the spirit or dream world is as material as the material world.
In Ben Okri's masterpiece novel *The Famished Road*, this transition

---

* Quoted in *Woven and Graphic Art*, 11.

occurs seamlessly on nearly every page. In the following scene, the "he" is the protagonist's dad, who has just learned that "Mum nearly died":

> He released a long sigh. Then he got up, looked down at
> Mum, placed his palm on her forehead, and shut her eyes.
> He went back to the chair and smoked some more and
> I could measure the sadness of his thoughts by the way
> he dragged on the cigarette and the way he sighed while
> exhaling.
> 　　I watched the bright point of his cigarette in the dark and
> it eventually lulled me into Madame Koto's bar. Dad was
> there. The bar had moved deep into the forest and all her
> customers were animals and birds. I sat on a bench which
> was really the back of a goat.
> 　　　　　　　　　　　(Ben Okri, *The Famished Road*, 59)

AND, BUT, OR SO AT THE BEGINNING

I begin this section with a deep sigh. Only pity for my neighbors keeps me from wailing and pounding my chest and pulling out my hair. Writers! You can and often should begin a sentence with *and* or *but* or *so*. These make excellent transitions, and first-rate writers use them copiously.

So why is it that well-meaning teachers keep teaching that this is incorrect or at best, casual? Haven't these English teachers read first-rate writers? Haven't they read the entertaining and perceptive Fowler's *Modern English Usage*, the original one or any of its later (somewhat less entertaining) editions? The problem for writers shackled with the mistaken notion that beginning with *and*, *but*, or *so* is wrong or unsuited to formal prose is that they are forced back into the clunky however/moreover/furthermore/therefore School of Transition.

The use of conjunctions at the beginning of a sentence is neither new, nor informal, nor slipshod, nor slang. Every stylebook, usage manual, and grammar on the shelf that treats the subject is utterly clear on this point. But don't take it from me. For your enjoyment I here present a few leading authorities on the topic. *The Chicago Manual of Style*:

> There is a widespread belief—one with no historical or grammatical foundation—that it is an error to begin a sentence with a conjunction such as *and*, *but*, or *so*. In fact, a substantial percentage (often as many as 10 percent) of the sentences in first-rate writing begin with conjunctions. It has been so for centuries, and even the most conservative grammarians have followed this practice.*

Garner's Modern American Usage:

> It is rank superstition that this coordinating conjunction cannot properly begin a sentence. . . . The very best writers find occasion to begin sentences with *and*.

> It is a gross canard that beginning a sentence with *but* is stylistically slipshod. In fact, doing so is highly desirable in any number of contexts, as countless stylebooks have said (many correctly pointing out that *but* is more effective than *however* at the beginning of a sentence).†

Charles Allen Lloyd, *We Who Speak English: And Our Ignorance of Our Mother Tongue*:

> Next to the groundless notion that it is incorrect to end an English sentence with a preposition, perhaps the most widespread of the many false beliefs about the use of our language is the equally groundless notion that it is incorrect

---

*   *Chicago Manual of Style*, 289.
†   Garner, *Modern American Usage*, 44, 121.

to begin one with "but" or "and." As in the case of the super-stition about the prepositional ending, no textbook supports it, but apparently about half of our teachers of English go out of their way to handicap their pupils by inculcating it. One cannot help wondering whether those who teach such a monstrous doctrine ever read any English themselves.*

The New Fowler's Modern English Usage:

> There is a persistent belief that it is improper to begin a sentence with *And*, but this prohibition has been cheer-fully ignored by standard authors from Anglo-Saxon times onwards. An initial *And* is a useful aid to writers as the narrative continues. The *OED* provides examples from the 9c. to the 19c.

> The widespread public belief that *But* should not be used at the beginning of a sentence seems to be unshakeable. Yet it has no foundation.†

Whew! Now we have that straight. If you've been burdened with this mistaken notion, you may now set that burden down. Begin your next sentence with *and*. And be happy.

Hands On: Making Transitions

But be forewarned. You have crossed the threshold into a new writ-ing strategy. At first, any new strategy feels awkward. If you've never before begun a sentence with *and*, if you've never repeated a word to leapfrog from one thought to the next, it will take practice to learn to do so gracefully. Every new strategy involves comprehending it in

---

* Quoted in *Chicago Manual of Style*, 289.
† Fowler, *Modern English Usage*, 52, 121.

principle and then practicing until it gets into your ear. To develop your ear, read your paragraphs out loud.

- Take a piece of writing that you are in the midst of and simply go through and work the transitions. Over the next few work sessions, review and make sure you've incorporated into your process every transition strategy explored in this chapter.
- Take a paragraph that narrates an event or occasion. Then write a following paragraph that reflects on its meaning.
- Venture from the real to the surreal, from the mundane to the magical or mythical. Set your timer for five minutes and write a scene in which an action takes place. Then decide what the emotion of the scene is. Then set the timer for another five minutes and using one sentence as a stem, generate similes. (She felt light as a feather, she felt light as a kite, she felt light as a piece of paper . . .) Choose a fitting one and turn it literal: She felt light as a butterfly. She lifted her wings, floated into bright air.

21.

The Practice of Punctuation

> Why do I avoid, as much as possible, using the semi-
> colon? Let me be plain: the semi-colon is ugly, ugly as a
> tick on a dog's belly.
> —*Donald Barthelme*

> Overseen by the semi-colon, the well-tended sentence can
> hold any number of things: apples, prunes, persimmons;
> linen and lace; pheasant, roast beef, goose; eggnog,
> brandy.
> —*Barbara Mallonee*

Are your punctuation skills up to par? It's not about pleasing your English teacher. It's not about wearing kid gloves or being proper or obeying rules. It's about becoming entirely familiar with your medium so that you can shape it the way a master potter shapes clay. Here's a perfect beauty of a sentence. It would be entirely beyond the range of a writer innocent of the structure of the compound sentence:

> I had no friends I made no friends I didn't care.
>
> (Lauren Slater, *Lying*, 141)

And here is a paragraph, perfectly punctuated considering the chaos of a train station in India and a farewell scene in which a small boy is seeing his mother for the last time:

Around them the hostling-jostling crowd.

Scurrying hurrying buying selling luggage trundling porter paying children shitting people spitting coming going begging bargaining reservation-checking.

Echoing stationsounds.

Hawkers selling coffee. Tea.

Gaunt children, blond with malnutrition, selling smutty magazines and food they couldn't afford to eat themselves.

(Arundhati Roy, *The God of Small Things*, 284)

In this chapter, you will not find a review of all the forms of punctuation; nor will you find a rant against the punctuation errors proliferating like rats in the attic as we speak. To brush up your skills, go to any standard usage manual, keeping in mind that American and British punctuation conventions differ radically.

Here we look at just a few moves that first-rate writers have under their belts and other writers don't.

COMMAS AND SEMICOLONS IN A LIST

Whether you adore or deplore the semicolon, know where it *should* go, *should* you want to use it. Knowing this, you can use it or refuse it without looking inept.

In a list, if any one item has a comma within it, then semicolons must separate the different items—all of them:

Mondrian's loves were Paris, France; London; Amsterdam; and New York.

Here's a form: a list of lists. Each "item" in the larger list is a smaller list. Within the smaller list, the items are separated by commas. The commas within the lists force the semicolons between them:

And I have been, as a Catholic, variously devout, lukewarm, outraged, and indifferent; comforted, contemptuous, pious,

and proud; ashamed, lazy, zealous, and amazed.
(Thomas Lynch, "The Dead Priest," 147–48)

PHRASAL ADJECTIVES

A phrasal adjective is an adjective made of two or more words: real estate broker, or better, real-estate broker. Except for *ly* words (nearly white walls) and proper nouns, phrasal adjectives should be hyphenated—to make reading easier and to avoid misreadings: small business owner (that tiny person). Bryan A. Garner puts it this way:

> General rule. When a phrase functions as an adjective preceding the noun it modifies—an increasingly frequent phenomenon in 20th- and 21st-century English—the phrase should ordinarily be hyphenated. Hence *the soup is burning hot* becomes *the burning-hot soup*; *the child is six years old* becomes *the six-year-old child*. Most professional writers know this; most nonprofessionals don't.*

Here are a couple of good ones:

> Where once I had been a quick-to-take-offense hothead, I was now docile and thoughtful.
> (Rick DeMarinis, "Weeds," 44)

> He was just a stock helper or some such bottom-of-the-ladder type.
> (Octavia E. Butler, *Kindred*, 53)

DASH AND COLON

To the writer, small skills are endlessly useful. At one point during my long apprenticeship, I studied how to use the dash (technically,

---

* Garner, *Modern American Usage*, 625.

the em-dash). Ever since—I must admit—I've been addicted to them.

One use of the dash is to set off an appositive. Appositives clarify and expand the meaning of nouns. Keep in mind the notion that the end of the sentence is the most emphatic place in the sentence. To make the end of a sentence even more emphatic, set off its appositive with a dash.

> What cruelty has not been glossed over with the white man's word—enterprise!
>> (Luther Standing Bear, "From *Land of the Spotted Eagle*," 177)

> In the great Central Valley of California there are only two seasons—spring and summer.
>> (John Muir, *My First Summer in the Sierra*, 1)

Now let's take a look at the colon. The colon is a gateway: two big eyes looking at what's ahead.

> We can agree with Bachelard on this: we all dream of houses.
> (Karsten Harries, *The Ethical Function of Architecture*, 209)

> I have my amulets: words.
>> (Henri Bosco quoted in Bachelard, *The Poetics of Reverie*, 27)

There are three ways to punctuate an appositive, moving from least emphatic to most emphatic.

> Lou was the prize of Kent County, a sleek black racehorse.
> Lou was the prize of Kent County—a sleek black racehorse.
> Lou was the prize of Kent County: a sleek black racehorse.

INTERRUPTERS

An interrupter is a cool way to create emphasis or pack in information. An interrupter can be a phrase or an entire sentence interjected into another sentence. In this Gretel Ehrlich sentence, the project in question is a Public Broadcasting film on Wyoming sheepherders:

> I had come alone because my partner in the project—also the man I loved—had just been told he was dying.
> (Gretel Ehrlich, *The Solace of Open Spaces*, 34)

> The outsized passions and eccentricities of the Abstract Expressionists—enacted on a tiny, obscure, ragamuffin scene—seem exotic in our jaded age.
> (Peter Schjeldahl, "Barnett Newman," 117)

> I am visible—see this Indian face—yet I am invisible.
> (Gloria Anzaldúa, *Borderlands/La Frontera*, 108)

The interrupter *well* came into journalism at some point during the 1980s and was so effective that you started seeing it everywhere, to the point of annoyance.

> The market smelled of fresh fish and basil and, well, dog poop.

Yes, you do include the question mark or exclamation point in an interrupter sentence. And, no, you don't include the period.

PART IV

Honing, Deepening, Stretching

Mauve takes offence at my having said "I am an artist"—
which I do not take back, because that word of course
included the meaning: always seeking without absolutely
finding. It is just the converse of saying, "I know it, I
have found it." As far as I know, that word means: "I am
seeking, I am striving, I am in it with all my heart."
—*Vincent van Gogh to Theo, May 1882*

22.

Metaphor and Simile

Is the bluing of the hills then a metaphor for distance?
—*John Hollander*

We look at the world through metaphorical glasses. As George Lakoff and Mark Johnson explicate in *Metaphors We Live By*, we see good as up (we climb corporate ladders, get high, enter high society), and bad as down (we speak of an uncle's downfall, the pit of despair). Lakoff and Johnson's illuminating book (knowledge as light) is enlightening. It may be intrinsic to our *Homo sapiens* way of perceiving to look at *A* by comparing it to *B*. Consider the Milky Way (comparing the white light of our galaxy to milk); dead end (comparing the end of a road to the end of life); a dog-eared book (comparing bent page-corners to a dog's ears).

But our concern as writers is to create metaphors that clarify and make vivid, metaphors we have never heard before. This last point is crucial, since many clichés are metaphors (to buy a house for a song, to cry over spilt milk, to run around like a chicken with its head cut off). And as Ben Yagoda observes in his excellent book *The Sound on the Page*, "Clichés are prominent features of *everyone's* first draft, whether we write it down or keep it to ourselves. How could they not be? We hear and read them all the time and our brains are filled with them. The key to avoiding them in the second and succeeding drafts is recognizing them and casting them out."*

A good metaphor is an original metaphor. It intensifies an emotion

---

* Yagoda, *Sound on the Page*, 233.

or clarifies a concept. It makes an abstract notion visual or visceral. It turns something unknown into something familiar.

Writers who make metaphors fluidly and aptly—and these are our best writers—practice making metaphors the way musicians practice scales. They practice making similes, which are a form of metaphor. Jonathan Raban, speaking of the notebook he takes on his travels, writes of his "daily target-practice of a dozen or so experimental similes."*

AVOIDING LITERARY SHIPWRECKS

Good metaphors clarify. Rotten metaphors attempt to decorate, to be poetic. They distract and confuse. Be willing to freely try out metaphors and to freely discard the rotten ones. Watch out for "out" images. What is an out image? On a sweltering hot beach, don't make the sand snow-white: snow doesn't belong on a hot beach. A metaphor should intensify the scene rather than distract from it by introducing a foreign object.

Some subjects defy comparison. Pablo Neruda wrote, "Y por las calles la sangre de los niños / corría simplemente, como sangre de niños." (And through the streets the blood of the children / ran simply, like blood of children.)† There's nothing to compare with the blood of children running in the streets, so don't try. Metaphors can weaken, trivialize, and falsify. As you set out to become more skilled at making metaphors, keep in mind that some things are beyond comparison. The practice of making metaphor ought to include the practice of eschewing metaphor.

How to avoid mixing metaphors? A metaphor compares two things. "Dora Maar became Picasso's doormat" compares a person to an object that is frequently stepped upon. A (Dora Maar) compares to B (door mat). A mixed metaphor compares A to two things.

---

*   Raban, "Keeping a Notebook," 233.
†   Quoted in Hills, *May Stevens*, 81.

"Dora Maar became Picasso's doormat, never yapping or nipping his hand" is a mixed metaphor in that it compares Maar to both a doormat and a dog. Mixed metaphors confuse rather than clarify. They usually come about because the writer is unaware of using a metaphor. "The window gaped open, beckoning the thief to enter" is mixed because it compares the window to both a mouth (gaping) and a hand (beckoning).

DEFINITIONS AND PRINCIPLES

A metaphor compares two things. Often it characterizes something abstract (memory, childhood, panic, death) by comparing it to something concrete (violets, volleyball, firestorm, tombstone).

> Panic in me now blacker than old tea.
>> (Sebastian Barry, *The Secret Scripture*, 34)

Panic is abstract. You can't see it or hear it or touch it. But you can see black tea.

A simile compares two things (white as snow, black as a crow's wing) using the connector "like" or "as." Similes typically compare just one aspect of a thing with one aspect of something else.

> Vermeer is blatant and ineffable, like the Sphinx.
>> (Peter Schjeldahl, "Vermeer," 157)

> It was blacker than olives the night I left.
>> (Anne Carson, *Plainwater*, 39)

It's a mistake to think of metaphors and similes as surprising gifts or as something only literary writers use. Certainly, an apt metaphor is a pleasing thing, but it also works as a conceptual tool. The best writing, whether memoir, science, history, or philosophy, uses metaphor to clarify ideas. The French philosopher Gaston Bachelard writes:

So, like a forgotten fire, a childhood can always flare up again within us.

> (Bachelard, *Poetics of Reverie*, 104)

The English historian E. P. Thompson, author of the monumental *The Making of the English Working Class*, writes:

> The working class did not rise like the sun at an appointed time.
>
> (Thompson, *The Making of the English Working Class*, 9)

In Anaïs Nin's novel *Collages* the Consul's wife speaks of their marriage:

> Then she talked about the Consul. The pattern of their marriage was frayed. The silver, gold, purple, red and green threads were worn away.
>
> (Anaïs Nin, *Collages*, 89)

Metaphor works not as ornament but to deepen, to clarify, and to extend meaning. Metaphors make ideas more vivid. Here is the opening passage of Faulkner's story "Dry September." To intensify the terror of his story about a lynching, Faulkner compares the red of the sunset to blood.

> Through the bloody September twilight, aftermath of sixty-two rainless days, it had gone like a fire in dry grass—the rumor, the story, whatever it was. Something about Miss Minnie Cooper and a Negro.
>
> (William Faulkner, "Dry September," 169)

If Faulkner had made the evening light "rosy" or "flushed," that would have set up a different story—perhaps an erotic story. For this story it would have been inapt and certainly inept. If the rumor had run like a dancing nymph . . .

Metonymy exists in the realm of metaphor. Metonymy names an associated object to stand for the object, "the crown" to stand for the king, "a uniform" to stand for a police officer. "The pen is mightier than the sword."

Synecdoche also exists in the realm of metaphor. A synecdoche names a part to stand for the whole. Do you have wheels? He worked as a hired hand. She was the brain of the class.

FORMS OF METAPHOR

A good way to approach working with metaphor is to practice, not metaphor in general, but metaphor as it occurs in particular syntactical forms. That way you can practice one form at a time. Here are seven ways of making a metaphor.

1. Adverbial clause of manner. The adverbial clause of manner, beginning with "as if" or "as though," compares one action or one object to another. It is found ubiquitously in literary writing, but not so much elsewhere. One way to begin working with metaphor is to begin working with the adverbial clause of manner. Keep in mind that all adverbial clauses of manner are not metaphorical. Metaphor compares one thing to something entirely different. So "He trudged into the kitchen as if he was exhausted" contains an adverbial clause of manner, but no metaphor.

    > His thoughts clogged **as if a comb working through his mind had stuck against a snarl.**
    > (Annie Proulx, "The Half-Skinned Steer," 24)

    > Joined in mutual admiration they watched each day **as though it were a movie arranged for their amusement.**
    > (Toni Morrison, *Sula*, 55)

There's also such a thing as an adverbial *phrase* of manner. Here the protagonist has just arrived from a war zone, so it is fitting that he would see huddled beer bottles as doomed persons. The phrase is a participial phrase:

> On the kitchen table was a throng of beer bottles with their labels torn off, huddled together **as if awaiting execution.**
> (Aleksandar Hemon, "Blind Jozef Pronek," 168)

2. X does something the way Y does something else.

> There are four hundred finches on the island at this moment, and the Grants know every one of the birds on sight, **the way shepherds can tell every sheep in their flocks.**
> (Jonathan Weiner, *The Beak of the Finch*, 3)

> Songbirds fly in and out of towering cottonwoods **the way people throng office buildings.**
> (Gretel Ehrlich, *The Solace of Open Spaces*, 90)

3. Appositive as metaphor. (An appositive defines a noun: Mr. Brown, the janitor . . .) In the first model, Roger Angell, age 93 at its writing, is speaking of the knowledge of impending death:

> It must be this hovering knowledge, **that two-ton safe swaying on a frayed rope just over my head,** that makes everyone so glad to see me again. "How great you are looking! Wow, tell me your secret!"
> (Roger Angell, "This Old Man," 269–70)

> But after the bottle was empty sometime that night, I was

finally left with nothing but myself and my thoughts, **devious cabdrivers that took me where I did not want to go.**
                    (Viet Thanh Nguyen, *The Sympathizer*, 186)

And all love that had overtaken her would have to be a memory, **a truck on the interstate roaring up from the left,** a thing she must let pass.
                    (Lorrie Moore, "The Jewish Hunter," 140)

4. It is like . . . It was like . . . It would be like . . .
       In the first model, the speaker is a girl and "the companions" are either ghosts or figments of her imagination.

       For a while after the disaster with Catherine, I tried to avoid the companions, but my loneliness **was like the slow gas bubbling up from the pond in the woods, poisoning even the sweetest of days.**
                    (Margot Livesey, *Eva Moves the Furniture*, 31)

       In its most basic form, a plant **is like a drinking straw,** drawing water and nutrients out of the soil and up through the stems to the leaves, where the water is lost through evaporation (properly termed "transpiration").
                    (Geoff Hodge, *Practical Botany for Gardeners*, 85)

       Looking for goshawks **is like looking for grace: it comes, but not often, and you don't get to say when or how.**
                    (Helen Macdonald, *H Is for Hawk*, 5)

5. X is Y.
       Keep in mind that all *X is Y* statements are not metaphorical. "The beach is hot" describes the beach. It does not compare the beach with something entirely different. "Happiness

is going to lunch with a friend" specifies one sort of happiness. It does not compare happiness (*A*) with something else (*B*). But our first model below is metaphorical. It compares a bed (*A*) to a completely different thing, a vehicle (*B*):

The bed is a mode of transport. It is our vehicle, our spaceship into oblivion.
(John Olson, *In Advance of the Broken Justy*, 195)

Memory is a house with ten thousand rooms; it is a village slated to be inundated.
(Anthony Doerr, "Village 113," 131)

Creative writing, like any art, **is a kind of fishing.**
(John Daniel, "In Praise of Darkness," 44)

6. Word substitution: bringing in a word or phrase from a different world.

You can't grasp the unknown even when **it's pissing in your face.**
(John Edgar Wideman, "Sightings," 161)

For a moment, all that remained in the sky was the **watermark stain** of the moon's dark side.
(Craig Childs, *The Secret Knowledge of Water*, 14)

The storm **came on a wild horse** and rode over us.
(Norman Maclean, *A River Runs Through It*, 47)

7. Similes. A simile compares by using *like* or *as*. Similes compare one *aspect* of a thing with the same *aspect* of another thing. Be aware that any random use of *like* or *as* does not necessarily result in a simile.

The sun rose yellow **as a lemon**.
(Ray Bradbury, *Something Wicked
This Way Comes*, 60)

In a badly designed book, the letters mill and stand **like
starving horses in a field**.
(Robert Bringhurst, *The Elements of
Typographic Style*, 19)

In an early Woody Allen film, a poor and lovely girl sits
opposite him at a table, her skin flawless **as a petal**.
(Rebecca McClanahan, "Considering the Lilies," 181)

Hands On: Making Metaphor

I suggest a three-part program. First, study the concept. Read the
warnings. Understand definitions and principles. Second, collect sentences that use metaphor. Collect the different forms and write them
in your sentence book to use as models. Third, practice making metaphors using a specific syntax, working on one form at a time (rather
than trying to think of metaphor in general).

Remember that you are comparing an unfamiliar thing to a familiar
thing. She ate the chocolate cake (the reader doesn't yet know how)
as if she were a starving person (something easily imagined). If you
wrote: "She ate the chocolate cake as if she were cibophobic," that
would compare something unfamiliar (how she was eating) to something equally unfamiliar except to an extreme minority of readers who
know that cibophobia means fear of food.

- Choose one of the forms, say, *X* is *Y*. *A barn, in day, is a small
  night* (John Updike). Then take an abstraction that is key to the
  piece you are working on. Set the timer for some excruciating
  amount of time—perhaps ten or twenty minutes. Write using
  the phrase over and over, spinning off comparisons using only

your chosen form. For example, for a piece on the Human Genome Project, I might write: "The human genome project is a modern-day Lewis and Clark expedition. The human genome project is the twentieth century's search for the Northwest Passage. The human genome project is exploration in the outer space of the infinitesimal. The human genome project is a modern-day search for the philosopher's stone." And so on. You keep going, never minding that some will be awful. While you are writing you are meditating on the thing you are writing about, sinking into the ambiance of it, the emotion of it. This is an exercise in association, so that, to use the Faulkner example again, if you were using a simile and a color (red as . . .) to describe the kind of evening on which a murder was to take place, your words might run to "red as gut, red as blood, red as hot lava."

- When the time is up, look over the result and choose an appropriate one. This is not an arbitrary choice, but one that deepens meaning. ("She had leopard eyes, narrow and yellow at the rims" does not describe a sweet silly person.) Turn some of your similes into metaphors. Turn "twilight red as blood" into "the bloody September twilight."

- Over the course of several weeks, practice using all the forms of metaphor. Don't get stuck on just one. Take one at a time and make it your own.

- As you become more fluid, become more rigorous. Keep questioning your metaphorical language. Is this apt? Does the comparison make literal sense? A dog may run as fast as a train but can a dog run like a train? I don't think so. But perhaps a rumor can run through town fast as a grass fire.

A writer in one of my classes recently wrote an excellent piece on living on a cul-de-sac. In it she wrote that during the 1950s, in suburban developments, culs-de-sac spread like a virus. Well, actually, culs-de-sac and viruses spread in entirely different ways. But perhaps culs-de-sac became as popular as white bread. (Both are manufactured things, both are made by companies, both were seen in the 1950s as being superior to their previous forms—the grid, whole-grain bread. Both were later criticized as being inferior to their previous forms.)

You see how it works.

23.

Extending Connections, Deepening Insight

I love words but I love the world more.
—*Scott Russell Sanders*

I sometimes ask myself: Why do the works that grab me grab me? What is it about the pieces I reread and pass around and quote from and teach from that hold me within the world they have created? Certainly, I love language. Certainly, I am drawn to writers who have a good ear, who play language as if it were a musical instrument. But beyond that, I am drawn to works that to me have significance, that offer insight. Alternatively, I shy away from works that seem slight, even if well-written.

In my own work I have been trying to extend my philosophical reach, to ask questions that matter to me but also to the world, to realize pieces that may be quite personal but that also weave connections to a wider circle. It is my desire, whether or not I succeed, to increase the philosophical weight of my work and to deepen any insight it can bring to bear. Does this strike a chord? Is insight something dispersed by the heavens or can a writer strive for it? Are such matters susceptible to intention and to conscious work? The answer I think is yes. Here are some approaches.

ASK QUESTIONS

One way to deepen and extend our work is to ask questions.

Michael J. Gelb's *How to Think Like Leonardo da Vinci*, written not for writers but for anyone wishing to enrich his or her life, suggests writing out—in your writer's notebook in the writing-practice manner, continuously without stopping—one hundred questions. These can be personal questions, questions about the world, questions about science, about nature, about society, about your mother, your life, your spouse, your dog, your car engine. After writing out your questions freely and without censorship or even much contemplation, circle the ten that seem to you to be the most important. On a clean page, write down your ten most important questions.

How do these ten questions relate to your body of work as it is developing right now? Are your most important questions reflected in your work? Do your questions suggest areas into which you might extend your work?

There are no right or wrong questions. Each writer's concerns and core questions will be different and a writer's questions will shift over time. Questions do not necessarily have answers and the best questions—examples might be, *How does a bird fly?* or *Why was my mother so silent?*—do not have simple answers. Rather, they open doors into areas of inquiry. The question, *Why was my mother so silent?* might lead me to write a memoir, or an exploration of expressiveness and communication, or a mother-daughter story, or a piece on family dynamics.

It seems right that our work as creators should reflect our deepest questions, concerns, and values. It seems obvious. Yet if we've never articulated these concerns or if we are professionally oriented to completing assignments generated by someone else, this dream can get lost. Allowing your own values to shape a piece does not preclude balance. Balance means you represent both sides of a question fairly and with respect. David Foster Wallace's "Consider the Lobster" is balanced, in that he takes care to fully express the viewpoint of the Maine lobster industry. Yet he also introduces his own questions. The piece appeared in *Gourmet*—not an animal rights venue. In it, Wallace manages to insert and even bring to the fore his question of whether or not dropping a live lobster into boiling water causes the creature to die in terror and agonizing pain, and if so, do we want to do that?

Asking questions can help to shape our whole body of work and can extend and deepen individual pieces. An entire essay might articulate the essential questions facing some discipline or area of concern or interest. A piece titled "20 Questions on our Minds" by neuropsychiatrist Richard Restak, which appeared in *The American Scholar*, consists of nothing more (or less) than twenty questions on the human brain, taking into account the revolution in neuroscience currently under way.

Fiction writers ask questions through their characters. In Sherwood Anderson's story "I Want to Know Why," an adolescent boy is smitten with horses and with a horse trainer who proceeds to degrade himself before the boy's very eyes. The boy wants to know, "What did he do it for?" In Penelope Fitzgerald's novel *Offshore*, Nenna, separated from her husband, who is living on the opposite side of London, is contemplating a move to Canada:

> After all, she thought, if she did go away, how much difference would it make? In a sense, Halifax was no further away than 42b Milvain Street, Stoke Newington. All distances are the same to those who don't meet.
>
> (Penelope Fitzgerald, *Offshore*, 165)

Characters, like people, have conundrums, things they want to understand, things they find incomprehensible. They seek. They query the universe, just as we ourselves do. Ask questions. Let your characters ask their questions. They want to know why.

CONNECT WITH A WIDER WORLD

Another way to deepen your writing is to spin threads to connect immediate personal experience with the big, wide, outside world. In an essay on dressing, I might articulate the current chaos of my closet, but also recall that Sappho was concerned with beauty, that there exists a history of costume, that the silkworm is a worm, that cotton is a plant requiring toil in a cotton field, that a fur garment was once a creature's skin, that the detective in Raymond Chandler's *The Big Sleep* steps out in a powder-blue suit.

In John Olson's "Home" we see how far you can travel to get home. In these twenty paragraphs we go from the view from the window to feeling at home in a book to the infrastructure necessary to make a home to the politics that disregards infrastructure to the abodes lived in during a lifetime (a school bus, a hotel . . .) to the mother's body as the first home to feeling at home in a personal sense and in a spiritual sense ("votive candles lit . . .") to feeling ill at ease, not at home within yourself due to remorse and anxiety and fear, to aging to Stoicism ("a home for realists") to the voyage of seeking philosophy, best undertaken at home.

I have composed a piece called "Housekeeping." It is based on my childhood experience growing up in an unkempt household, which stood in contrast to my maternal grandmother's household, which was vacuumed and polished to the point of fanaticism. What does my personal housekeeping experience connect to, out there in the wide world? Well. There is Hercules's fifth labor—cleaning the Augean stables. There are writers who are hyperkempt (May Sarton with her washed cups and cut flowers) and writers who are hyperunkempt (the poet Auden with his white wine-splattered suit; Iris Murdoch and John Bayley with their dustballs and dirt-desecrated dinner plates). There is fêng shui in which clutter clogs energy. There is "ethnic cleansing," God help us. There was my sister Susanne whose refrigerator full of rotting food revealed a life spiraling into mental illness. There are the ten random people I asked, "How do you keep your house (or your room) clean?" (My favorite answer came from my nephew Eric Messerschmidt: "This assumes I do keep my room clean.") There is Marilynne Robinson's brilliant novel *Housekeeping*. And no doubt there are other connections I haven't thought of yet.

Look at the piece you are working on. Where are its mirrors, out there in the world? Is there a way you can spin a thread to the moon? Back to the Middle Ages, to the black plague? Is your personal situation connected to a scientific or medical finding? (I am an identical twin. Twins are clones. Clones bring us to the first cloned mammal, Dolly, to the debate about cloning and stem cells, to the Human Genome Project).

You get the idea.

READING

"Reading is important," writes Yusef Komunyakaa. "I can't see how anyone can write and not read. I'm not just talking about only reading literature, but reading in the sciences, philosophy, mythology, history, about the arts, current events—everything that one can possibly read. This feeds the imagination."*

Reading is one of the absorbing pleasures of the writing life. Research is part of it. Say I have a character, an elderly photographer. How does her work fit into the history of photography? What does she herself know of this history? What were the influences on her? As a woman, was she an anomaly, a maverick? Or part of a long tradition? These questions may lead to happy hours in the library. And the internet has become another library whose riches multiply as the years roll on.

Reading carries us into wider worlds, sparks ideas for our own work, lets us rest from our own work, and provides shelter for mind and spirit. Just as visual artists spend hours and years looking at contemporary and past art, so we writers read.

One immediate way to let your reading inform your writing is to collect epigraphs—a quotation taken from your reading, placed at the beginning of a work, setting forth the theme. Whenever I read a passage that strikes me, and that can stand alone, I copy it into a small blank book I call my epigraph book, carefully noting the author, and

*   Miller and Anglesey, *Writer's Chronicle*, 16.

where I got the quote from. I do this with no preconceived notion of where to use it. It's remarkable how many of these quotations have found their way into something I'm working on. Here is a random list of epigraphs taken from a few pages of my epigraph book:

"I am working out the vocabulary of my silence."
    (Muriel Rukeyser)
"Darkness was hidden by darkness in the beginning."
    (*Rig Veda*)
"Anything could happen in the strange cities of the mind."
    (C. D. Wright)
"Honey, the gods are laughing at us."
    (Langston Hughes)
"You have to take freedom. No one will give it to you."
    (Meret Oppenheim)
"I am worn out with dreams."
    (William Butler Yeats)

Beginning a piece with an epigraph makes an immediate connection between what is to follow and something out there in the world that mirrors it.

INTENTION

After you've finished a draft of a piece, set your timer for ten minutes. In your writing-practice notebook, write the start line, "If I could bring 5 percent more insight to this matter, it would be that . . ." Write for ten minutes without stopping, letting anything that comes to mind go on the page.

You may be surprised at the further insights and understandings you can come to in this way.

24.

On Revision

Let's say it's a mess. But you have a chance to fix it.
You try to be clearer. Or deeper. Or more eloquent.
Or more eccentric. You try to be true to a world.
You want the book to be more spacious, more
authoritative. You want to winch yourself up from
yourself. You want to winch the book out of your balky
mind. You try to liberate it. You try to get this wretched
stuff on the page closer to what you think your book
ought to be—what you know, in your spasms of elation, it
can be. You read the sentences over and over.
Is this the book I'm writing? Is this all?
—*Susan Sontag*

Revision is about deepening, extending, elaborating, and only then burnishing and honing. Polishing a too-thin piece is to do the right thing at the wrong time. And most unrealized works are, basically, too thin. They don't extend far enough. Perhaps they lack insight. Perhaps the language is thin as weak tea. Perhaps the structure needs correcting for the piece is structured nonsensically or lacks a dramatic structure altogether. Perhaps the emotional ground is merely hinted at because the setting is not saturated with the emotion of the piece. Perhaps the character is engaged in some job or sport or activity that is scarcely on the page, no glimpse of the tools or odors or tasks of this trade. Perhaps someone comes on stage without portrayal. Or speaks but lacks body language. Perhaps the sentence forms bear no relationship to the meanings they are carrying.

For writers who make themselves students of the language—of words and word origins, of forms of the sentence and of the paragraph—revising becomes a pleasurable stage of composition. This is the time to play, to experiment, to enjoy the delicious sense of mastery that comes from growing skills.

As you revise, keep hold of the idea that you are working out your own thoughts in your own words. You're not trying to second-guess some teacher or mentor or reader. There's a time to focus on the demands posed by the work itself, the work in front of you. I've known writers who are so externally oriented, so fixed on whether anyone will ever like this thing or read it or publish it that they've lost track of what they want for the piece and are paying no attention to what the piece itself requires. There's a time to turn inward, to create an interior space in which the two forces interacting are the creative work and the creative worker.

Here are some approaches and strategies.

- You have a rough essay, with various blocks of type in place. Perhaps some of the segments are rather badly written, perhaps transitions are lacking. But, as far as you know, every piece is there. Do not, I repeat, *do not* go into the essay and begin hacking or thrashing about. Do not enter the premises with a wrecking bar. Instead, work on craft outside the essay itself. Work in your writing-practice notebook. Copy down a sentence or a paragraph that needs work and work on it there, in the notebook. Experiment with alternatives until you get one you like. Then type it back into the essay.
- There is no need to begin at the beginning, but when you do return to the beginning, remember to ground the reader in time and place, and in your connection to this material. Is there something surprising, or startling, or unusual that unfolds within the first few paragraphs? Try putting it in the first sentence:

François was killed on a Saturday night. Just as it was

getting dark. A car coming from behind knocked him
over.

(John Berger, "François, Georges and Amélie:
A Requiem in Three Parts," 413)

- Does the piece ask questions? Does it open up the key questions inherent in its subject matter? If it is fiction, what are the protagonist's questions?
- Structure: Look at complication/resolution (probably 85 percent of stories use this structure). Or look over the structures presented in this book or elsewhere, structures you've taken into your repertoire. Does the structure of the piece fit its content? If it is about baseball, could it have nine innings? If it is about twins, could it repeatedly double itself? If it is about beauty versus ugliness, could it fit into an A/B structure?
- Verbs carry the piece. Circle every verb. Question every verb. Can you make a verb more active, more accurate? Does at least one sentence have multiple verbs?
- Go through and circle areas that are vacant of images (gray areas). Rewrite the sentence to expel the gray and the drab. Make general words more specific. Change *casual attire* to *T-shirt and blue jeans*. Change *She packed her undergarments* to *She packed her black lace panties and matching bra*.
- Work on sentences. Make a sentence or a paragraph enact its own meaning.
- Body parts ground writing and increase its visual and visceral impact. Merely increasing the number of body parts can improve a story. Not, *He leaned against the doorjamb* but *He leaned his shoulder against the doorjamb*. Not, *He touched her face*, but *He touched her face with his fingertips*.
- What is the emotion of the piece? Is the setting saturated with this emotion? Can you put in an object that holds a love or a pain or a recurring dream or memory?
- Work on coloration. Color is not arbitrary but resonates metaphorically. Thus, *blood-red nail polish* will deepen a sense

of doom, whereas a *rose-silk gown* adds an erotic blush. It is important what you choose to color and what you choose to leave alone. Color what is significant to the story. Leave the rest alone. All this language work is about making a piece more visual and more sonorous. It is not about making it more flowery.

- Whenever a person comes onstage, he or she becomes visible and needs a portrait. Whenever a person speaks, he or she speaks from a body, moves the body, or holds it still.
- Voice: Do persons and characters each have their own voice, or do they sound generic?
- Go through and take out every lie (Grace Paley).
- Deepen insight, and deepen the connections of the piece with the outer world. What is the philosophy of a piece? How does it connect with the past, with history? What stories in mythology, fairy tale, or fable does this story carry? What are the icons, associations, archetypes? How does this relate to scientific findings? Do timed writes in your writing-practice notebook on each section, in which you ask yourself: What is the meaning of this? What further insight can I bring to this? Is there any story out there in the world that this is an instance of?
- There is a constant tension between accuracy and authenticity on the one hand, and language as music, as vision, as a palpable aesthetic object on the other. We are not in the decorating business but we are working to deepen our contact with the language, to engage it fully. Constantly measure the one—truth—against the other—color, odor, sound, sight.
- Finally, after each session, insert your new changes into the piece and print out a clean version. Always have at hand a clean version including all your most recent tweaks. Do not work for long periods with a scratched-up, emended mess.

WORK VS. TALENT

Here is a good place to question whether some people may just have more talent. Most people, when speaking of great artists—writers or painters or musicians—speak of talent (for the undeveloped) or genius (for the well-developed). Art students and apprentice writers often ask themselves, "Do I have it?" When I was in graduate school, a fellow graduate student in creative writing announced his intention to ask his faculty advisor whether he had "it." If not, he planned to quit. Some accomplished writers believe fervently that talent is fundamental to their own and other people's artistic achievement.

Perhaps because I did not grow up hearing the word *talented*, I've always belonged to the opposite school of artistic development, the practice-makes-perfect school. Pablo Picasso—the artist to whom the word "genius" most often sticks—may also have been in the practice-makes-perfect school because he was a prodigious, indefatigable worker, outworking all his friends, outworking probably every other artist in France. So, yes, he was a genius, but he may have come by that genius through his fanatical work habits.

Indeed, neuroscience and cognitive psychology have landed with both feet in the practice-makes-perfect school. The emerging picture, writes Daniel J. Levitin in *This Is Your Brain on Music*, "is that ten thousand hours of practice is required to achieve the level of mastery associated with being a world-class expert—in anything. In study after study, of composers, basketball players, fiction writers, ice skaters, concert pianists, chess players, master criminals, and what have you, this number comes up again and again. . . . But no one has yet found a case in which true world-class expertise was accomplished in less time. It seems that it takes the brain this long to assimilate all that it needs to know to achieve true mastery." *

Let's assume you have talent, whatever that means. If you want to write, why waste time wondering? We all have some abilities and propensities. We all have potential. Now we know that to realize that potential, all we have to do is—work for ten thousand hours.

---

* Levitin, *Your Brain on Music*, 197.

PART V

Getting the Work into the World

All of them want to know if they have enough talent
to become successful artists. This is always a difficult
thing to advise a student about. There are so many other
factors that determine the complete artist other than the
possession of artistic talent. Who can tell whether or not
the young artist can bear all the vicissitudes of the artist's
life, not only standing up under the blows, but turning
them to his own advantage.
—*Romare Bearden*

25.

Literary vs. Commercial Writing

> Anything that happens to me as a writer has been
> precipitated by an action of my own.
> —*Joyce Carol Oates, note kept on her desk*

I like the distinction made in the visual arts between commercial artists and fine artists. Commercial artists, whether freelance or employed, are working to earn a living and their product belongs to their employers. In general, before they begin they have a commitment to receive compensation. Fine artists want to make money, and some keep an eye on viable markets for their work, but their work belongs to themselves and they do it without regard to compensation. The fine artist may have a day job and the day job may be doing commercial art.

We writers are the same. The commercial writer—whether reporter, freelance journalist, grant writer, paid blogger, or publicist—writes to earn a living.

This writer would not write for free any more than a grill cook would flip hamburgers for free. It is a job. In contrast, the literary writer writes with no guarantee of compensation. But the reality is that many writers cross back and forth over this line. And the distinction is muddied by the fact that at least some "commercial" writers scrimp along making a rather inadequate income whereas some "literary" writers make good money, and a novelist whose novel sells well will very likely get a contract for the next one. Still, between the two, procedures and strategies differ.

Commercial freelance writers query editors for assignments, and write a piece only after they get an assignment. Commercial freelance writers write to a word count and they write to a deadline. They send the piece to the editor on the deadline. The editor works the piece in conjunction with the writer, and the piece sees the light of day shortly thereafter. These writers learn to write expeditiously and they learn to complete work.

All of these are reasons why any writer would benefit from doing this some of the time. Many of our finest writers are literary writers who work or once worked as commercial freelance writers. I think of Jonathan Raban, Annie Proulx, Donald Hall, and William Kennedy. On the other side, editors of commercial periodicals sometimes do a large amount of rewriting on pieces they buy from commercial freelance writers. Certainly they value their brilliant writers, but all of their writers are not brilliant. Anyone knows this who has ever worked on the editorial staff of a commercial magazine.

Literary writers send out completed works to literary journals with a note (including thanks and a short bio that mentions previous publications, if any). These days the submission process is commonly done online; only a few journals still accept (or require) the work to be mailed in an envelope that contains the piece, a note, and a self-addressed stamped envelope (SASE) to be returned to the writer with an acceptance or rejection. Literary writers do not query the journals, but they do read them constantly. Most journals post some of their contents online and many publish online exclusively.

At the literary journals, it's the quality of writing that counts above all. A literary journal does not take a poorly written piece containing good information and rewrite it. The writing has to be superb upon arrival, although small edits may be made. Of course, different editors have different tastes, and there are various aesthetics afloat. Literary journals also publish regular features and theme issues.

Although the writing found in the literary journals is not of course uniformly brilliant, some of the best work being done today can be found in their pages. Out of a random sample of journals stacked on my living room rug or perused online—*Agni, The Gettysburg Review, The American Scholar, North Dakota Quarterly, Brevity, Brick,*

Alaska Quarterly Review, *New England Review*—I see the works of these nationally acclaimed writers: Joyce Carol Oates, Paul Zimmer, Chase Twichell, Oliver de la Paz, Stanley Plumly, Emily Bernard, Doris Grumbach, Jane Hirshfield, Christian Wiman, Toi Derricotte, Don DeLillo . . . well, I could go on.

So don't look down on the literary journals, and do read them, even if they pay little. Think of it as a different career path—you are aiming for collected works, that coveted National Endowment for the Arts award, a Guggenheim. Many literary writers end up teaching, as do some journalists.

If you are a literary writer, you might consider also doing some commercial freelance writing. Why? To make some money, of course. But also to learn to write to a word count, to a deadline. To learn to complete a piece and let go of it and on to the next. If you are a commercial writer—an articles writer, newsletter writer, publicist, or the like—you might consider doing some literary writing. Why? You can write longer, more honestly, more deeply, and you can write on your own agenda. You can aspire to literature. Among my clients are successful commercial writers who are good at cranking out articles but have lost the knack for writing longer, more substantive pieces that have more depth than is required by an airline magazine. On the other hand, some amazing literary writers—Hemingway for example—learned at least some of their craft strategies as reporters.

Why not have it both ways? Why not cross back and forth over this line from the start?

26.

First Time Out

Writers feed off each other when they're in close
proximity. It's not competition. It's just that somebody
will read his poem to you, and you'll say, "Oh, man, that's
wonderful!" And then you'll get charged up. You'll want
to write something that's that effective.
—*Tommy Scott Young*

We are a community of writers. The better one of us does, the better the prospects for all the rest. This is not an idle thought or sentimental wish. Biographies and creativity studies too numerous to list reveal that master-creators from Renoir to Picasso to O'Keeffe had a knowledgeable support group, whose composition shifted over time, but from which they received lifelong support. The important point here is that they got not just support—"This is great, send it out!"—but *knowledgeable* support, including praise, challenges, questions, criticism, and the sustaining company of others who understood their ambitions, compulsions, and way of life.

You can see how this works in practical ways. Sharing resources, knowledge, and venues results in more resources, more knowledge, and more venues. If I get better at paragraphing and tell you what I learned and how you might improve your paragraph, then you might question what my antagonist really thinks and whether he would say what he thinks or lie or say nothing. Multiply this over years and you have an enormous helping force, especially if your peer artists are skilled. One of the challenges and tasks of a writer is to learn to be a skillful reader of another's work. This skill is similar to that of learning to read (as a writer) a published masterwork. It is the skill of looking at such a work and being able to unravel the technical means by which it achieves its effects.

WRITING BUDDIES

Many writers begin alone. They experience the clandestine pleasure of the blank page—often a journal or diary page—that seems to invite their words. Other writers begin within the shelter of parental praise or the encouragement of a teacher. But all of us are eventually out here on our own, more or less. (I include the many writers who start late.) We all grow up. We discover that one or another of our pals who also aspired to being a writer, who was at least as talented as we were, who had a lot more promise, who had everything going for him or her, even the support of a husband or a mother or a brother, has fallen by the wayside, has quit writing. We become aware that, although, to be sure, our dear relatives want us to be happy, they do not actually care whether or not we write. (Indeed, it may take entirely too much time, and for what?) Of course, if we make a mountain of money then it has all worked out in the end (according to them). But most of us don't make a mountain of money. (Is there a struggling writer in existence who has not been asked, Why don't you write a Harry Potter novel?) "Most good writing," says Edward Hoagland, "is done against the resistance of others—first parents, then spouses or colleagues at jobs. It's a candle you protect with both cupped hands."*

Under such circumstances, a writing buddy or two is not a luxury. We need a friend to meet every week in a café to write with for an hour. Or we need a workshop. Or we need to take a writing class or go to a writing conference or even enter an MFA program if and when appropriate. Writers and other artists simply do not accomplish excellent works year in and year out in a social vacuum. Those who

---

*   Hoagland, "Vermont 2002–2004," *American Scholar*, 151.

attempt it work at a disadvantage and risk producing a mountain of failed works due to the lack of stimulation, challenge, inspiration, and encouragement that artists get from peer artists.

Writers' conferences; writers' centers—the Loft Literary Center in Minneapolis, the Cambridge Center for Adult Education and Grub Street in the Boston area, Hugo House in Seattle, The Writer's Center in Bethesda, Maryland—and others; writing classes and programs associated with colleges and universities; and MFA programs provide many resources for writers: classes, critique groups, forums, lectures, readings, and resources such as a library or a place to work or a tutor. They provide introductions to other writers, connections.

Writing teachers—and many of us turn to teaching—have advantages: no one learns better or more deeply or more thoroughly than the teacher does. But because we live so much of the time in the bubble of our own classroom, we writers who teach have a particularly urgent need for peer writers: a literary and literate buddy or two, a workshop of our peers, or a writing-practice session that we don't lead or "teach" but attend just in order to write. It is useful for teachers to take a class now and then. I often have one or more writing teachers in my classes and I try to occasionally take a class, taking care to avoid the situation in which I must critique the work of my fellow classmembers (don't ask the carpenter to pound nails on holiday). There is that tragic, often secret situation: the teacher of writing who does not write. He or she is "blocked" or teaching has usurped all his or her time, or . . . If you are in that hole, begin your fifteen-minute practice today. And find a buddy—one of your equals—to write with.

Whatever your situation as a writer, whether you teach or write grant proposals or magazine articles, whether you are just beginning or have years of experience, it's a good idea to take the time now and again to evaluate the question of whether you have an excellent social context in which to grow and thrive as a writer. Give yourself a writing-practice session to think it through. Set your timer for five or ten minutes. First write: What is my present situation in terms of a social context that supports me as a writer? What is the reality? Then take ten minutes to answer the question: How might I improve this situation by 5 percent? Then do those one or two things.

CRITIQUE GROUPS

One way is to find and join a critique group, a workshop in which writers take turns sharing work, giving feedback on it, and getting feedback in return. There are two forms of this: workshops taught in writing programs led by teachers who are master-writers, and writing-critique groups composed of peers.

I admit that I am at odds with the workshop method utilized as the main way to teach and learn how to write. Too many hours are spent in scrutinizing unrealized work when we should be putting those hours into scrutinizing masterworks. "One learns nothing from others' bad work, only from one's own," writes Marvin Bell. "Would we attempt to learn to sing by listening to the tone-deaf? Do we imagine we could learn to fly by imitating the labors of a kangaroo?"*

And, although any feedback is useful, too often the blind are leading the blind. Hasty, and sometimes wrongheaded advice can be given—and worse, taken. Or, perhaps more common and just as useless, vague praise.

But working alone is not the answer either. And some workshops are superb. I've participated in my own once-a-month workshop for some twenty-five years, and I wouldn't do without it. It includes some very skilled writers as well as visual artists, and we help each other get better all the time.

Whether we "workshop" a little or a lot, there are ways we can improve our skill at giving feedback and receiving it. Here are some guidelines.

The Writer's Responsibility
Be open to feedback. Listen, and think about it. Don't argue.

---

* Bell, "Three Propositions," 4.

But do not accept advice if it doesn't feel right. I have seen writers flounder for years dutifully following the contradictory advice of their writing group, getting increasingly lost. This does not work.

The problem is that if you follow someone's advice, even a good teacher's advice, while not really "getting" it, then the captain has abandoned ship. The ship is tossing directionless at sea. This is the case even if the feedback is exactly right. (Sometimes we get advice that we don't really understand until later. Later then, is the time to put it to use in the piece. Other times, we get advice that is plain wrong.) When you are hearing something you don't agree with or don't really get, try to listen, try to understand, and again, don't argue. Sleep on it. Think about it. But be loyal to your process and to your work. Be loyal to your vision.

Sometimes we get a suggestion that we know instantly is exactly right. Other times a suggestion seems off, but clues us that something is amiss. We take note and get to work.

As readers for a writer who takes responsibility for his or her own work, we can be more free, less timid, less worried that we'll make a mistake and lead the writer astray. This writer follows only advice that feels right.

The Reader's Responsibility

How can you upgrade the quality of feedback you give to your peer writers? Your job is to try to help the writer fully realize this piece, which is a piece in process. Bring everything you know to bear.

Here are a few points to think about:

- Compare the work to masterworks. How can this piece be improved enough to get into *The Best American Essays* or *The Best American Short Stories* of the year? (This is not, by the way, how you would look at a young person's writing. You would never treat a child's writing or even a freshman college student's writing this way. This is for adult writers who are or aspire to be professional published writers.)

- Naturally we are not trashing pieces. Trashing is truly an amateur move—it takes far more skill to say, here is a good part (specified and why) and here's what could use some work (specified and why). Make a huge effort to understand what the writer is trying to achieve (the weaker the piece, the more important this is). Then help the writer get there.
- Kindness, always. Vague praise is not kindness; it's condescending laziness. Still, kindness is a crucial virtue in this interaction as in all others.
- Structure: Know what the structure of the piece is. Does the structure work?
- Beginnings: Is this a good beginning or is it a long windup? Can you find a better place to begin on page two?
- When someone comes onstage does he get a portrait? When someone speaks does she have body language, gesture? Are the characters dressed? Does the setting carry its share of the emotion?
- Take one paragraph and do a microanalysis of the sentences. Are they sturdy muscular sentences or are they weak and flabby? Is the diction conventional received diction (they buy a "home"; she is "a blonde")? Is the writer avoiding repetition or fragments or the compound sentence? Why? Is this a door that could be opened?
- Do the characters have voice? (To write: "My mother used to scold and nag all the time" is to talk about her without giving her voice. To write: "Every day my mother yelled, 'Why can't you get up and dress yourself and go to school! I'm a failure! I have a twenty-year-old living at home doing nothing! What's the matter!? Talk to me! What have I done?'" is to give a character voice.)
- Can the insight be deepened? Could a memoirist reflect on a past event from the perspective of the present? Did a character have some past trauma that causes her to be so close-mouthed?

Ask questions that will help the writer think more deeply about the matter at hand.

- Could the piece benefit from a story or reference from somewhere else—another person's parallel experience? A myth? An insight from science? A quote from a philosopher or from the grocer down the street?

Finally, it's not really useful to say, "This doesn't work for me." This implies that technical skill and literary mastery are a matter of personal taste: I like chocolate but you like vanilla. Not so, dear writers. Not so.

PRESENTING AND PERFORMING

Readings are proliferating in cities and towns around the country, and often they include an "open mic" where you can arrive a bit early and sign up to read for a short time, three or five or ten minutes. Many reading venues welcome not only poetry but also prose. And, in my experience, nothing is better for a piece, whether poetry or prose, than reading it out loud to an audience.

First, practice. Read your piece into a voice recorder and listen back. You will learn to slow down and to get comfortable with it. You will also see spots to improve, to work. Then go out and read it to an audience. Gradually you will get over any stage fright; you will get comfortable, and you will find that reading the piece out loud helps you to hear it.

You work on it as you are working up to reading it and afterward you work on it some more—especially the sounds. Then, another time, read it again. Reading to an audience allows you to *hear* the piece. Nothing could be better for your work. And the practice of sharing your work with an audience is one more way to connect to the community of writers.

Be courteous. Time your piece in your practice sessions so you know exactly how long it takes to read it. Don't hog the mic, don't go over your allotted time. And please use the microphone. When a writer asks, "Can you hear?" and several in the audience raise their hand, does that mean that everyone in the audience can hear? No it doesn't. Everyone cannot hear. Please use the mic. It's a skill that can be honed. And stay for the entire reading to listen while others read. Those who read only to promptly depart are noticed.

27.

Sending Your Work Out

My first novella was returned with the succinct note: "We found the heroine as boring as her husband had."
—prolific novelist Mary Higgins Clark

For the writer of stories or poems or literary essays, sending work out becomes part of the creative working process. Why? Because getting a personal essay or a poem or a story ready to send out is tantamount to completing it. Work never sent out is likely never completed. The author never has to stand by it, for better or for worse. It is never exposed to a stranger's eye. It is never received with love, hate, indifference, or with interest. It has no audience, no public. As a result, the writer is never obliged to see it through a reader's eye.

A dynamic process percolates in the interval between doing the work and exposing the work. You do that crucial read-through before sending the piece out for the first time. Suddenly the eye is more acute, aware of the imminent exposure. Adjustments are made, a sentence tweaked, the list of nouns in a list sentence jimmied to ratchet up colors and notes.

Your hard-won work is about to be exposed, with all the shame and actual humiliation that exposure can bring up, especially to writers still wet about the ears. We've all been there.

A writer's embarrassment about his or her short story says nothing whatever about its quality. A critical eye, the ability to see faults, has nothing to do with embarrassment. Embarrassment speaks, rather, to how exposed the writer feels in the piece. I once wrote a short story called "Storm." I worked it and reworked it. I went to the setting (the granitic seacoast of Massachusetts) and wrote on the setting. I made an extensive family tree for each character. And on and on. When I finished the story, I polished and polished. Finally, there was nothing more I could do. The story practically finished me off, but it too was finished.

There it was, all typed up. It caused me intense embarrassment. I put it on the mantelpiece in the living room to remind myself that I was a writer and that writers must send their work out. Every time I glanced over at the typescript propped behind the snapshot of my Grandma Henry, my face burned with further embarrassment. Finally, to get it out of my sight, I sent it to *The Southern Review*. I sent it to *The Southern Review* because it is one of the three or four best literary magazines published in the United States. No doubt these erudite editors read and reject the work of fools all the time, so one more story from one more fool could not possibly make a bit of difference. In about three weeks I received a letter from *The Southern Review*. They wanted the story.

But often a story does come back. Big deal. (Okay, sometimes it is a big deal. Nevertheless . . .) You look at it again, perhaps rework the sentences or deepen the insight or extend a thought or recast the beginning. Study the rejection note for any hint of a specific response. But even if it's only that inscrutable printed note, you have your own fresh eyes and improving craft skills to bring to the task. Thus is the endeavor of creating a work served by the rather different endeavor of getting it published.

If you are immersed in a writers' community, you know writers who seldom if ever send out work. Some of these writers have been working for years. They don't feel ready, personally. They don't feel the work is ready. Or they send out a piece and it is rejected, so they go into a major funk. That's it—nothing more goes out for two more years. Then maybe they send something else out. Again they are full of high hopes mixed with trepidation. Again they get a rejection. Now what?

Nobody gets published this way.

When I first began to send out my poems, the idea of getting one published seemed to me virtually an impossible dream. I had loved poetry since childhood, since "Now We Are Six" and "The Raggedy Man." Starting when I was sixteen, I began writing "poems." Very late in the day, it now seems to me, I took a poetry workshop, Harold Bond's ten-week poetry seminar at the Cambridge Center for Adult Education. I owe the late Harold Bond a tremendous debt of gratitude. He taught us to look at lines and to ask what made this line a line of poetry. He taught us what enjambment was, as well as many other strategies and moves. Harold Bond also taught us to send out our poems, three to five poems per envelope.

After taking his workshop three times for a total of thirty weeks, I began sending out my poems, three to five poems in an envelope with a short cover letter. I would make up a set and send out two or three identical sets simultaneously, as Harold Bond taught us to do. Perhaps I had three or four different sets of poems circulating at any one time. (This was in the long-ago days before the internet.)

My plan was this. I intended to send out five hundred different envelopes before I would reconsider my strategy, much less quit. (By the time I started sending out, I had written a fairly large number of poems.) Notice that my goal essentially was to open myself to receiving five hundred rejections. My goal was not: Get a Poem Published. Of course, Get a Poem Published *was* my goal. But that goal does not require any action, except the action of sending out one envelope, which is virtually a waste of time.

My goal was to energetically accumulate five hundred rejections by sending out that many envelopes as intelligently as I could ("intelligent" meaning, read the journal before you send poems). I wanted the number to be a large number, because I wanted time and I wanted room and I didn't want to fail. With this setup, a rejection wasn't a failure; it was progress toward the goal.

So what happened? It took me several months and seventy rejections before I received an acceptance. That acceptance was one of the thrilling moments of my life.

I have no idea what made me think of that strategy, but years later

I am still impressed by it. It reduces the weight of any one rejection and it requires the writer to submit and submit and submit. For many years thereafter I kept probably ten or fifteen works, including prose and poetry, in circulation at all times. Whenever a piece was accepted for publication, this required me to complete another piece and get it out the door.

Then I thought of a strategy similar to my original one, a strategy that entertains me quite a bit. (Entertainment is important. Why be miserable?) It is to send out a certain preestablished number of "envelopes" (now more often an electronic submission) a year. My first marathon year of doing this I sent out three hundred "envelopes" and got eleven acceptances: you can do the math on the number of rejections! These days my yearly quota of send-outs is one hundred. This is my version of an athletic competition (for one who could not be less athletic). It ups the ante. It pushes me to be more productive. I've even experienced a twinge of anxiety upon an acceptance because that meant I had to fling another piece into circulation. The result, though, is that more works get accepted sooner. The cause is a matter of mathematics. A certain percentage of work gets accepted: the more you send out, the more gets accepted. I probably get more rejections than anyone else in the room. But, hey, my list of published works is seven feet high—so far.

The process of unloading (read publishing) can happen in several stages and each one can further the process of finishing a work. First the writer readies a piece to send out. (If you never send your work out, you never get to this stage of the creative work process.) Let's call this "Quote Finished," because its rejection (no big tragedy) becomes an opportunity to look at it again, to see its faults with clear eyes (the fickle writer embroiled in the current work-in-progress has now gained distance from this old thing). The job is to read it out loud again, to finish it again, to send it out again. Even first publication is not the end of the road for many pieces. As poets, fiction writers, essayists, we always hope for the collection of poems or stories or essays. Therefore, we indulge ourselves in postpublication revisions.

And what if you just don't like it anymore? It no longer interests you. It's stupid and you never want to see it again.

Here I want to quote from a perceptive essay on "Learning to Work" that psychologist Virginia Valian published some thirty years ago. It's a reminder that losing interest in a piece may be nothing more than a bad work habit.

> Attitudes toward finishing work most distinguish successful from unsuccessful workers. I discovered that I resisted working my ideas out to the end. Many times I caught myself putting something away once the end was in sight. This was true both of writing papers and of doing more menial tasks. Sometimes, when I went back to a task, I would discover that I had as little as thirty minutes' work left. This resistance to the end product contrasts sharply with what I have seen of or read about successful workers, who always finish everything, even after they have lost interest in it. Successful workers are also always thinking about the next project, planning ahead, integrating their current work into a larger picture which is constantly being revised. I tended not to do this. One consequence of viewing work as a continuing process is that one wants to finish the present project to get on to the next. Although one could conceivably just go on to the next without finishing the present piece of work, important learning occurs in putting the finishing touches on a paper or project, learning that may govern the direction of the next work. One is gratified by the feeling of closure that comes with finishing a project, but aside from this feeling, the finishing touches to make what one has done presentable, to make sure the idea is expressed, puts the project in perspective, aligns it with what one has done so far and what one is going to do next.
>
> (Virginia Valian, "Learning to Work," 173)

It may be rarely true that some works should be abandoned. But mostly we should plan to finish what we've started, even if, upon occasion, it is a struggle to do so.

Should you submit a single work to more than one journal at the same time? This is the question everyone asks. The answer is simple: Yes and No.

Every literary magazine in existence today is reading simultaneous submissions. The journals that forbid them (fewer and fewer each year) are nonetheless reading them. More and more journals see fit to accept them, as long as they are informed immediately if a piece is accepted elsewhere. That does not answer the question, but it is an important fact of the matter.

Pose the question to all manner of writers, teachers, editors. You will get the same two answers.

Answer Number 1: Don't do it.

Answer Number 2: Do it.

So in the end, you decide. Here is what I do.

I simultaneously submit to the numerous journals, such as *Ploughshares* and *The Missouri Review*, that accept simultaneous submissions.

I simultaneously submit to journals that take a year to turn a piece around, no matter what their policy is. Life is short! I do not have a year to find out if my story, one of fifty received every day by the average literary journal, is going to make it!

To editors with whom I have a relationship, I often single-submit. Sometimes I single-submit a piece to a top-drawer venue because I think it's the best thing written to date in Western Civilization and therefore it will not be denied. After it comes back a few times I get over that. I work on it some more, and I may start sending out a few at a time.

There are a few journals to which I have submitted for years, without a word of response, without a hint that there is a living, breathing human being at that address. I am one of the plebeians, one of the masses. They are too busy to toss me a kind nod, a *Sorry!* or a *Thank you!* One advantage of being completely ignored is that you are then free to make up your own rules.

That's what I do.

Now you decide what you are going to do.

READ THE MARKET

Smart writers read the target journal or target magazine. Fools send out blind. Of course we're all fools some of the time, but we try to keep it to a minimum. I consider reading literary journals as an indispensable part of my life in a writers' community. I might read *Boulevard* edited by Richard Burgin, and think about writers and music (the theme of a recent issue). I might read *Conjunctions* or *The Gettysburg Review*. My quest is partly to know where my work is going, to know with whom I'm speaking. It's partly to read some of the world's best writing—Brian Doyle or Francine du Plessix Gray or Aimee Bender or Cynthia Ozick.

Of course, some works found in literary journals aren't especially good. And some isn't to my taste, and some I don't get. Sometimes I read a journal and I feel compelled to rise from my chair in disgust and flip this dog of a rag into the recycle bin. But I also find models, assignments, challenges, inspirations. American literature, as it is being written today, may be found, to a very great extent, in literary journals, plus in a very few mass-circulation magazines such as *The New Yorker*.

I enjoy grazing aesthetics and literary points of view. I enjoy reading poems and stories written by the editors of literary journals and published in other literary journals (usually not in their own). I enjoy opening a journal and finding one or two things to read, then putting it away or giving it away.

Sometimes too many journals pile up. There's too much paper in the house. I give the big pile away, or I might dump the lot into the recycle bin. Then I begin again.

WHAT ABOUT SELF-PUBLISHING?

It's an idea. It's a possibility. It has always been a possibility. It was a possibility before print-on-demand, before the digital age, before there were seven hundred thousand books self-published in the United States (in 2015, latest figures from Bowker).* Here I present no answers but only considerations and questions—and a few personal experiences.

With some regularity I hear folks relating success stories about best-selling or at any rate nicely selling self-published books. True stories. What we hear little about are poorly selling self-published books. Much more common.

The process of getting a book published by a "real" publisher can be long, arduous, and even at times tortuous. Why put up with it?

I have witnessed many writers put up with it. And I have put up with it. What I note is that in the process, which can take years, the work gets better and better. It gets rejected and revised and rejected and revised again, rethought, revised, rejected, and finally accepted. And then it succeeds. It is well-published and it takes its place in the world. If this writer had given up after a year, after a few rejections, if this writer had self-published instead, it would not have been so accomplished. And—perhaps—it would not have found much of a place in the world.

But there is another side to this story. Or, maybe, several other sides. The success stories are true stories. And maybe some books should be self-published. If you have a work that is complete and polished and no one in sight to put it out and there is a pressing reason why it should appear this year rather than next year or the year after, why not educate yourself as to how to do it properly and go for it?

What would be a pressing reason? One is our own mortality. I have a good friend, Geri Gale, who composed a gorgeous nonmainstream

* Steven Piersanti, "The 10 Awful Truths about Book Publishing," Berrett-Koehler Publishers, accessed September 2017, https://www.bkconnection.com/the-10-awful-truths-about-book-publishing.

work (a blended genre she calls a "poemella"). *Patrice: A Poemella* was ready to go. About then, the author, Geri Gale, came up with breast cancer. She sent *Patrice* on its rounds, received ninety rejections, but no takers. She self-published the work. Her stunning prose is presented within a stunning design, and it's available—information on her website. Now the cancer is gone, thank goodness. And *Patrice* is out in the world. And Geri Gale is at work on further works of literary art. As her work becomes gradually better known, it's important that *Patrice* is out there, available, not sitting in a box under the bed.

Or take the first edition of this book. The manuscript of the first edition was agented, shopped around, and rejected by acquiring editors, who felt, mostly, that the market for how-to-write books was saturated. But I knew that writers needed this book and I knew its own market was *not* saturated. I founded Wallingford Press for the purpose of publishing it. The first edition of *The Writer's Portable Mentor* was printed (on demand) by Lightning Source. It was distributed by Partners-West (before that firm went out of business) and also by Ingram Book Co. (I did all the marketing work.) It sold more than eight thousand copies. I declare it a success story.

But I have four other books (to date) that are published by other publishers. And I am working on further books that I do not wish to self-publish. I want the affirmation of another publisher. I want to write the books and help to market, but I don't want to be entirely responsible.

So I present this idea. Some works should be self-published. Other works should be sent out, revised, sent out, revised . . . They should wind through that arduous—but ultimately rewarding—process of finding a home away from home.

"IT'S WHO YOU KNOW"

It's human nature to pay more attention to the work of someone you've had coffee with or played tennis with or had a beer with. So yes, to some extent who you know could matter to your career as a writer.

What does that have to do with you and me?

Whoever we are, and wherever we live, it's important for us to connect on a regular basis with people in the publishing world. Begin by being connected to other writers in your community. Take your place at the table. Go to writing practice or present your work at an open mic.

Go further. Write a note to someone whose work you admire. Shake an author's hand and thank her for her work. Buy the book of your fellow writer from time to time. Read the book. Write a note thanking this writer for this good work.

To this I would add that it's important to keep to good values, to be honest, to respect yourself, to retain your dignity, to keep your head up, to be proud, to keep priorities straight, to shun sycophantism.

That's right, *shun sycophantism!* Sycophantism sucks. Who wants to be a toady, a lickspittle? Instead, respect the working person, the janitor, the working mother, the clerk, the soldier. Respect the person who may not be in the limelight, but whose struggle to survive contributes to the survival of our communities.

But back to the publishing world. You are a writer. You are part of the publishing world. It is never too soon to take your place in this world. Your work deserves your best effort to connect. Yes, hobnob. Gad about.

It's time to overcome shyness and social dread. It's time to get out there and look around, look for allies, be an ally to other deserving writers. It might even be fun.

I used to be terribly shy about introducing myself to anyone who could conceivably aid me in my career. In fact I was so paranoid about appearing to suck up to a person "higher up on the food chain"—an expression I detest—that I must admit to having upon occasion actually left the premises rather than shake hands with such a person or thank him or her for his or her work or God forbid, actually initiate a conversation, suggesting by this action that this person might be just another human being with his or her own life to live.

Mind you, I grew up on a dairy farm where we had our best

conversations with the cows. If I can change, so can you. We all live in a community (not only in the sense of our neighborhood or town, but we live in a writers' community). We, each of us, have a place in this community. It is better to value ourselves highly, to respect ourselves completely, to help when we can, and to ask for help when appropriate. Envy is natural. We all feel it at times. But kindness, generosity, getting out there, saying hello, saying thank you for this good work (if it is good work) goes a lot further a lot faster.

Then of course, we work on our work. We get better. We work on craft, on sentencing. We help each other whenever we can. Did I mention that we work on our work? We work on our work every day.

28.

The Practice of Productivity

How much time you spend on your writing will depend
on how serious you are about it. For the serious writer,
writing is not merely an assignment. It is a way of life,
an everyday habit.
—*Richard Marius*

"The creative life happens," writes researcher Howard Gruber, "in a being who can continue to work."* Continuing to work through uncertainty, through lack of recognition, through innumerable interruptions and alternatives, and yes, even through success, is a core attribute of high-achieving creators. As a writer, you can decide to be productive. It is a decision that can open many doors. As we know, high-achievers in the arts are more *productive* than average achievers. They achieve more masterworks but they also make more messes, create more duds.†

I like the story told in that essential book, *Art & Fear*, written by visual artists David Bayles and Ted Orland. A ceramics teacher divides the class in half. Potters on the right need only make one pot, but to get an *A*, it must be a perfect pot. Potters on the left will be graded by quantity alone. Their output will be weighed on a scale, and the heavier the output the higher the grade. And here is what happened:

Well, came grading time and a curious fact emerged: the

---

*   Quoted in John-Steiner, *Notebooks of the Mind*, 78.
†   Simonton, "Historiometric Perspective," 122.

works of highest quality were all produced by the group
being graded for quantity. It seems that while the "quantity"
group was busily churning out piles of work—and learning
from their mistakes—the "quality" group had sat theorizing
about perfection, and in the end had little more to show for
their efforts than grandiose theories and a pile of dead clay.*

In the end what matters to the ambitious dreamer is a steady and
even rather plodding stream of work. Poems, stories, novels, creative
nonfictions do not emerge as perfect art-objects. They emerge rough,
awkward, contrived, and arguably awful. "Artists get better," write
Bayles and Orland, "by sharpening their skills or by acquiring new ones;
they get better by learning to work, and by learning *from* their work."

One strategy toward increased productivity is to set forth on a project whose success is to be gauged not by quality but by quantity. I
have, during certain periods, composed "one bad poem a day," an idea
I got from my good friend, the poet Bethany Reid. Why a bad poem?
Because, frankly, it's impossible, at least for me, to write a good poem
every day or even every week. But to write a "bad" poem every day
is quite possible, even for such a busy and overbooked person as me.
What I am providing for myself is a new body of work to work on.

THE LIST OF WORKS

Record-keeping is another strategy toward increased productivity. I
have long studied the lives and practices of high-level creators, including visual artists like Georgia O'Keeffe. These predecessor creators
inspire me. Perhaps, I thought, I could ratchet up my strategies and
techniques—do whatever they did—to realize my own dreams as a
writer. One rather odd thing I discovered is that they keep track of
their works. They keep records and these records account for all their
works—not just works sold or commissioned or published.

---

*   Bayles and Orland, *Art & Fear*, 29.

In contrast, average creators tend to forget works, abandon works, reject works, and lose works. Because of this trail of lost pieces (poems, stories, essays, paintings, or whatever), they have a weak sense of what actually constitutes their body of work, and each new piece is brand new. Their lost writing is essentially devalued writing. (And if the writer does not value his or her own work, who will value it?) This is not to say that every piece is a good piece, but that any piece, whether poem or story, might be worked on and eventually driven into the barn of finished work. Writers who work on their craft gain a bit of skill each year and that skill is available for honing past work. A lost poem loses its chance at art. It is lost to the possibility of revision. The creative energy expended on it, which may have been considerable, is also lost (or at least dissipated). In contrast, Yeats (for example) continued to revise his entire body of work, including his juvenilia, throughout his lifetime.

Considering all of the above, I've worked out a system for tracking the body of work I've created over the past four decades. It is remarkable how my creative inventory has helped me to deepen and extend my creative efforts. I now require all the writers in my classes to do the same, and they too find it a useful and even remarkable tool.

Each writer will devise his or her own system for keeping track of works. But for any system, a few principles should be kept in mind. The first is that the creative inventory should include all works brought to the point of first draft, not just works deemed worthy. This is a creator's tool, not a résumé.

The second is that the inventory should be organized chronologically, with the most recent at the top, so that you can see at a glance what you were doing ten years ago or twenty years ago, and so that you will have an ever-growing record of your output for the current year. Georgia O'Keeffe's system was to keep a page in a notebook for every painting she started, in which she included materials, notes, title, dimensions, where the work was located, and so on. Because she did this as she went, the notebooks, which are dated, proceed chronologically. For visual artists such a notebook will become the basis for an eventual catalogue raisonné. A visual artist will typically include a visual representation of the work as part of the inventory.

The List of Works forms the core of my own inventory system. When I first started making my list, I was astonished at how much work I was sitting on. This, it turns out, is a common astonishment for writers who undertake to make a chronological list of every piece of work that has reached the point of first draft or beyond. If you've been writing for a number of years, you'll find that it will take some time to complete your list (you open another drawer only to find one more forgotten poem, one more forgotten story). However, the minute you begin to construct your list, the benefits start accruing, and once the system is set up, it's simple to maintain.

I keep two Lists of Works, one for prose and one for poetry. (For me this double list came about for reasons of personal history: I had begun the Complete Inventory of Poems years earlier and it is, alas, ordered from early to late—a lot of work to reverse. Most writers should simply make one list for all works.) My two lists literally contain every piece I've ever brought to the point of first draft or beyond. Among the items on my "List of Works—Prose" are my published history book, the draft of a novel, and a rather dreadful story I wrote in 1964, more than fifty years ago. On the "List of Works—Poetry," the earliest poem is dated summer 1970. (It's the first poem I typed out of my journal. May the untyped "poems" of the sixties Rest in Peace in their respective journals.) My two Lists of Works tell me that to date I've written 501 poems (some published, some in circulation, some in draft, some inept) and 310 prose works (some published, some in circulation, some in draft, some inept).

What is this, quantity over quality? Exactly. But the speed of work is not at issue. I for one am a slow writer. And I resist the idea of churning out slight pieces. The actual numbers matter only to the poet or writer. This is your private working tool, and the numbers it reveals are nobody's business but your own.

The list allows you to see the work you've done and it signifies respect for work done. It allows you to track your yearly production.

It allows you to find any given piece to take up again. The list gives you a practice that you now share with those high-achieving creators who do quantify their works. Georgia O'Keeffe, 2,045 objects. Edouard Manet, 450 oil paintings among other works. The American painter Alice Neel, about 3,000 works. Dare we mention Picasso?—26,000 works. The remarkable short-story writer Edith Pearlman has published, according to her website, more than 250 works of short fiction and short nonfiction. That of course, does not tell us how many works Pearlman has *composed*.

How to Set Up Your List of Works

Force each title on the list and all associated information to take up one and only one line (you can clearly see the items at a glance).

Order the list chronologically by year, beginning with the present and working backward. Works done long ago with fuzzy dates go under decade dates (like "1980s"). As you continue to make new poems or stories it's easy to update the list, using exact dates. Every time I complete a first draft of a new work, I put it on the list, with its date of original composition (the date the first draft was completed).

Your list includes the title of the piece. It includes the date of original composition. That is, when did you complete the first draft? That's the date you want. Date of "final" completion is not of interest and in any case it floats. As you move backward in time you will no doubt have to guess at some dates. The date you achieve that first draft is autobiographically interesting and once fixed, never has to move. (Visual artists do it a bit differently since they typically do not consider a work a work until it is finished.)

Put after each title the word "published" or the word "circulating," unless it is neither published nor circulating, in which case put nothing after it. Literary writers such as poets, who are not working on commission, typically have several pieces working and some lying dormant, ready to be taken up at a later date.

Finally, and this is important: The one line of information per title does not say where a published piece appears, it does not say where a circulating piece it is circulating *to*, and it does not contain any sort of judgment or assessment or plan (such as "abandon?" or "revise" or "shorten"). This is not a work plan. It is a record.

A piece you may never revise just sits there, like my short story written in 1964. It is part of your body of work. It shows you where you have been. For me, that first story of mine, however amateur, is a remarkable repository of threads I find woven into subsequent writing. Thus may a creator's preliminary works have interest and value. (Besides, some day I may revise that old story.)

Here is a literal copy of a segment of my list.

List of Works—Prose

2017
Fourteenth Avenue NW Bridge—November 6, 2017 **Published**
Blue Note—October 2017
Home—August 8, 2017
Complementary Colors—August 2, 2017
Agnes Denes—August 2, 2017
My Seattle Garden—June 15, 2017 **Circulating**
Guernica—February 13, 2017 **Published**
Ballard Bridge (Seattle)—March 10, 2017 **Published**
Beauty and the Beast—January 30, 2017 **Circulating**
Seeing Green—January 17, 2017 **Circulating**
Dwelling Spaces / Urban Places—March 17, 2016 **Published**

2016
Hedgebrook: An Appreciation—December 28, 2016
On Happiness—October 2016 **Circulating**
Becoming a Poet—July 20, 2016 **Published**
Michael of Rhodes—July 10, 2016 **Published**
et cetera . . .

Where are these works, physically? I keep one digitalized copy, latest version only, on the computer and I keep its printed-out hard copy in chronologically ordered three-ring binders (one for poetry, one for creative nonfictions, one for short stories). Previous drafts and marked-up workshopped copies are put far away in archive boxes or in the recycle bin. The hard copies of current versions have their date of original composition written on them.

As you begin this process of listing your works, you will make interesting discoveries, the first being the actual extent of your work to date. Another surprise for me was to find works I considered vastly inferior, requiring (I thought) massive revision, which in actuality were close to complete. A lyrical essay I wrote had been gathering dust for five years. I worked on it for two hours and sent it out. It's a lovely piece (I now think). It appeared in a lovely literary journal and was that year nominated for a Pushcart!

Constructing your List of Works will help you become a more aware writer. Each year it will give you a measuring stick of your annual progress—defined not by the external world of prizes and publications but by you, the creator.

Finally, the List of Works stands as an emblem of respect for the work. It is a creator's tool that can help artists, poets, and writers realize their dream of creating a meaningful body of work.

WORKING AND PLAYING WITH THE WORK

There are a number of ways to stay productive and many are fun. Take an evening writing class at an adult education center or writer's center and then do your assignments. (You would be embarrassed not to!) There are well-published writers who continue to take courses from time to time. Consider the assignments to be more than mere make-work: plan yours to result in a published piece.

Make a schedule with a buddy to do such-and-such an amount of work by such-and-such a date on which date you will meet again at a café. Take a book of short creative nonfictions and write one piece a week using each structure in turn (following carefully the guidelines laid out in part II, so as not to create an imitative piece but to use the deep structure only). Or, do what poet Marvin Bell begs us to do:

> Stay up half the night for a week and write one hundred poems. Write badly, rawly, smoothly, accidentally, irrationally . . . join the disparate. Make the like unlike and the unlike like. When you can't write, read. Use the word "window" in every line. Write about colors. Set out to write a poem "like a sweater." It makes no difference. The coherence is already within you. Afterward, you will have learned more about writing than an entire semester of classes can teach you.*

All this works its alchemy because work grows out of work. Productive writers have more fun. The stakes on each piece are lower, because you are making more pieces. Another lucky thing: when you learn to be really productive, you begin coming into more surprises and more interesting turns. As your craft skill becomes more acute, you come to see that you can turn any piece—at least any piece written from the heart—into a fine finished piece. It all becomes so much more engrossing and entertaining and it is the road to that charmed country we call success.

---

* Bell, "Three Propositions," 10–11.

29.

Success

My ambition was relatively modest.
I just wanted to be part of literature.
—Frank Conroy

Success is sweet. Your first publication is sweet. Your first poem published, or your first article—sweet. Suddenly the world is nodding in agreement. The world is saying, yes. You are a writer. You are a poet. You are a novelist. And then the world nods again, and then again (never mind those rejection slips). Your dream is coming true. Perhaps a novel begins to sell. Perhaps you are nominated for one of those big awards. Perhaps some actual money drops on your head from afar. Sweet.

Still, every position presents its challenges. The more famous a writer becomes, the greater number of interruptions he or she sustains. (I know, I know. We all sustain interruptions. But this is a kind of interruption that is difficult specifically because it coincides with your ambition. Can you come and speak? . . . May I interview you? . . .) To become a well-known writer is to become to some extent a public figure. Some writers take happily to the choppy waters of public life, but others struggle with it. One novelist, whose gripping and beautiful novels I've read avidly, received that coveted MacArthur Foundation "genius award." Make no mistake, the award just about saved his artistic life. But I read somewhere that he was immediately so inundated with literary and public-service duties and requests that he wrote nothing at all for two years. Another example: an old friend of mine from college days became a renowned scientist whose exquisite and profound essays became bestsellers. He told me once that, beginning about the time he was emerging from relative obscurity, he lost five years of work before he figured out how to deal with the tsunami of invitations and requests.

Another type of challenge is visited upon the moderately successful writer. It is that of having our second book on the midlist and our third book homeless. (This problem increases as publishers turn into multimedia conglomerates willing to switch from books to bling-bling if doing so will help their bottom line.) Perhaps, as Donald Maass allows in *Writing the Breakout Novel*, these third books are just not good enough. Then the task is to make them better. But perhaps they are good enough. A writer can start to receive an encouraging series of publications and prizes, and then, suddenly, fall into a trough, the zero trough, the nothing-doing trough, the *nada* trough. The well-known, thirty-eight-book novelist James Lee Burke writes:

> The most difficult test for me as a writer came during the middle of my career, when, after publishing three novels in New York, I went 13 years without a hardback publication. My novel "The Lost Get-Back Boogie" alone received 110 rejections during nine years of submission, supposedly a record in the industry.
>
> It was during this period I had to relearn the lesson I had learned at 20 . . . you write it a day at a time and let God be the measure of its worth; you let the score take care of itself; and most important, you never lose faith in your vision.*

Never lose faith in your vision. But what if we do? Who among us does not fall, from time to time, into the terrible anxiety of ambition? One day Tolstoy wrote in his diary: "I am doing nothing and thinking about the landlady. Do I have the talent to compare to our modern

---

*   Burke, "Writers on Writing," E2.

Russian writers? Decidedly not."* And here is Kafka in a funk: "I will write again but how many doubts have I meanwhile had about my writing. At bottom I am an incapable, ignorant person."†

We are all incapable, ignorant persons. Still, we must keep on. If confidence fails, which it may, the task is to continue working without confidence. Writing does not require confidence: it requires only a pen and a notebook. Get discouraged but don't quit. Writers who write when they hope and quit writing when they don't hope don't get far. ("I'm going to write this novel, and if it succeeds, then . . .")

There is the special problem of writers blessed and later saddled with early success: "Will I ever be able to do that again?" ("Undoubtedly not. I am an incapable, ignorant person.") The necessity in this case is to turn inward again, to shut out the too-bright light of the limelight—to appreciate its warmth, to be sure, its praise, its remunerations, and then to return to the blank page. Success is sweet, but it turns us inside out, it puts a smile on our face. To make new work we need to return to the interiority inside of which we did our first work. We need to listen to the muses, to take the risk of failing, to return to the desk where once we wrote in a notebook hidden from all other eyes. In this way, we need to begin again.

Agents and editors frequently pressure successful authors to repeat the previous book in a slightly different form, to become a manufacturing enterprise, churning out what is essentially another version of that mass-produced commodity that sold so well. I once attended a panel on "How to Get a Literary Agent," which featured literary agents. One agent encouraged her writers to follow up on a previously successful work with a second one along the same lines designed to fit the same market. She said, with some irritation in her voice, "I do this to help your career!" Apparently she had run into resistance.

Certainly, we should do whatever is feasible to help our careers. And we should listen closely to our helpers—peer writers, mentors,

---

* Quoted in *Writer's Life*, 181.
† Kafka, *Diaries*, 308.

teachers, editors, agents. But shouldn't we also use our own values and make our own choices about what to produce in the time allotted to us? About what we think is important? About what we hope to leave behind in a body of work?

Here Scott Russell Sanders—that master-writer—speaks of his own progression as a writer:

> As though I had not already violated enough boundaries by writing science fiction, historical fiction, criticism, fables, and contemporary short stories, during the 1980s I added personal essays, documentary narrative, biographical fiction, and children's books to my profusion of forms. And why not a profusion? The world is various. Nature itself is endlessly inventive, trying out one form after another. How dull, if birds had stopped with sparrows and not gone on to ospreys and owls. How dull, if plants had not spun on from ferns to lilacs and oaks. Why squeeze everything you have to say into one or two literary boxes for the convenience of booksellers and critics?*

Speed of production is another contested issue. We should all be concerned with completing work. But speed of production ought to be balanced against quality of product. Charles Frazier's novel *Cold Mountain* took him more than ten years to write and his next novel, *Thirteen Moons*, took him eight years—most of a decade. I recently read an interview in which an agent suggested that an author, for the sake of maximum marketability, extrude a book every two years. For a writer, this depends very much on what you want your legacy to be. Some writers are just fast and original and great. But a great many writers who produce a book every two years are writing the same book over and over again. My own choice is to try for work that has a chance of lasting, a chance of becoming part of literature. Whether I

---

* Sanders, "Letter to a Reader," 249.

succeed or not is not mine to know. But if you've read the brilliant and profound *Cold Mountain* you will understand that no writer could possibly have written it in two years.

Poet and novelist James Dickey wrote: "I think the tragedy of my poetic generation is that people are willing to let stuff go and be published simply because there are people who can and will publish it. The bookstores are flooded with forgettable books that are good but not good enough. They just don't make it around the bend into the area of being good, or memorable, or with luck, even unforgettable."*

I find it useful to preserve the distinction between worldly success— any worldly recognition or publication whether honorary or monetary—and artistic success (my judgment). If I am receiving a flood of rejection slips, if my agent has skipped town or if I can't find an agent, if my phone has mislaid its ring, if my email is 99 percent spam, still, I am composing a poem or an essay or a story that may succeed artistically. The value of this distinction is that I am not leaving it up to the world to tell me whether or not I am an incapable, ignorant person. That is for me to decide.

Still, getting an acceptance letter or an award or a check in the mail is thrilling. Getting a note from someone who has read your book and found it moving is thrilling. Getting the recognition you feel your work deserves is thrilling. But gaining more technical skill, more depth, more range is also thrilling. The joy of realizing a poem or a story—is there anything like it?

It is also gratifying to find yourself part of a vibrant community, reading to audiences, getting published, getting readers, getting more readers. Of course, rejections continue as well. But acceptances come more often now. Your writing is improving . . .

But perhaps the greatest pleasure of all is to put aside the striving and anxiety of ambition, if only for a while, and to sit down to the blank page, clean and empty and inviting. And then you begin again.

---

*   Hillman, "James Dickey," 183.

I am grateful to my mother, the late Dr. Barbara H. Long, and to my father, Winslow Long, for reading to us children every day—from the bible to *Oliver Twist* to *Pride and Prejudice* (this last a bit mystifying to a six year old). Their focus on reading was for me a sustaining foundation in life as in literature. I'm grateful, too, to my Uncle Rodney Henry for honoring my fourteen-year-old writing, no matter which way spelled. Miss Edna Bergey, my ninth-grade English teacher at Quakertown High School, dubbed my "Autobiography" the best in the class and required me to stand up and read it to the class. These caring adults (and my young uncle was barely an adult) made it possible for me to realize my greatest dream: to become a writer.

My first poetry teacher was the late Harold Bond of the Cambridge (Massachusetts) Center for Adult Education. At the same indispensable institution I took two entertaining and enlightening courses, The Art of the Sentence and the Art of the Paragraph, taught by engineer Buchanan Ewing. I am grateful to these teachers and to my first fiction teacher, Charles Brashear, of San Diego State University.

In my view the best time to pursue an MFA (Master of Fine Arts) degree is after you've written for a decade or two, after you've published your first book, after you already know a lot, after you know— or sense—how much there is yet to learn. The Creative Writing Program in the English Department at the University of Washington in Seattle sheltered my writing for two years in the late 1980s. It gave me two years of exhilarating talk about literature. It gave me two years in which to write and in which to instruct (as a teaching assistant with a class of her own) a new batch of fresh composers each quarter. It gave me as mentors David Bosworth, Lois Hudson, and the poets Colleen McElroy and Heather McHugh. It gave me Hazard Adams who gave me Yeats. It gave me two fabulous years of writing. Thank you.

Perhaps every writer hits a low point, the less said about which the better. As for my low point, two grants, one from The Authors League Fund and the other from the Carnegie Fund for Authors, provided crucial funds and also what felt like a tap on the shoulder from the community of writers, as if to say, "You are one of us. Stick it out. We need you here." I am very grateful.

I owe my longtime workshop more than thanks. I believe these poets and artists were dispatched to my door by the muse. As we work, reflect, perform, and work some more, I am sustained and inspired to do better. I am grateful to Jack Remick, M. Anne Sweet, Geri Gale, Gordon H. Wood, Irene Drennan (1922–2008), Kevin Coyne, Don Harmon, Joel Chafetz, Jo Nelson (1947–2001), Francia Recalde, and Jim Karnitz.

For many years I've sent poems, stories, and essays hot off the printer to my old friends Saul Slapikoff, Louis Kampf, Howard Zinn, and Roz Zinn. Their own essential work and their support of mine has meant more than a few words can express; that Roz had to leave us in 2008 leaves a great hole in the world. And as we go to press in 2010, Howard is gone. Goodbye, old friends.

The dearest of Dear Readers are first readers. These pages originated as study sheets presented to writers I mentor and teach, writers who over the years have amazed me with their development and who have nurtured my own. First readers of *The Writer's Portable Mentor*, the book, include peer poets, dear friends, and the writers who roll up their sleeves and work like bricklayers in my classes. They include Bethany Reid, Scott Driscoll, Ralph Keyes, and Jay Schlechter. They include Carol Ann Miraben (formerly Shade), Rabbi Elana Zaiman, MaryLee Martin, Corry Venema-Weiss, Patricia Smith, and Neil Mathison. Professor Maya Sonenberg scrutinized the text and gave valuable suggestions. Jennifer Wong and my sister Pamela O. Long have been unflagging supporters. To each of these writers I give fervent thanks.

When I began preparing this book for actual publication, as opposed to photocopying the latest version for a class, I had a moment of trepidation. Here was a book I was passionate about, a book that would provide untold benefits, I knew, to the conscientious writer who took it to heart. How then to help it out into the world? There were many tasks, too many tasks, and did I even know what they all were? I soon realized "it takes a village." My committee of advisors is composed of five superb writers with book savvy and energy to boot. Grateful thanks to Andrea Lewis, Suzan Huney, Susan Knox, Kathie Werner, and Waverly Fitzgerald. Add my fellow poet Geri Gale, copyeditor par excellence. May I find a way down the road to repay you in kind. And thanks to Ms. James Kessler for cheerful, competent assistance in all departments.

During the decade of writing this book, I was also editing that fat internet volume, HistoryLink.org, the free online encyclopedia of Washington state history. HistoryLink has become a pride to our state. It was my great good luck to hook up with the history-obsessed, creative, argumentative, hardworking, quirkily copacetic team that runs it.

Book design, happily, is not a lost art. This comely book was designed by Nancy Kinnear (interior) and Tracy Wong (cover). Thank you.

My sister Elizabeth Long, in the midst of her exacting and demanding work as a Critical Care Unit nurse, in the midst of raising her children and reading to them constantly, in the midst of climbing mountains with her dear husband, David Messerschmidt, and their aforementioned offspring, in the midst of running marathons, in the midst of pedaling to work and back, in the midst of doing whatever it is one does in triathlons, in the midst of training her dogs and keeping their tails wagging joyously, in the midst of tending her garden, in the midst of reading novels and science and natural history, my little sister, I say, has also found time to bring me a bag of groceries once or twice a month. No writer could wish for more. Although Liz declines to write anything more lengthy than a grocery list, or so she says, I dedicate this book to her.

BIBLIOGRAPHY

Adrian, Kim. "Questionnaire for My Grandfather." *Gettysburg Review* 22, no. 4 (Winter 2009): 523–36.

Agee, James. *A Death in the Family*. New York: Vintage Books, 1956.

Albers, Anni. Quoted in *The Woven and Graphic Art of Anni Albers*, 11. Introduction by Lloyd E. Herman. Washington, DC: Smithsonian Institution Press, 1985.

Allison, Sue. "Taking a Reading." In *The Best American Essays 2009*, edited by Mary Oliver, 1–2. Boston: Houghton Mifflin Harcourt, 2009.

Almond, Steve. "A Dream of Sleep." In *God Bless America: Stories*, 195–211. Wilmington, NC: Lookout Books, 2011.

Alsop, Stewart. *The Center*. Quoted in Tufte, *Artful Sentences: Syntax as Style*, 6.

Anderson, Sherwood. "I Want to Know Why." In *The Egg and Other Stories*, 1–8. Mineola, NY: Dover, 2000.

Andrews, Tom. "Codeine Diary." In *Random Symmetries: The Collected Poems of Tom Andrews*, 111–29. Oberlin, OH: Oberlin College Press, 2002.

Angell, Roger. "This Old Man." In *This Old Man: All in Pieces*, 267–82. New York: Anchor Books, 2015.

Angelou, Maya. *I Know Why the Caged Bird Sings*. New York: Baltimore Books, 2015.

Anzaldúa, Gloria. *Borderlands/La Frontera*. 4th ed. San Francisco: Aunt Lute Books, 1999.

Armitage, Simon. *Walking Home: A Poet's Journey*. New York: Liveright, 2013.

Aristotle. *Poetics*. Translated by S. H. Butcher, Internet Classics Archive website, http://classics.mit.edu/Aristotle/poetics.html.

Bachelard, Gaston. *The Poetics of Reverie*. Translated by Daniel Russell. Boston: Beacon, 1969.

———. *The Poetics of Space*. Translated by Maria Jolas. Boston: Beacon, 1964.

Baker, J. A. *The Peregrine*. New York: New York Review of Books, 1967.

Baldwin, James. "Sonny's Blues." In *Going to Meet the Man*, 101–40. New York: Vintage Books, 1995.

Banks, Russell. "Sarah Cole: A Type of Love Story." In *The Best American Short Stories 1985*, edited by Gail Godwin, 1–23. Boston: Houghton Mifflin, 1985.

Banville, John. *The Sea*. New York: Vintage International, 2005.

Barry, Sebastian. *The Secret Scripture*. New York: Penguin Group, 2009.

Barthelme, Donald. Quoted in *The Sound on the Page* by Ben Yagoda, 68.

Bayles, David, and Ted Orland. *Art & Fear: Observations on the Perils (and Rewards) of Artmaking*. Santa Cruz, CA: Image Continuum, 1993.

Bearden, Romare. "Diary, September 8, 1947." In *Origins and Progressions*, edited by Cynthia Jo Fogliatti, 29–30. Detroit: Detroit Institute of the Arts, 1986.

Bell, Marvin. "Three Propositions." In *Writers on Writing: A Bread Loaf Anthology*, edited by Robert Pack and Jay Parini, 1–14. Lebanon, NH: University Press of New England, 1991.

Berger, John. "Drawing." In *John Berger: Selected Essays*, edited by Geoff Dyer, 10–14. New York: Vintage Books, 2001.

———. "Drawn to that Moment." In *John Berger: Selected Essays*, 419–23.

———. "François, Georges and Amélie: A Requiem in Three Parts." In *John Berger: Selected Essays*, 413–18.

———. "The Hals Mystery." In *John Berger: Selected Essays*, 393–98.

———. "Wanting Now." In *Hold Everything Dear: Dispatches on Survival and Resistance*, 7–8. New York: Vintage Books, 2007.

Bergman, Robert L. "Blue Notes: Poetry and Psychoanalysis." In

Mindless Psychoanalysis, Selfless Self Psychology and Further Explorations, 184–90. Seattle: Alliance Press, 2008.

Berlin, Lucia. "Mourning." In *A Manual for Cleaning Women: Selected Stories*, 236–41. New York: Farrar, Straus and Giroux, 2015.

———. "Tiger Bites." In *A Manual for Cleaning Women: Selected Stories*, 69–87.

Berriault, Gina. "Don't I Know You?" In *Passion and Craft: Conversations with Notable Writers*, edited by Bonnie Lyons and Bill Oliver, 60–71. Urbana: University of Illinois Press, 1998.

Biss, Eula. "Babylon." In *Notes to No Man's Land: American Essays*, 105–14. Minneapolis: Graywolf Press, 2009.

Boland, Eavan. "Letter to a Young Woman Poet." *American Poetry Review* 26, no. 3 (May/June 1997): 23.

———. "A Fragment of Exile." In *Object Lessons: The Life of the Woman and the Poet in Our Time*, 35–51. New York: W. W. Norton, 1995.

———. "Subject Matters." In *Object Lessons: The Life of the Woman and the Poet in Our Time*, 175–201.

Bollas, Christopher. *Being a Character: Psychoanalysis and Self Experience*. New York: Hill and Wang, 1992.

Bosco, Henri. Quoted in *The Poetics of Reverie: Childhood, Language, and the Cosmos* by Gaston Bachelard. Translated by Daniel Russell. Boston: Beacon, 1969.

Boyd, William. "Anton Chekov: An A–Z." In *Bamboo*, 245–55. London: Penguin Books, 2006.

Boyle, T. Coraghessan. "Chicxulub." *New Yorker*, March 1, 2004, 78–83.

Bradbury, Ray. *Something Wicked This Way Comes*. New York: Avon Books, 1996.

Brande, Dorothea. *Becoming a Writer*. New York: Tarcher/Putnam, 1981.

Brashear, Charles. *Elements of the Short Story*. Santa Rosa, CA: Books, etc., 2005.

Bringhurst, Robert. *The Elements of Typographic Style*. Vancouver, BC: Hartley & Marks, 2012.

Brooks, Gwendolyn. *Maud Martha*. In *Blacks*. Chicago: Third World Press, 1987.

Brown, Norman O. *Love's Body*. New York: Vintage Books, 1966.

Burke, James Lee. "Writers on Writing: Seeking a Vision of Truth, Guided by a Higher Power." *New York Times*, December 2, 2002, E2.

Burroway, Janet. *Writing Fiction: A Guide to Narrative Craft*. 5th ed. New York: Addison Wesley Longman, 2005.

Butler, Octavia E. *Kindred*. Boston: Beacon, 1979.

Butler, Robert Olen. *From Where You Dream*. New York: Grove, 2005.

Buzbee, Lewis. *The Yellow-Lighted Bookshop*. Minneapolis: Graywolf Press, 2006.

Byatt, A. S. "The Chinese Lobster." In *The Matisse Stories*, 29–86. New York: Vintage Books, 1996.

Carson, Anne. *Plainwater*. New York: Vintage Books, 1995.

Carson, Rachel. *The Sea Around Us*. New York: Oxford University Press, 1989.

Carter, Karen Rauch. *Move Your Stuff, Change Your Life*. New York: Simon & Schuster, 2000.

Castillo, Ana. *Black Dove*. New York: Feminist Press, 2016.

Chandler, Raymond. *The Big Sleep*. In *The Raymond Chandler Omnibus*. New York: Alfred A. Knopf, 1976.

Childs, Craig. *The Secret Knowledge of Water*. Boston: Little, Brown, 2000.

Christie, Alix. *Gutenberg's Apprentice*. New York: HarperCollins, 2014.

Cisneros, Sandra. *The House on Mango Street*. New York: Vintage Books, 2009.

Clark, Mary Higgins. "Touched by an Angel." In *The Writing Life: Writers on How They Think and Work*, edited by Marie Arana, 35–38. New York: Public Affairs, 2003.

Conroy, Frank. "A Final Conversation." Transcript of an audio inter-
view by Lacy Crawford, March 2004. *Narrative Magazine*,
Winter 2009, http://www.narrativemagazine.com/node/552/.
———. *Midair*. New York: Dutton, 1985.
Daniel, John. "In Praise of Darkness." In *The Far Corner: On Land,
Life, and Literature*, 37–45. Berkeley, CA: Counterpoint,
2009.
Delacroix, Eugène. *Painter of Passion: The Journal of Eugène Dela-
croix*. Edited by Hubert Wellington. Translated by Lucy
Norton. London: Folio Society, 1995.
DeLillo, Don. "Midnight in Dostoevsky." In *The Angel Esmeralda*,
119–45. New York: Scribner, 2011.
———. "The Starveling." In *The Angel Esmeralda*, 183–211.
DeMarinis, Rick. "Seize the Day." In *Borrowed Hearts: New and
Selected Stories*, 287–94. New York: Seven Stories Press,
1999.
———. "Weeds." In *Borrowed Hearts: New and Selected Stories*,
42–51.
Dick, Philip K. *Do Androids Dream of Electric Sheep?* New York:
Random House, 1968.
———. *A Scanner Darkly*. New York: Vintage Books, 1977.
Dickey, James. Quoted in "James Dickey" by Bruce Joel Hillman. In
On Being a Writer, edited by Bill Strickland, 180–86. Cincin-
nati: Writer's Digest Books, 1989.
Doerr, Anthony. "Village 113." In *Memory Wall: Stories*, 125–56.
New York: Simon and Shuster, 2010.
Doyle, Brian. "Grace Notes." In *Leaping: Revelations and Epipha-
nies*, 41–58. Chicago: Loyola Press, 2013.
———. "A Sturdy Man." In *Spirited Men: Story, Soul, & Substance*,
129–39. Cambridge, MA: Cowley, 2004.
Dufresne, John. "Holdalls." In *Writers and their Notebooks*, edited
by Diana M. Raab, 113–120. Columbia: University of South
Carolina Press, 2010.

Durrell, Lawrence. "Lawrence Durrell." In *Writers at Work*, edited by George Plimpton, 259–82. New York: Penguin Books, 1959.

Ehrlich, Gretel. *The Solace of Open Spaces*. New York: Penguin Books, 1985.

Eiseley, Loren. *The Immense Journey*. New York: Vintage Books, 1957.

Elbow, Peter. *Writing Without Teachers*. New York: Oxford University Press, 1973.

Ellroy, James. *The Black Dahlia*. New York: Mysterious Press, 1987.

Erikson, Joan M. *Wisdom and the Senses*. New York: W. W. Norton, 1988.

Ernst, Max. Quoted in *Max Ernst*. Directed by Peter Schamoni, 2002; Chatsworth, CA: Image Entertainment, 2002. DVD.

Faulkner, William. "Dry September." In *Collected Stories of William Faulkner*, 169–83. New York: Vintage Books, 1977.

Ferris, Joshua. *To Rise Again at a Decent Hour*. New York: Little, Brown, 2014.

Fitzgerald, Penelope. *Offshore*. Boston: Houghton Mifflin Harcourt, 1979.

Ford, Richard. "Communist." In *100 Years of the Best American Short Stories*, edited by Lorrie Moore and Heidi Pitlor, 395–408. Boston: Houghton Mifflin Harcourt, 2015.

Fountain, Ben. "Near-Extinct Birds of the Central Cordillera." In *Brief Encounters with Che Guevara*, 1–32. New York: HarperCollins, 2006.

Fowler, H. W. *A Dictionary of Modern English Usage*. London: Oxford University Press, 1926.

———. *The New Fowler's Modern English Usage*. 3rd ed. Edited by R. W. Burchfield. Oxford: Oxford University Press, 1996.

Franklin, Jon. *Writing for Story*. New York: Penguin Books USA, 1994.

Frazier, Charles. *Cold Mountain*. New York: Vintage Books, 1997.

Gaitskill, Mary. "Daisy's Valentine." In *Bad Behavior: Stories*, 10–30. New York: Vintage Books, 1989.

Gale, Geri. *Patrice: A Poemella*. Seattle: PK & Alex, 2014.

Gardner, John. *The Art of Fiction*. New York: Alfred A. Knopf, 1983.

Garner, Bryan A. *Garner's Modern American Usage*. 3rd ed. New York: Oxford University Press, 2009.

Gass, William H. "Lust." In *Life Sentences*, 291–300. New York: Alfred A. Knopf, 2012.

———. *Reading Rilke: Reflections on the Problems of Translation*. Victoria, TX: Dalkey Archive, 2015.

Gates, Henry Louis, Jr. "In the Kitchen." In *The Best American Essays 1995*, edited by Jamaica Kincaid, 117–124. Boston: Houghton Mifflin, 1995.

———. "Lifting the Veil." In *Inventing the Truth: The Art and Craft of Memoir*, edited by William Zinsser, 101–18. Boston: Houghton Mifflin, 1998.

Gautreaux, Tim. "Idols." In *Signals*, 3–23. New York: Alfred A. Knopf, 2015.

Gawande, Atul. "Trumpcare vs. Obamacare." *New Yorker*, March 6, 2017, 21.

Gelb, Michael J. *How to Think Like Leonardo da Vinci*. New York: Random House, 1998.

Gilb, Dagoberto. "Brisa." In *Woodcuts of Women*, 101–11. New York: Grove, 2001.

———. "Maria de Covina." In *Woodcuts of Women*, 3–15.

———. "Mayela One Day in 1989." In *Woodcuts of Women*, 17–27.

Goldberg, Natalie. *Long Quiet Highway*. New York: Bantam Books, 1993.

———. *Writing Down the Bones*. New York: Shambhala, 1986.

Gordon, Karen Elizabeth. *The Deluxe Transitive Vampire*. New York: Pantheon Books, 1993.

Gourevitch, Philip. "Mr. Brown." *New Yorker*, July 29, 2002, 46–65.

Gray, Francine du Plessix. "The Work of Mourning." In *The Best American Essays 2001*, edited by Kathleen Norris, 60–72. Boston: Houghton Mifflin, 2001.

Greene, Melissa Fay. "On Writing Nonfiction." In *The Confidence*

Woman, edited by Eve Shelnutt, 227–40. Atlanta: Longstreet Press, 1991.

Groff, Lauren. *Fates and Furies*. New York: Riverhead Books, 2015.

Grosholz, Emily. "On Necklaces." In *The Best American Essays 2008*, edited by Adam Gopnik, 75–89. Boston: Houghton Mifflin, 2009.

Gruber, Howard E. Quoted in *Notebooks of the Mind* by Vera John-Steiner. Albuquerque: University of New Mexico Press, 1986.

Haines, John. "Spring." In *The Stars, the Snow, the Fire: Twenty-Five Years in the Alaska Wilderness*, 80–84. Minneapolis: Graywolf Press, 2000.

Hall, Donald. "Out the Window." *New Yorker*, January 23, 2012, 40–43.

Hanh, Thich Nhat. *Being Peace*. Berkeley: Paralax Press, 2005.

Harries, Karsten. *The Ethical Function of Architecture*. Cambridge, MA: MIT Press, 2000.

Harrison, Jim. "Is Winemaking an Art?" In *A Really Big Lunch*, 128–30. New York: Grove Atlantic, 2017.

———. "My Problems with White Wine." In *A Really Big Lunch*, 31–43.

Hazzard, Shirley. *The Great Fire*. New York: Picador, 2003.

Hemon, Aleksandar. "Blind Jozef Pronek." In *The Best American Short Stories 2000*, edited by E. L. Doctorow, 166–81. Boston: Houghton Mifflin, 2000.

Hendrickson, Robert. *The Literary Life and Other Curiosities*. San Diego: Harcourt Brace, 1994.

Hesse, Hermann. *Siddhartha*. Translated by Joachim Neugroschel. New York: Penguin Books, 1999.

Hillman, Bruce Joel. "James Dickey." In *On Being a Writer*, edited by Bill Strickland, 180–86.

Hills, Patricia. *May Stevens*. San Francisco: Pomegranate, 2005.

Hoagland, Edward. "Journal: Vermont 2002–2004." *American Scholar* 73, no. 4 (Autumn 2004): 151–55.

Hodge, Geoff. *Practical Botany for Gardeners*. Chicago: University of Chicago Press, 2013.

Hollander, John. *The Poetry of Everyday Life*. Ann Arbor: University of Michigan Press, 1999.

Hughes, Langston, and Arnold Rampersad, eds. *The Poems 1921–1940*. The Collected Works of Langston Hughes, vol. 1. Columbia: University of Missouri Press, 2001.

Hurston, Zora Neale. *Dust Tracks on a Road*. New York: Harper-Collins, 1991.

The I Ching: Or, Book of Changes. Edited by Hellmut Wilhelm. Translated by Cary F. Baynes. Princeton: Princeton University Press, 1977.

Irons, Peter. *God on Trial*. New York: Viking, 2007.

Irving, John. "Getting Started." In *Writers on Writing: A Bread Loaf Anthology*, edited by Robert Pack and Jay Parini, 98–104.

Ivey, Eowyn. *The Snow Child*. Boston: Little, Brown, 2012.

Jahren, Hope. *Lab Girl*. New York: Vintage Books, 2016.

Jarman, Derek. "Into the Blue." In *Chroma*, 103–24. Minneapolis: University of Minnesota Press, 1995

Kafka, Franz. *Diaries, 1910–1913*. Edited by Max Brod. Translated by Joseph Kress. New York: Schocken Books, 1965.

Kerouac, Jack. *The Dharma Bums*. New York: Penguin Books, 1958.

Keyes, Ralph. *The Courage to Write*. New York: Henry Holt, 1995.

Kincaid, Jamaica. *Lucy*. New York: Farrar, Straus, and Giroux, 1990.

Kingston, Max Hong. *The Woman Warrior*. New York: Vintage International, 1989.

Kitchen, Judith. "Requiem." In *Distance and Direction*, 173–78. Minneapolis: Coffee House Press, 2001.

Kramer, Jane. "The Reporter's Kitchen." In *The Best American Essays 2003*, edited by Anne Fadiman, 146–59. Boston: Houghton Mifflin, 2003.

Kupperman, Kim Dana. "Relief." In *The Best American Essays 2006*, edited by Lauren Slater, 96–106. Boston: Houghton Mifflin, 2006.

Laing, Olivia. *To the River*. Edinburgh: Canongate Books, 2011.

Lakoff, George, and Mark Johnson. *Metaphors We Live By*. Chicago: University of Chicago Press, 1980.

Leduc, Violette. *La Bâtarde*. New York: Riverhead Books, 1964.

Levitin, Daniel J. *This is Your Brain on Music*. New York: Penguin Group, 2007.

Livesey, Margot. *Eva Moves the Furniture*. New York: Picador, 2001.

Long, Priscilla. "Archaeology of Childhood." In *Fire and Stone*, 128–38. Athens: University of Georgia Press, 2016.

———. "The Color Orange." *Pacifica Literary Review*, no. 6 (Summer 2015): 41–46.

———. "Composition in Yellow." *Tahoma Literary Review*, no. 10 (Summer 2017): 93–98.

———. "Genome Tome." In *Fire and Stone*, 94–114.

———. "House." *Cold Mountain Review* 42, no.1 (Fall 2013): 28–31.

———. "Living for Robert." *Chaffin Journal*, 2008, 145–56.

———. "My Brain on My Mind." In *Fire and Stone*, 13–36.

———. "Snapshots: The Eastern Shore of Maryland." *North Dakota Quarterly* 55, no. 4 (Winter 1987): 93–99.

———. "Solitude." In *Fire and Stone*, 146–53.

———. "Stonework." In *Fire and Stone*, 139–45.

Lopez, Barry. *Desert Notes: Reflection in the Eye of a Raven; River Notes: The Dance of Herons*. New York: Avon Books, 1979.

———. "A Passage of the Hands." In *About This Life*, 211–22. New York: Vintage Books, 1999.

Lutz, Gary, and Diane Stevenson. *Writer's Digest Grammar Desk Reference*. Cincinnati: Writer's Digest Books, 2010.

Lynch, Thomas. "The Dead Priest." In *Bodies in Motion and at Rest*, 139–48. New York: W. W. Norton, 2000.

———. "Sweeney Revisited." In *Bodies in Motion and at Rest*, 39–48.

Maass, Donald. *Writing the Breakout Novel*. Cincinnati: Writer's Digest Books, 2001.

Macdonald, Helen. *H Is for Hawk*. New York: Grove, 2014.

Macfarlane, Robert. "Limestone." In *The Old Ways: A Journey on Foot*, 209–31. New York: Penguin Books, 2012.

Maclean, Norman. *A River Runs Through It*. Chicago: University of Chicago Press, 1976.

Madden, Patrick. "Laughter." In *Quotidiana*, 11–28. Lincoln: University of Nebraska Press, 2010.

Mailer, Norman, and John Buffalo Mailer. "Generations." In *The Big Empty*, 3–11. New York: Nation Books, 2006.

Majmudar, Amit. "The Servant of Two Masters." *Kenyon Review* 34, no. 2 (Spring 2012), https://www.kenyonreview.org/kr-online-issue/spring-2012-2/selections/the-servant-of-two-masters.

Mallonee, Barbara. "Semi-colon." In *Short Takes*, edited by Judith Kitchen, 188–91. New York: W. W. Norton, 2005.

Manguel, Alberto. *A History of Reading*. New York: Viking, 1996.

Marius, Richard. *A Writer's Companion*. 1st ed. New York: Alfred A. Knopf, 1985.

Martin, Alexander C. *Golden Guide to Weeds*. New York: Golden Press, 1987.

Martone, Michael. "Contributor's Note." In *Short Takes*, edited by Judith Kitchen, 176–80.

May, Cindi. "A Learning Secret: Don't Take Notes with a Laptop," *Scientific American*, June 3, 2014, https://www.scientificamerican.com/article/a-learning-secret-don-t-take-notes-with-a-laptop/.

McCann, Colum. *Let the Great World Spin*. New York: Random House, 2009.

McCarthy, Cormac. *All the Pretty Horses*. New York: Vintage International, 1993.

———. *The Road*. New York: Vintage International, 2006.

McClanahan, Rebecca. "Considering the Lilies." In *In Brief*, edited by Judith Kitchen and Mary Paumier Jones, 180–85. New York: W. W. Norton, 1999.

Michaels, Leonard, "My Yiddish." In *The Essays of Leonard*

Michaels, 187–204. New York: Farrar, Straus and Giroux, 2009.

Miller, E. Ethelbert, and Zoe Anglesey. "An Interview with Yusef Komunyakaa." *The Writer's Chronicle* 33, no. 2 (October/November 2000): 13–17.

Miller, Henry. *To Paint Is to Love Again*. Alhambra, CA: Cambria Books, 1960.

Millman, Lawrence. "Bookless in Biak." In *Short Takes*, edited by Judith Kitchen, 169–70.

Moody, Rick. "On Celestial Music." In *The Best American Essays 2008*, edited by Adam Gopnik, 163–75.

Moore, Dinty W. "Son of Mr. Green Jeans." In *Short Takes*, edited by Judith Kitchen, 283–91.

Moore, Kathleen Dean. "The Little Stoney River." In *Riverwalking: Reflections on Moving Water*, 41–50. New York: Harcourt, 1995.

———. "The Maclaren River." In *Riverwalking: Reflections on Moving Water*, 187–93.

———. "Winter Creek." In *Riverwalking: Reflections on Moving Water*, 31–37.

Moore, Lorrie. "The Jewish Hunter." In *Like Life*, 116–41. New York: Penguin Books USA, 1991.

———. "Two Boys." In *Like Life*, 3–19.

Morrison, Toni. *Sula*. New York: Vintage International, 2004.

Morton, Danelle. "Setting Achievable Goals and Meeting Them." In *Finishing School* by Cary Tennis and Danelle Morton, 179–86. New York: TarcherPerigee, 2017.

Mosley, Walter. *Always Outnumbered, Always Outgunned*. New York: Simon & Schuster, 1998.

———. "For Authors, Fragile Ideas Need Loving Every Day." In *Writers on Writing: Collected Essays from The New York Times*, compiled by John Darnton, 161–64. New York: Henry Holt, 2001.

————. *This Year You Write Your Novel*. New York: Little, Brown, 2007.

Muir, John. *My First Summer in the Sierra*. Mineola, NY: Dover, 2004.

Nemerov, Howard. "On Poetry and Painting, with a Thought on Music." In *Poets on Painters*, edited by J. D. McClatchy, 177–84. Berkeley: University of California Press, 1988.

Nguyen, Viet Thanh. *The Sympathizer*. New York: Grove, 2015.

Nims, John Frederick. *Western Wind: An Introduction to Poetry*. 2nd ed. New York: Random House, 1983.

Nin, Anaïs. *Collages*. Chicago: Swallow Press, 1964.

————. *Ladders to Fire*. Chicago: Swallow Press, 1959.

Oates, Joyce Carol. "Joyce Carol Oates in the Studio." *American Poetry Review* 32, no. 4 (July/August 2003): 15.

O'Connor, Flannery. "Writing Short Stories." In *Crafting Fiction in Theory and Practice*, edited by Marvin Diogenes and Clyde Moneyhun, 11–19. Mountain View, CA: Mayfield, 2001.

Okri, Ben. *The Famished Road*. New York: Anchor Books, 1993.

Oliver, Mary. "A Man Named Frost." In *Winter Hours*, 49–54. Boston: Houghton Mifflin, 1999.

————. "Of Power and Time." In *Blue Pastures*, 1–7. San Diego: Harcourt Brace, 1995.

Olson, John. "Home" (original title "Yesterday's Rain"). In *Raven Chronicles Journal* no. 24 (2017): 165–68.

————. *In Advance of the Broken Justy*. Niantic, CT: Quale Press, 2016.

Oppenheim, Meret. "Acceptance Speech for the 1974 Art Award of the City of Basel, January 16, 1975." In *Meret Oppenheim*, by Bice Curiger, 130–31. Cambridge, MA: MIT Press, 1989.

Orr, Gregory. "Return to Hayneville." In *The Best American Essays 2009*, edited by Mary Oliver, 125–39. New York: Mariner Books, 2009.

Orringer, Julie. "Neighbors." In *The Paris Review*, no. 221 (Summer 2017): 147–61.

Ozick, Cynthia. "On Being a Novice Playwright." In *The Writing Life: Writers on How They Think and Work*, edited by Marie Arana, 250–57.

Paley, Grace. "Goodbye and Good Luck." In *Grace Paley: The Collected Stories*, 3–13. New York: Farrar, Straus and Giroux, 1994.

Parms, Jericho. "A Chapter on Red." In *Lost Wax: Essays*, 87–95. Athens: University of Georgia Press, 2016.

Pearlman, Edith. Edith Pearlman website, http://www.edithpearlman. com.

Perry, Michael. "The Big Nap." In *Short Takes*, edited by Judith Kitchen, 322–27.

Pilcher, Rosamunde. "The Tree." In *The Garden of Reading*, edited by Michele Slung, 29–44. New York: Overlook Duckworth, 2012.

Pollitt, Katha. "Webstalker." In *Learning to Drive*, 21–24. New York: Random House, 2007.

Porter, Katherine Anne. Quoted in Tufte and Stewart, *Grammar as Style*, vii.

Proulx, Annie. "The Half-Skinned Steer." In *Close Range: Wyoming Stories*, 19–41. London: Fourth Estate, 1999.

———. "The Mud Below." In *Close Range: Wyoming Stories*, 43–88.

———. "The Perfect Word: Interview by Michael Upchurch." In *The Glimmer Train Guide to Writing Fiction*, 248–49. Cincinnati: Writer's Digest Books, 2006.

Proverbs. *Holy Bible King James Version*. London: Collins Clear-Type Press, 1949.

Psalms. *Holy Bible*. Translated by George M. Lamsa from the Aramaic of the Peshitta. San Francisco: Harper & Row, 1968.

Raab, Diana M. *Writers and Their Notebooks*. Columbia: University of South Carolina Press, 2010.

Raban, Jonathan. "Keeping a Notebook." In *Driving Home: An American Journey*, 233–36. Seattle: Sasquatch Books, 2013.

———. "Last Call of the Wild." In *Driving Home: An American Journey*, 202–14. Seattle: Sasquatch Books, 2013.

———. "The Waves." In *Driving Home: An American Journey*, 184–90. Seattle: Sasquatch Books, 2013.

———. Quoted in Yagoda, *The Sound on the Page*, 132.

Randall, Lisa. *Warped Passages: Unraveling the Mysteries of the Universe's Hidden Dimensions*. New York: Harper Perennial, 2005.

Ray, Janisse. "Whither Thou Goest." In *The Woods Stretched for Miles*, edited by John Lane and Gerald Thurmond, 203–13. Athens: University of Georgia Press, 1999.

Ray, Robert J., and Bret Norris. *The Weekend Novelist*. New York: Watson-Guptill, 2005.

Ray, Robert J., and Jack Remick. *The Weekend Novelist Writes a Mystery*. New York: Dell, 1998.

Remick, Jack. *Trio of Lost Souls*. Seattle: Coffeetown Press, 2015.

———. *Valley Boy*. Seattle: Coffeetown Press, 2012.

Restak, Richard. "20 Questions on our Minds." *American Scholar* 75, no. 2 (Spring 2006): 16–17.

Rhys, Jean. *Wide Sargasso Sea*. New York: Popular Library, 1966.

The Rig Veda. Translated by Wendy Doniger O'Flaherty. London: Penguin Books, 1981.

Robinson, Marilynne. *Housekeeping*. New York: Picador, 1980.

Roy, Arundhati. *The God of Small Things*. New York: Harper-Perennial, 1997.

Rukeyser, Muriel. *The Life of Poetry*. Ashfield, MA: Paris Press, 1996.

Sacks, Oliver. *On the Move: A Life*. Toronto: Vintage Canada, 2015.

Sadoff, Ira. "Ben Webster." In *An Ira Sadoff Reader*, 254–58. Hanover, NH: Middlebury College Press, 1992.

Sanders, Scott Russell. *Hunting for Hope: A Father's Journeys*. Boston: Beacon, 1998.

———. "Letter to a Reader." In *My Poor Elephant*, edited by Eve Shelnutt, 239–53. Atlanta: Longstreet Press, 1992.

Sarton, May. *After the Stroke*. New York: W. W. Norton, 1988.

———. *Plant Dreaming Deep*. New York: W. W. Norton, 1983.

Schjeldahl, Peter. "Barnett Newman." In *Let's See*, 116–18. New York: Thames & Hudson, 2008.

———. "Runaway: Paul Gauguin." In *Let's See*, 30–32.

———. "Vermeer." In *Let's See*, 157–59.

Shulman, Seth, et al. *Cooler Smarter: Practical Steps for Low-Carbon Living*. Washington, DC: Island Press, 2012.

Silko, Leslie Marmon. *The Turquoise Ledge: A Memoir*. New York: Penguin Books, 2010.

Simonton, D. K. "Creativity from a Historiometric Perspective." In *Handbook of Creativity*, edited by Robert J. Sternberg, 122–24. Cambridge: Cambridge University Press, 1999.

Slater, Lauren. *Lying*. New York: Penguin Books, 2000.

Smith, Annick. "Sink or Swim." In *In Brief*, edited by Judith Kitchen and Mary Paumier Jones, 221–23.

Sontag, Susan. "Directions: Write, Read, Rewrite. Repeat Steps 2 and 3 as Needed." In *Writers on Writing: Collected Essays from The New York Times*, 223–29.

———. "Writing Itself: On Roland Barthes." In *Where the Stress Falls*, 63–88. New York: Farrar, Straus and Giroux, 2001.

Spragg, Mark. "Wind." In *Where Rivers Change Direction*, 208–20. Salt Lake City: University of Utah Press, 1999.

Standing Bear, Luther. "From *Land of the Spotted Eagle*." In *Bedrock: Writers on the Wonders of Geology*, edited by Lauret E. Savoy, Eldridge M. Moores, and Judith E. Moores, 176–77. San Antonio: Trinity University Press, 2006.

Stevenson, Robert Louis. Quoted in *The Literary Life and Other Curiosities*, by Robert Hendrickson. San Diego: Harcourt Brace, 1994.

Talese, Gay. "New York." *Esquire*, October 1973, 396.

Tennis, Cary, "The Winchester Mystery Novel." In *Finishing School* by Cary Tennis and Danelle Morton, 83–93. New York: TarcherPerigee, 2017.

Tharp, Twyla. *The Creative Habit*. New York: Simon and Schuster, 2003.

Thompson, E. P. *The Making of the English Working Class*. Westminster, MD: Random House, 1966.

Tolstoy, Leo. Quoted in *The Writer's Life*, edited by Carol Edgarian and Tom Jenks. New York: Vintage, 1997.

Toomer, Jean. *Cane*. New York: W. W. Norton, 1988.

Towles, Amor. *A Gentleman in Moscow*. New York: Viking, 2016.

Tufte, Virginia. *Artful Sentences: Syntax as Style*. Cheshire, CT: Graphics Press, 2006.

Tufte, Virginia, and Garrett Stewart. *Grammar as Style*. New York: Holt, Rinehart and Winston, 1971.

University of Chicago Press. *The Chicago Manual of Style*. 17th ed. Chicago: University of Chicago Press, 2017.

Updike, John. "Pigeon Feathers." In *100 Years of the Best American Short Stories*, edited by Lorrie Moore, 242–59. Boston: Houghton Mifflin Harcourt, 2015.

Valian, Virginia. "Learning to Work." In *Working It Out*, edited by Sara Ruddick and Pamela Daniels, 162–78. New York: Pantheon Books, 1977, http://maxweber.hunter.cuny.edu/psych/faculty/valian/valian.htm.

van Gogh, Vincent. *The Letters of Vincent van Gogh*, edited by Mark Roskill. New York: Macmillan, 1963.

Wallace, David Foster. "Consider the Lobster." *Gourmet*, August 2004, 50–64.

Walser, Robert. "A Discussion of a Picture." In *Looking at Pictures*, 133–36. Translated by Susan Bernofsky, Lydia Davis, and Christopher Middleton. Christine Burgin Series. New York: New Directions, 2015.

Weiner, Jonathan. *The Beak of the Finch*. New York: Vintage Books, 1994.

White, E. B. "Bedfellows." In *Essays of E. B. White*, 80–89. New York: Harper & Row, 1977.

Wideman, John Edgar. "Fanon." In *God's Gym: Stories*, 120–37. Boston: Houghton Mifflin, 2005.

———. "Sightings." In *God's Gym: Stories*, 153–75.

Wilkins, Joe. "Eleven Kinds of Sky." *Orion* 31, no. 1 (January/February 2012): 32–40.

Williams, David B. *The Street-Smart Naturalist*. Portland, OR: Westwinds Press, 2005.

Williams, Joy. "The Visiting Privilege." In *The Visiting Privilege*, 264–74. New York: Vintage Contemporaries, 2016.

———. "Winter Chemistry." In *The Visiting Privilege*, 89–103.

Winterson, Jeanette. *The Passion*. Toronto: Vintage Canada, 2000.

Wolff, Tobias. *This Boy's Life*. New York: Harper & Row, 1989.

Woodrell, Daniel. *Winter's Bone*. New York: Little, Brown, 2006.

Wright, C. D. *Cooling Time*. Port Townsend, WA: Copper Canyon Press, 2005.

———. "69 Hidebound Opinions, Propositions, and Several Asides from a Manila Envelope Concerning the Stuff of Poets." In *By Herself: Women Reclaim Poetry*, edited by Molly McQuade. Minneapolis: Graywolf Press, 1999, http://www.english.illinois.edu/maps/poets/s_z/cdwright/opinions.htm.

Wulf, Andrea. *The Invention of Nature: Alexander von Humboldt's New World*. New York: Vintage Books, 2016.

Yagoda, Ben. *The Sound on the Page*. New York: HarperCollins, 2004.

Yeats, W. B. "Men Improve with the Years." In *W. B. Yeats: The Poems*, edited by Richard J. Finneran, 136. New York: Macmillan, 1983.

Young, Gary, and Christopher Buckley. *One for the Money: The Sentence as a Poetic Form*. Spokane, WA: Lynx House Press, 2012.

Young, Tommy Scott. Quoted in "Tommy Scott Young" by Gayle R. Swanson and William B. Thesing. In *Conversations with South Carolina Poets*, edited by Gayle R. Swanson and

William B. Thesing, 139–58. Winston-Salem, NC: John F.
    Blair, 1986.
Yuknavitch, Lidia. *The Chronology of Water*. Portland, OR: Haw-
    thorne Books & Literary Arts, 2010.
Zacharias, Lee. "Buzzards." In *The Only Sounds We Make*, 186–213.
    Spartanburg, SC: Hub City Press, 2014.
Zinn, Howard. "Failure to Quit." In *Failure to Quit*, 157–64. Mon-
    roe, ME: Common Courage Press, 1993

CREDITS

INDEX